W9-CSE-267

Praise for *Gentle Birth, Gentle Mothering*

I have not seen a more penetrating analysis with thorough documentation from the scientific literature. I wish every obstetrician, family physician, midwife, and obstetric nurse would read this book. In addition, this book would be a wonderful primer for women and families searching for a better childbirth.

Marsden Wagner MD (perinatologist;
former WHO regional director, Maryland)

Sarah Buckley is one of the few people in this world telling the truth about pregnancy and birth. Now in this book you will read her well-researched work. Sarah's words are truly a gift to the midwifery and birthing community.

Jan Tritten (midwife; editor *Midwifery Today*, Oregon)

A fascinating, deeply moving and wide-ranging exploration of different aspects of birth and mothering, drawing on research evidence and vivid personal experience.

Sheila Kitzinger (author; social anthropologist, Oxford)

I love your book. It is delightfully easy to read, inspiring and incredibly informative. You speak to women from a gentle yet empowering voice. The book brilliantly combines mind/body wisdom with medical information, which cultivates awareness and provides us with a path to awakening. Your own personal stories create a soft loving touch. Thank you Sarah – you have provided a gentle yet powerful framework for change and I am grateful.

Vicki Abrams (co-author, with Deepak Chopra, of *Magical Beginnings,
Enchanted Lives*; director prenatal programmes, Chopra Centre, San Diego)

Sarah Buckley marries the medical mind and the birthing woman's body wisdom. Her writing comes from the unique perspective of a holistic integration of these often-poles-apart realities. Her writing opens up new possibilities for those lucky enough to imbibe.

Gloria Lemay (midwifery educator;
contributing editor *Midwifery Today*, Vancouver)

Sarah Buckley's work is unique: as a health professional AND a hands-on mother, Sarah exquisitely demonstrates how science affirms the intuitive wisdom of mother love, as well as how gentle parenting works in practice – not just in theory.

Pinky McKay (author of *Parenting By Heart;
100 Ways to Calm the Crying*, Melbourne)

Gentle Birth, Gentle Mothering *is the book Hygieia College can fully endorse. Sarah Buckley is a true birthkeeper. As a mother, she knows what having two hearts feels like. Yet as a birthkeeper, she has soul. I am honored to be Sarah's colleague. Moreover I am blessed that Sarah is my dear friend, indeed she is a spiritual sister.*

Jeannine Parvati Baker (midwife; author; birthkeeper, Utah)

Gentle Birth, Gentle Mothering *is compelling reading for all midwives, medical and midwifery students and anyone interested in the innate ability of women during pregnancy, labour, and birth, providing essential information and presented in a way that gives wisdom back to women and knowledge to those who provide care.*

Robyn Thompson (midwife, Melbourne)

All of the gentle mothering articles (and the whole collection, in fact) affirms the feminine, affirms our ability to mother well, affirms our choice to invest ourselves in our children and imbues a general sense of confidence in ourselves as mothers.

Lea Mason (childbirth educator; mother, Sydney)

Dr Buckley has a beautiful way of weaving the primal and meaningful emotion of birth with the scientific facts that support instinctual normal birth.

Hilary Shirven (natural childbirth educator/doula; mother, Illinois)

Your information has had a key role in many of the decisions we have made for our family, and we are so grateful to have you as a source of knowledge.

Melissa Bruijn (Birthtalk convenor; mother, Brisbane)

I aim to set your book as compulsory reading for my students.

Sandy Kirkman (midwifery tutor, Glamorgan, UK)

Dr Sarah J Buckley

Gentle Birth, Gentle Mothering

*The wisdom and science of gentle choices
in pregnancy, birth, and parenting*

ONE MOON PRESS BRISBANE AUSTRALIA

One Moon Press
245 Sugars Road, Anstead, QLD 4070
Australia
www.sarahjbuckley.com

© Sarah J Buckley 2005

First published 2005. Reprinted 2006.

Cover illustration © 2005 Durga Bernhard
durgabernhard.com

The author has made every effort to provide accurate information, but there may be errors, omissions, and information that is, or becomes, out of date. This book is not intended as a sole source of information, or as a substitute for medical or midwifery care. Readers are encouraged to read widely and to consult a health care professional who can provide individualised information and advice.

The author and One Moon Press shall have neither liability nor responsibility to any person or entity with respect to any loss or damage caused, or alleged to have been caused, directly or indirectly, by the information contained in this book.

All rights reserved. Without limiting the rights under copyright above, no part of this publication shall be reproduced, stored in or introduced into a retrieval system, or transmitted in any form or by any means (electronic, mechanical, photocopying, recording or otherwise) without the prior permission of the publisher of this book.

However, permission is given to purchasers of the book to copy and circulate articles to friends (to a maximum of 10 percent of the book, as copyright law allows) and permission for birth professionals to use these articles, exactly as printed, for clients, or for childbirth education class participants. Note, however, that no article may be published in a magazine, stored in an electronic medium, or posted on a formal or informal Internet site without express permission.

Produced by Literal Ink
Edited by Soni Stecker
Text design by Mark Myszka
Cover design by Peter Buchholz
Typeset in 11pt Berkeley Oldstyle Book by
    SilverLining Design Pty Ltd (www.silverlining.com.au)
Printed by Finsbury Green Printing, Melbourne, Australia www.finsbury.com.au
Printed with non-toxic vegetable-based inks on Cyclus 100% recycled,
    total chlorine-free paper made from 100% post-consumer waste (ISO 14001).

National Library of Australia
cataloguing-in-publication data:
Buckley, Sarah J, 1960
Gentle Birth, Gentle Mothering: the wisdom and science of gentle choices
    in pregnancy, birth, and parenting
Bibliography.
Includes index.
ISBN 0-9758077-0-6
1. Childbirth. 2. Pregnancy. 3. Motherhood. 4. Parenting.
I. Title
618.24

Foreword

Hooray for Sarah Buckley! Her broadly informed, authoritative voice is sorely needed in these trying times when there is so much fear, ignorance, and confusion surrounding childbirth and the decision-making and organisation of maternity care. Never has there been a time when there was so much at stake for women giving birth, in terms of age-old knowledge and wisdom that may be lost for decades or longer, if current trends continue unabated.

In many countries, it is only the middle-aged and the elderly who remember the time when only four or five women out of every hundred had their babies by caesarean. How will people of the future even know that uninterfered-with birth is safer than surgical birth? Will women of the future believe today's birth activists, or will they believe the obstetricians who are far more comfortable with surgery than with physiological processes that have their own timing?

Fear can make for irrational decision-making, and here we have a good example of this phenomenon at work. In many areas of the world, women have become sufficiently afraid of Nature's plan for labour and birth that they are literally clamouring for surgical birth when there is no medical reason to justify the added risk to them and their babies posed by such surgery. There is no historical precedent for a phenomenon such as this. We have mass hysteria spreading over the planet – a rather strange development, considering it comes after the second wave of the women's movement, since it involves women being afraid of their own wombs.

Ironically, this widespread fear leads countless women to agree to deliberate injury of their uteri by caesarean section, although we don't commonly speak of these acts in such stark language as I have just used. Women, like most of the rest of our society, are not given the amount of information necessary to fully understand the risks of many of the decisions they are called upon to make around the time of birth. While all this is going on, the confusion grows even deeper, and it becomes ever more difficult for young women to learn about the gifts and capacities of their bodies.

Horrible birth stories can now be sent around the world at lightning speed via satellite television and movies, with the result that uninformed attitudes (many of which arose originally in the United States) that promote ever more routine medical intervention in birth for healthy women are threatening to make the ancient way of birth viewed as a selfish or irresponsible act on the part of the woman who wishes to make this choice. Most women have little awareness of how important an autonomous midwifery profession is when it comes to retaining age-old wisdom of women's true capacities in labour and birth. When midwives no longer have the ability to honour women's right to labour as long as they are willing to continue, and when their and their babies' vital signs are good, in the birth site of their choice; when hospital-based midwives are forced to divide their attention among several labouring women in a busy maternity unit; when student midwives and physicians are no longer assured the opportunity of witnessing the normal physiological process of labour during their training – we lose the meaning of birth, step by step, and myths take further precedence over physiological realities.

Here's what makes Sarah Buckley's writing so authoritative and compelling. She knows medicine because of her years of medical training and experience, and that of her husband. But unlike 99 percent of her medical colleagues in the wealthy countries, she also knows unmedicated birth in a way that only one who has experienced it can. She has lived her education in the most real way possible – by giving birth at home four times. That fact alone speaks volumes.

Her knowledge is in her bones, but she also knows where it is corroborated by scientific research that you can rely upon. You'll find rich resources in this book on each subject discussed in relation to pregnancy, antenatal diagnostic testing, giving birth, various birth practices, breastfeeding, weaning, childcare, and gentle discipline.

Young feminists, are you listening? Remember, here we have a physician who actually knows more, and has a broader range of experience, than those of her profession who disagree with her, those who have never themselves tried out the birth-giving capacities of their bodies. Feminism is about courage and strength and celebration of feminine power. True feminism does not disrespect the woman who finds power in giving birth without medication or unnecessary interference. Few women who have such an experience will come away from birth subscribing to a belief in a creator who, some maintain, deliberately created women's bodies to be poorly designed for giving birth. Rather, they are far more likely to gain new respect for the heretofore hidden and mysterious powers of their bodies.

INA MAY GASKIN, CPM

Contents

For mothers, babies, fathers,
and families everywhere.

Introduction

T HE seeds for *Gentle Birth, Gentle Mothering* were sown in the blissful days and weeks following the birth of my son, Jacob Patrick. Jacob's birth, my third at home, had been intense and yet ordinary, challenging but joyous, and ultimately ecstatic and fulfilling. Holding my new baby in my arms, I wished that every mother, baby, father, and family could be so blessed by birth.

With this wish, I began to write. My first article, "Reclaiming every woman's birth right" was published in *The Age*, Melbourne, in 1996, and has been updated as the first chapter in this book. This article asks the question: Why is birth seen in such a negative light in our culture and what can we, as women and as a culture, gain through reclaiming birth?

In the years that followed Jacob's birth, I took an extended break from my work as a GP (family physician), gaining more opportunities to explore my path as a mother and to write about my experiences. I became especially interested in exploring the nexus between biomedical perspectives and gentle approaches in birth and mothering, and this became a cornerstone of my writing.

I was excited to discover that many gentle birth and parenting practices that I had instinctively chosen – for example homebirth, carrying my baby, and child-led breastfeeding – were well supported by evidence from science, anthropology, psychology, and evolutionary medicine. I felt strongly that parents deserve to know this, so that they can distinguish cultural disapproval from genuine risks when they evaluate birth and parenting choices.

I also learned that there are still major questions about, for example, the long-term safety of ultrasound; and that long-term studies of almost every other medical procedure in pregnancy and birth are lacking. I learned, contrary to medical belief, that a mother's feelings and experiences during pregnancy and birth can have major, and possibly life-long, consequences for her baby and herself, which highlights the importance of gentle, loving care for women in pregnancy, birth, and mothering.

Through my research and writing, I also learned about the evolutionary wisdom of co-sleeping and long-term breastfeeding, and of the innate ability of babies to communicate their elimination needs, all of which inspired and supported me as a mother. I also came to see, from my reading, my observations, and my own experiences, just how profound the imprint of birth and early mothering on child development and family relationships is.

With the birth of my fourth baby Maia Rose in 2000, I experienced giving birth as our foremothers may have: birth as pure instinct and pleasure. This amazing experience inspired me to look at the ecstasy of birth from a scientific perspective, and I began to develop the material on ecstatic and undisturbed birth that you will read here, first published in *Mothering* magazine.

In this book, you will find a collection of my best articles, written from 1996 to 2005. Almost all of these articles have been previously published in parenting and professional publications, and I have been touched by the rich feedback that I have received. Many of you, my readers, have contacted me to let me know how much my writing has supported you in your journey to parenthood. Birth professionals have been appreciative that they can now cite positive proof for their gentle approaches, and many have asked to distribute my articles to their clients and contacts.

Every article has been updated for publication in *Gentle Birth, Gentle Mothering*, with the intention that each one can stand alone. For this reason you may find some of my favourite themes repeated through the book, especially the information on hormonal systems of birth, which I see as one of the most powerful arguments for gentle birth.

You may also notice, with these updates, that I have used a mixture of Australian, UK and US spellings and terms, which reflects my international audience, and which I hope is at least reasonably tolerable to you all.

"Gentle Birth", the first part of *Gentle Birth, Gentle Mothering*, focuses on gentle approaches to pregnancy and birth. These articles are straightforward and largely unreferenced, and incorporate some of my own experiences in pregnancy and birth. These include the homebirth of Emma, my first child, who was born almost a month early (as well as arriving unexpectedly posterior), the waterbirth of Jacob, my third child, who was born almost three weeks past his due date, and the unassisted (and also surprising) semi-waterbirth of Maia, my fourth baby. Maia's birth is the foundation of the article "Ecstatic Birth", also featured in this section.

My second child Zoe's posterior birth, my most challenging, is the focus for my reflections on instinctive birth. This essay includes many ideas and tools to help prepare for birth. I also share my own inspiration for birth through the popular essay, "Healing Birth, healing the Earth". Zoe's birth is also mentioned in my articles on the practice of lotus birth (non-severance of the cord) and homebirth.

The middle section, "Gentle Birth – the Evidence", looks at pregnancy and birth from medical and scientific perspectives, providing substantial and well-referenced information supporting informed and gentle choices. I include articles about ultrasound and prenatal diagnosis because I feel that parents are generally not given sufficient accurate information to make an informed choice about these very new technologies. I also express my concerns about the possible long-term physical and emotional side effects for both parents and offspring. In a similar vein, the essay "Leaving well alone" explores the possible sequelae of early cord clamping (including cord blood banking), which again is rarely discussed with parents, but can have a major impact on mother and baby.

The centrepiece in this section, and in the book as a whole, is my article, "Undisturbed Birth: Mother Nature's blueprint for safety, ease and ecstasy". This is an expansion of my previously published ecstatic birth material, and features a wealth of scientific research that supports the ecstasy, and the evolutionary wisdom, of gentle birth. I also detail some of the possible consequences of disturbing birth with intense monitoring and with medical interventions. The power of this article lies in the extensive material (and I am always finding more to add!) and its resonance with many women's cellular memories of giving birth, and with the experiences of those who support undisturbed birth.

My own experiences, again, have inspired me to look at the medical evidence around breech birth and homebirth, concluding that the evidence supports women who wish to make gentle choices in these areas. This section includes well-referenced facts on caesareans, which will assist women making informed choices when offered this major birth intervention.

The final section, "Gentle Mothering", features my favourite articles on gentle parenting choices. For new parents, there are introductions to attachment parenting and co-sleeping, with information that will ensure safe sleeping in any setting. I also explore choices such as controlled crying in the article, "Getting a Good Night's Sleep", and share more of my own experiences as a co-sleeping parent.

You can also read about my journey – almost 15 years, in total – as a breastfeeding mother, and the benefits of prolonged breastfeeding for mother and child. "Mothering, Mindfulness, and a Baby's Bottom" describes the amazing process of raising my fourth baby without nappies/diapers. I also share the richness and support that yoga has brought me, in pregnancy and mothering, and hope to inspire and support more yoga-mamas!

"Gentle Mothering" concludes with some very practical parenting information to support gentle discipline. This material can be used with children of any age, but is especially relevant from ages two to ten.

Birth and mothering have truly blessed me, and in turn I am passing that blessing to you through this book. May you be inspired, informed, nourished and supported by what you read, and may your parenting have a firm and gentle foundation, based on instinct, wisdom, and love.

Gentle Birth

Reclaiming every Woman's Birth Right

BIRTH is a women's issue, birth is a power issue; therefore birth is a feminist issue. My logic may be correct, but the issue of birth has been at the bottom of the feminist agenda in western countries for some years, well behind matters such as equal opportunity, sexual harassment, bedroom politics, abortion, and body image, to name but a few.

Feminism has championed many other women's health issues and resisted the medicalisation of menopause, the other major rite of passage in our culture; however, there seems to have been no equivalent analysis of birth. Yet most women in our culture will give birth at some time in their lives, and for the majority it is their first experience as a hospital patient, with the loss of autonomy implied in that role. Many will feel the conflict between their own desires, needs, and ways of knowing, and the technology-does-it-better approach that the medicalisation of birth has produced.

This medical approach, which I believe reflects our culture's infatuation with technology in general, has not benefited birthing women. Australia has one of the highest rates of operative birth (caesarean, forceps or vacuum delivery) in the world; in 2002, 37.8 percent of birthing women experienced an operative delivery.[1] In the US in 2002, 32 percent – around one in three – women gave birth by operative delivery,[2] and this figure was almost identical (33 percent) in the UK[3] and in Canada (34.9 percent)[4] in 2002–3. In Queensland, Australia, caesarean section rates in private hospitals (which serve around one-third of birthing women) are approaching 50 percent,[5] compared to World Health Organization recommendations of 10 to 15 percent.[6]

Even women who have a so-called normal birth are experiencing significant interventions. One study of first-time mothers in Melbourne in 1997 found that only nine women out of 242 gave birth without any medical procedures during labour and delivery.[7] In the US, according to the authors of the 2002 *Listening to Mothers* survey, "…there were virtually no 'natural childbirths' among the mothers we surveyed. Even mothers having a vaginal birth experienced a wide array of medical interventions…"[8]

And all of this is happening in an extremely healthy population, where some estimate that at least 70 to 80 percent of women should be giving birth without intervention.

As a GP (family physician) and a mother, I ask myself why women are tolerating this situation. Why are educated, articulate women, who are prepared to battle for their rights in their personal and professional lives, so accepting of the high intervention rates that characterise this group in particular?

Why are we not at least advocating for ourselves and our babies, at a time when science is discovering what mothers have known for years: that a newborn baby is a highly sentient being, exquisitely sensitive to its emotional and physical environment; and that a baby's experiences during labour and birth – for example, exposure to some drugs – can have life-long consequences?[9]

Perhaps there is a perception among women that there has been improvement. After all, there are now birth centres in many countries; even though they are politically precarious in almost every setting, demand for public birth centres can outstrip supply by more than seven to one,[10] and up to two-thirds of women using a birth centre may be transferred to a labour ward before the birth.[11]

Labour wards are looking more comfortable and homely, with fathers' presence being allowed – even expected – during labour and birth. However, cosmetic changes do not guarantee a low-technology philosophy and the father's presence at birth may be a mixed blessing. Some men may be disturbed and frightened by seeing their partners in the endorphin-altered state that is natural for a labouring woman, and is due to high levels of these naturally produced pain-killing chemicals. It has even been suggested that the increased use of epidurals for pain relief parallels the advent of men into the labour room, reflecting a subtle pressure on women to behave more "normally" in labour.

Perhaps the lack of birth activism also reflects our small families and our busy working lives, which give each of us less motivation to lobby for improvements. A bad birth experience can be forgotten in the intensity of the early months, and then we go back to our careers where we feel safe and life is more predictable. Yet I feel that there is an enormous amount of disappointment and hurt among mothers around giving birth. As a pregnant woman I noticed that other women told me overwhelmingly negative stories about their own birth experiences. I wonder, too, about depression after birth, which affects up to one in five women, and which Australian researchers have linked to forceps and caesarean births,[12] and early separation of mother and baby.[13]

However, I am not advocating one particular type of good birth, nor even birth without intervention. A woman's satisfaction with her birth experience is related more to her involvement in decision-making than to the outcome.[14] But women need all the information to make informed decisions, and this requires that doctors and midwives take time to listen and explain, and that women and their partners take their share of responsibility.

This informed approach to birth is a prescription for lower rates of litigation, which at present are frightening obstetricians into defensive and often interventionist practices, benefiting neither doctors nor women.

This approach also implies that parents can be trusted to make good decisions, and is a radical departure from the paternalistic attitude that has been prevalent in obstetrics. It is welcome, too, because many current obstetric practices are not supported by evidence of effectiveness or cost-benefit ratio. For example, an evidence-based analysis, based on the best of international research, shows that models of care that prioritise women's choices such as homebirth and midwife-only care are as safe as conventional obstetric care, while offering high rates of satisfaction.[15, 16]

Consumers now have access to evidence-based information through the work of the UK-based Cochrane Collaboration. This group produces the regularly updated book *A Guide to Effective Care in Pregnancy and Childbirth*[17], and their information is available on the Cochrane library website,[18] which is freely accessible in many countries. Both resources provide an excellent base from which to assess choices in birth anywhere in the world.

Perhaps the most exciting aspect of evidence-based obstetric care is the possibility for institutional change that it implies. Murray Enkin, one of the authors of *A Guide to Effective Care in Pregnancy and Childbirth*, states:

> The only justification for practices that restrict a woman's autonomy, her freedom of choice, or her access to her baby, would be clear evidence that these restrictive practices do more good than harm.[19]

If all involved in birth were to take these premises seriously, profound changes would take place in the birth room.

Birth is women's business; it is the business of our bodies. And our bodies are indeed wondrous, from our monthly cycles to the awesome power inherent in the act of giving birth. Yet in our culture I do not see respect for these extraordinary functions: instead we diet, exercise, abuse, conceal, and generally punish our bodies for not approximating an unrealistic and unobtainable ideal.

This lack of trust and care for our bodies can rob us of confidence in giving birth. Conversely, an experience of the phenomenal potential of our birthing bodies can give us an enduring sense of our own power as women.

Birth is the beginning of life, the beginning of mothering, and of fathering too. We all deserve a good beginning.

A previous version of this article was published in The Age *(Melbourne), 29 November 1996. This version updated March 2005.*

References

1. Laws P, Sullivan E. *Australia's mothers and babies 2002*. Sydney: AIHW National Perinatal Statistics Unit, 2004.

2. Martin J, et al. *Births: Final data for 2002. National vital statistics reports*. Hyattsville MD: National Center for Health Statistics, 2003.

3. Department of Health. *Statistical bulletin: NHS maternity statistics, England: 2002–3*. London: DoH, 2004.

4. Canadian Institute for Health Information. *Giving Birth in Canada*. Ontario: CIHI, 2004.

5. Queensland Health. *Perinatal data collection quarterly report, Anonymous Private Hospital, Jan to March 02*. Brisbane: Queensland Health, 2001.

6. World Health Organization. Appropriate technology for birth. *Lancet* 1985; 2(8452):436–7.

7. Fisher J, et al. Adverse psychological impact of operative obstetric interventions: a prospective longitudinal study. *Aust N Z J Psychiatry* 1997; 31(5):728–38.

8. Declercq E, et al. *Listening to Mothers: Report of the First U.S. National Survey of Women's Childbearing Experiences. Executive Summary and Recommendations*. New York: Maternity Center Association, October 2002, p 4.

9. Jacobson B, et al. Opiate addiction in adult offspring through possible imprinting after obstetric treatment. *Br Med J* 1990; 301(6760): 1067–70.

10. Health Department Victoria. *Having a Baby in Victoria: Final Report of the Ministerial Review of Birthing Services in Victoria*. Melbourne: Health Department Victoria, 1990.

11. Hodnett ED, et al. Home-like versus conventional institutional settings for birth. *Cochrane Database Syst Rev* 2005(1):CD000012.

12. Boyce PM, Todd AL. Increased risk of postnatal depression after emergency caesarean section. *Med J Aust* 1992; 157(3):172–4.

13. Rowe-Murray HJ, Fisher JR. Operative intervention in delivery is associated with compromised early mother–infant interaction. *Br J Obstet Gynaecol* 2001;108(10): 1068–75.

14. Hodnett ED. Pain and women's satisfaction with the experience of childbirth: a systematic review. *Am J Obstet Gynaecol* 2002; 186(5 Suppl Nature):S160–72.

15. Waldenstrom U, Turnbull D. A systematic review comparing continuity of midwifery care with standard maternity services. *Br J Obstet Gynaecol* 1998; 105(11):1160–70.

16. Olsen O, Jewell MD. Home versus hospital birth. *Cochrane Database Syst Rev* 2000(2):CD000352.

17. Enkin M, et al. *Effective Care in Pregnancy and Childbirth*. 3rd edn. Oxford: Oxford University Press, 2000.

18. Cochrane Collaboration. The Cochrane Library: John Wiley, 2005 www.thecochranelibrary.org

19. Enkin M, et al. *Effective Care in Pregnancy and Childbirth*. 3rd edn. Oxford: Oxford University Press, 2000, p 486.

Ecstatic Birth ~
natural childbirth
and its ecstasy-inducing
hormonal cocktail

A WOMAN gives birth to her second baby – a rapid birth in the back of the car en route to hospital. "That was..." she says, "absolutely ecstatic."

A fourth baby is born, unexpectedly breech, in the family bathtub. The mother, who catches her own baby, describes the minutes after birth as "the purest bliss".

In a small clinic in France, a young mother gives birth to her footling-breech baby without drugs or intervention. A BBC cameraman asks her, half an hour later, how she felt as she pushed her baby out. She replies unhesitatingly to the camera, "It was like an orgasm."

These true stories reflect an aspect of birth that is almost unknown in our culture; one that contradicts our cultural belief that giving birth is a traumatic experience. The ecstasy that these new mothers have experienced is not only possible; it is an intrinsic part of the birth process. Ecstatic birth has kept our species flourishing for more than two million years, bonding mothers and babies in love and pleasure, and rewarding new mothers for their crucial role in reproduction.

Ecstasy – an experience that takes us outside (*ec*) our usual state (*stasis*) – is every woman's genetic blueprint for birth. This blueprint includes the release of an ecstatic cocktail of hormones, our bodies' chemical messengers, which are released from the middle part of the brain during labour, peaking at the moment of birth. These hormones include oxytocin, the hormone of love; beta-endorphin, hormone of pleasure and transcendence; adrenaline and noradrenaline (epinephrine and norepinephrine), hormones of excitement and fight-or-flight; and prolactin, the hormone of tender mothering.

As well as inducing feelings of love, pleasure, transcendence, excitement, and tenderness, this hormonal cocktail is also responsible for many of the actual processes of labour.

Oxytocin, for example, is the hormone that causes a labouring woman's uterus to contract, and adrenaline/noradrenaline catalyse the final powerful contractions at the end of a natural labour. The orchestration of these hormones also provides important safeguards for mother and baby. For example, adrenaline/noradrenaline give the baby protection against the powerful contractions of late labour and, after the birth, oxytocin acts to prevent maternal bleeding.

Oxytocin

Oxytocin is known as the hormone of love because it is released from our pituitary gland, deep inside our middle brain, during sexual activity, orgasm, birth, and breastfeeding, as well as when we are touching, hugging, and sharing a meal. When our oxytocin levels are high we feel loving and positive towards others.

During a natural labour a woman's oxytocin level gradually increases, reaching a peak around the time of birth. This oxytocin peak – the highest in her life – occurs because of the stretching of her lower vagina as her baby descends, and causes the strong contractions that will help her to birth her baby as efficiently as possible.

The baby also produces increasing amounts of oxytocin in labour, also peaking at birth. In the minutes after birth, both mother and baby are saturated with oxytocin, the hormone of love. Both will enjoy increased levels of oxytocin through skin-to-skin and eye-to-eye contact and through the baby's first attempts at suckling. Good oxytocin levels at this time will also assist the mother in delivering her baby's placenta, and protect her against bleeding by keeping her uterus well contracted. Oxytocin is an important hormone of bonding in all mammals, and oxytocin levels are elevated in the baby for at least four days after birth.

In breastfeeding, oxytocin causes the let-down (or milk ejection) reflex, and pulses of oxytocin are released from the mother's pituitary gland as her baby suckles. During the months and years of lactation, oxytocin continues to keep the mother well nourished and relaxed. The anti-stress effects of oxytocin, which are also prominent in pregnancy, have been shown to persist for several months after weaning.

Synthetic oxytocin

The oxytocin system, designed to aid labour and produce love and bonding after birth, is a major casualty of medicalised birth. In Australia almost half of all labouring women are administered synthetic oxytocin (Syntocinon/Pitocin) in labour to induce or speed up (accelerate, augment) their labour. In the US, 38 percent of labouring women are induced or augmented in their labour and around 20 percent of labouring women in the UK are induced; most inductions will involve Syntocinon.

This can create significant problems for mother and baby. First, when a woman is given Syntocinon by intravenous drip (IV), oxytocin levels in her bloodstream may become much higher than she would naturally produce in labour. As well as this, Syntocinon is administered by continuous IV infusion, whereas oxytocin is naturally released in pulses. For both of these reasons, IV Syntocinon makes a labouring woman's contractions longer, stronger and closer together than a she would naturally experience, and all of these factors can cause the baby to become distressed.

US birth activist Doris Haire says, "The situation is analogous to holding an infant under the surface of the water, allowing the infant to come to the surface to gasp for air, but not to breathe." For these reasons, every woman with a Syntocinon drip is under continuous monitoring to detect fetal distress. Fetal distress implies that the baby has insufficient oxygen and needs to be treated promptly – usually by caesarean – to avoid brain damage and death.

A second problem with Syntocinon is that it cannot, for physiological reasons, cross from the bloodstream back into the brain. This means that it cannot reach the labouring woman's middle brain, and therefore cannot act as the hormone of love. However, it may interfere with the natural oxytocin system of mother and baby in other ways.

For example, there is solid evidence that a woman who has a Syntocinon infusion in labour will be at higher risk of bleeding after the birth. This is due to over-stimulation of the oxytocin receptors in her uterus, leading them to decrease in number and become unable to respond adequately (to stop bleeding) in the critical minutes after birth.

Natural birth pioneer Michel Odent believes that the functioning of the oxytocin system, which is still developing in the baby at the time of birth, reflects our ability to love ourselves and others. Odent has suggested that many of our society's problems – our current epidemics of drug addiction and teenage suicide, for example – may be traced back to the widespread and unprecedented interference with the oxytocin system of mothers and babies at birth. His theory, which is a powerful indictment of practices such as inducing and augmenting labour, is increasingly being supported by scientific research on oxytocin and other brain-hormone systems. (For more about this, see chapter 13, "Undisturbed Birth".)

Beta-endorphin

Beta-endorphin is a naturally occurring opiate, with properties in common with other opiates (drugs derived from the opium poppy) such as heroin, morphine and pethidine (meperidine, Demerol), and is known to act in the same areas of the brain. Beta-endorphin, like oxytocin, is secreted from the pituitary gland in the middle brain and levels are high during sexual activity, pregnancy, birth, and breastfeeding.

Beta-endorphin, like the other opiates, induces natural pain relief (analgesia) as well as feelings of pleasure and connectedness. Beta-endorphin levels increase throughout a natural labour and peak at the moment of birth. Beta-endorphin helps the labouring woman to transcend pain and enter the altered state of consciousness that characterises a natural birth. After birth, high levels of beta-endorphin enhance bonding and mutual pleasure between mother and baby. Beta-endorphin is also released during breast-feeding.

Beta-endorphin systems are also interfered with through medicalised birth, especially through the use of drugs for labour pain. As with oxytocin, pain-relieving drugs may be given as compensation for hormones that a labouring woman would naturally release if she felt safe and undisturbed. The use of opiate drugs such as pethidine will decrease a woman's natural release of beta-endorphin, reducing the help that her body can give her with the stress of labour, and diminishing her feelings of pleasure and transcendence at the moment of birth.

The long-term sequelae of such interference has been poorly researched but what we do know is very concerning. Swedish researcher Dr Bertil Jacobson looked at the birth records of 200 opiate addicts and compared them with the birth records of their non-addicted siblings. He found that, when the mothers had received opiates, barbiturates (sedating drugs which are no longer used in labour), and/or nitrous oxide gas during labour, especially in multiple doses, the offspring were more likely to become drug addicted in adulthood. For example, when a mother had received three doses of opiates in labour, her child was almost five times more likely to become addicted to opiate drugs in adulthood. This study was recently repeated with a US population, with very similar results.

Adrenalin and noradrenaline

The fight-or-flight hormones adrenaline and noradrenaline (epinephrine and norepinephrine) are part of a family of hormones called catecholamines (CAs), and are released by the body in response to stresses such as hunger, fear, and cold. As well as stimulating the sympathetic nervous system for fight or flight, CAs also give feelings of excitement, such as we might experience during extreme sports, or riding a theme park roller coaster.

During a natural labour, a woman's CA levels will gradually rise. However, if she is fearful, cold, hungry, or in excessive pain, she will release unnaturally high levels of CAs, which will act in her brain to reduce her oxytocin release. This will cause her contractions to slow or even stop. CA release will also cause blood to be diverted away from her uterus, and baby, to her large muscle groups in preparation for fight or flight. This CA response enhances safety for animals that give birth in the wild who, when under threat, need a delay in labour and the muscular energy to flee to safety.

An instinctive CA response continues to operate in modern birthing environments. For example, when a labouring woman moves from her own familiar home environment to a hospital, the unfamiliarity of the hospital can trigger feelings of anxiety. She may sense, at an instinctive level, that she (or her baby) is in danger and her labour may slow or even stop. This fight-or-flight response can also reduce the blood supply to her uterus, putting her baby at risk of distress.

However, these hormones are designed to benefit both mother and baby at the end of labour, when CA levels naturally increase, especially noradrenaline. For the mother, this hormonal surge can activate what has been called the fetal ejection reflex. This reflex begins during the transition between the first and second stages of labour and gives the mother a rush of energy; she will become alert and will usually want to be upright. She may have a dry mouth and shallow breathing and perhaps the urge to grasp something. She may express fear, anger, or excitement, and the CA surge will, paradoxically at this time, increase her release of oxytocin.

With high levels of both oxytocin and CAs, the mother's uterus will produce several very strong contractions, and she will birth her baby quickly and easily. Such a dramatic yet easy birth is uncommon in our culture, because the fetal ejection reflex will only operate when a woman has felt private, safe, and undisturbed in her labour. The fetal ejection reflex is common, for example, in mothers who give birth before arriving in hospital.

For the baby also, labour is an exciting and stressful event, and the baby's CA levels rise as labour progresses. High CA levels – specifically noradrenaline – in late labour provide important safeguards for the baby by protecting against the lack of oxygen (hypoxia) that arises when the mother's contractions are at their strongest. High CA levels help to keep blood flowing to the baby's most important organs – brain and heart – and make all of the baby's tissues more tolerant to low oxygen levels.

CA levels peak just before birth for the baby as well; this has been called the catecholamine surge. This hormonal surge ensures that the baby is well prepared for life outside the womb by raising the baby's blood sugar and fat levels, which are both important fuels for the newborn brain. High CA levels also clear fluid from the lungs; promote heat production; stimulate heart and breathing functions; and make the baby more alert and responsive at first contact with the mother. The CA hormone noradrenaline is also known to be an important bonding hormone in other mammals, and almost certainly in human mothers as well.

Prolactin

Prolactin, the hormone of tender mothering, also peaks at the moment of birth for both mother and baby. Prolactin is known to play an important role in reorganising the mother's brain, hormones, and behaviours in preparation for motherhood. According to Michel Odent, the presence of prolactin in the ecstatic hormonal cocktail ensures that a new mother's feelings of love, pleasure, transcendence, and excitement will be directed towards her baby.

After birth, prolactin is the main hormone of breast milk synthesis. Prolactin is also present in breast milk and is thought to be important for optimal brain and neuroendocrine (brain-hormone) development in the growing baby. As our human brains are not fully developed for several years, this new finding provides scientific support for prolonged breastfeeding.

Optimising the ecstasy

A labouring woman needs to feel private, safe, and undisturbed so that she can enter the altered state of consciousness that will ensure a smooth and safe orchestration of her ecstatic birth hormones. Ideal conditions for birth are similar to those of lovemaking or meditation but any place can, with forethought (and a lot of cushions and fabric), be converted to a comfortable birth nest.

Ecstatic birth is also more likely when the chosen carer has an understanding of these basic needs, and will respect the woman's choices. This implies an established and trusting relationship, and one-on-one care with a holistically minded carer during pregnancy, labour and birth. A midwife is the ideal person to give such high quality and personalised care.

Making choices that enhance our chances of ecstasy will, as described, increase safety and ease in birthing. Such choices also optimise our transition to motherhood, because they enhance the release of our mothering hormones.

Our babies also benefit, experiencing a more gentle and safe transition from womb to world, as well as the full processes of labour and birth, which are important in switching on their own bodily and hormonal functions.

Birth is ultimately mysterious and unpredictable yet, like our female bodies, intrinsically trustworthy. The outcome of birth cannot be guaranteed in any situation, but "birth is", as they say, "as safe as life gets". And just as we trust our lungs to take the next breath, and our heart to keep pumping, so can we trust our instincts, our bodies and our babies in birth.

A previous version of this article was published in Wellbeing *magazine, February 2005. This version updated March 2005. More details and all references can be found in chapter 13, "Undisturbed Birth".*

Instinctive Birth ~ vision and tools

instinct [*instinkt*] *n* congenital and unreasoned tendency to specified reactions, behaviour etc.; elaborate pattern of actions occurring as a whole in response to stimuli; natural, unreasoned impulse or response.

instinctive [*instinktiv*] *adj* promoted by instinct; involuntary.[1]

A VISION of Birth came to me in the months after I gave birth to Zoe, my second baby. As I meditated on the challenges that I had encountered during my labour, I began to see my experience, and Birth herself, as a huge multi-faceted crystal. I saw that the different aspects of Zoe's birth, like facets of a crystal, would not add up to one clear picture but would reflect at many different angles.

For me, each of these exquisite facets was worthy of many months of meditation, or alternatively I could stand back and appreciate the beauty and wholeness of Birth, and of my own experience. I also saw that, to paraphrase poet Walt Whitman, "Birth can contradict herself because she is vast, she contains multitudes", and that I could not expect rationality or even consistency as I worked to integrate my experience.

This vision comes back to me when I think about some of the more complex and controversial aspects of birth. I see all of us, with our unique experiences, beliefs, and skills, as different parts

– facets if you like – of this birth crystal. Although we may not share the same angle on birth, our differences are necessary and our dialogues essential.

Birth as an instinctive act

When I think of instinctive birth, I imagine myself as occupying one or more facets of this birth crystal. From my perspective as a GP (family physician) and writer on gentle and undisturbed birth, I can say that birth is essentially an instinctive act; that is, "...an elaborate pattern of actions occurring as a whole in response to stimuli..."[1]

As a physician I know that important hormones, such as oxytocin, the hormone of love; endorphins, hormones of pleasure and transcendence; adrenaline/noradrenaline (epinephrine/norepinephrine), hormones of excitement; and prolactin, the mothering hormone, are all naturally produced and mediate the "elaborate pattern of actions" of birth and of instinctive mothering behaviour in humans, as well as in our mammalian cousins.

Like other mammals, human mothers, too, need a safe and private space so that our labour and birth instincts can unfold with ease. Sometimes I imagine how difficult it would be for a pregnant cat or ape to give birth in a large, brightly lit room, surrounded by strangers, as most labouring women do today. The excellent outcomes at Michel Odent's clinic in Pithiviers, France, where women gave birth in quiet, semi-dark, and private conditions highlight the importance of an undisturbed environment.[2] In these circumstances, a labouring woman can let down her guard, switching off her higher brain and opening to the "unreasoned impulse" of her instincts.

But if I look from another angle, I could also ask, "Is birth any less instinctive than, for example, eating or making love?" We are all hard wired to perform these enjoyable activities but our hard wiring does not guarantee easy digestion, ecstatic sex, or instinctive birth. And there are many women who have had ideal environments – at home with loving support, for example – who have still encountered difficulty and needed assistance in birth. (This may also reflect our negative cultural beliefs and our lack of exposure to normal birth, over several generations.) So even as I state from one perspective that birth is instinctive, I find contradictions.

Helping our instincts

I can imagine myself in a dialogue with my friend Wintergreen, body worker and developer of *The Pink Kit*,[3] who has another valuable perspective. Wintergreen would tell me that birth may be an instinct, like sex, but we can learn to give birth just as we can learn to be good lovers.

She would agree that it is important to look at the external circumstances of birth, but she would also say that we can influence our internal circumstances by learning to work with our birthing bodies. She might mention the importance of the internal work of *The Pink Kit* – a multimedia kit that takes us into our own body knowledge, teaching us to map and work with our anatomy, to massage ourselves internally in preparation for birth, and to feel inside our own vaginas during late pregnancy and labour.

These tools are invaluable, helping us to be in touch with our own bodies – which, even in birth, may be seen as the province of professionals – and assisting us to birth instinctively in whatever birth setting we choose.

I see that there are other levels to be cleared in order to be able to birth instinctively. This facet of birth – which I could ascribe to my friend, director of the International College of Spiritual Midwifery Shivam Rachana,[4] and which has been validated through many women's experiences – looks at our past experiences and beliefs, all of which are stored in our bodies, and concentrates on freeing us up emotionally, physically, and spiritually for birth.

Here we can use movement, counselling/psychotherapy, re-birthing, bodywork, yoga, and other therapies in order to clear out all the emotional and psychological issues that can arise for us in labour and birth. For example, counselling/psychotherapy was my ally when giving birth to my first baby, Emma; and the Osho meditation CD, *Chakra Breathing*, which combines breath and movement, was superb preparation for my subsequent births. Clearing out was a very powerful facet for me with Zoe's birth and I realised, in retrospect, how much my own childhood experience of being displaced by the birth of my younger sister had affected this birthing.

Connecting with the Earth

We are also creatures of the Earth and our bodies need the Earth's nourishment to work efficiently in any instinctive behaviour. Good nutrition is a very important aspect of instinctive birth, as any animal breeder will affirm.

Australian naturopath and author Francesca Naish ascribes much of our modern difficulties in labour and birth to poor nutrition, and it is certainly true that our modern western diets are generally not wholesome or replete with all the nutrients that our bodies and our babies need. Her books, co-written with Janette Roberts, including *The Natural Way to Better Babies*;[5] *The Natural Way to Better Birth and Bonding*;[6] and in the US, *Healthy Parents, Better Babies*,[7] contain valuable information to help us enhance our birth experience, and the long-term health of our babies, through optimal nutrition.

There are also deeper levels to our connection with the Earth. For some women, pregnancy brings an urge to garden or to go walking, to hike or just to gaze at the scenery of earth and sky. All of these activities help align us with the Earth, our great mother, and teach us respect and love for the natural order.

If we want to birth instinctively, we can prepare ourselves by beginning to live more instinctively. We can, for example, make an effort to live less by the clock, which UK birth activist Sheila Kitzinger calls "…an unevaluated technological intervention that has major impact on the conduct of birth."[8] When we live without a clock – or simply stop wearing a watch – we can more easily tune into our own instinctive and earth-based rhythms, which are much gentler on mothers and babies.

Spiritual beliefs and practices are another important facet of pregnancy and birth. In a practical sense, having faith helps us to believe in our bodies and in birth, and prayer is a beautiful way to prepare for birth and motherhood. Belief systems that venerate the feminine as well as the masculine principle have a special place in my heart as I see, from a spiritual perspective, that much damage can been done to women when religions fail to honour the female body and feminine authority. Through the ages we have also had our birthing goddesses and saints, from Artemis to Mary (who gave birth unassisted and surrounded by mammals), to remind us that birth is a natural and instinctive act for all women.

Using our bodies

What about the ways we use our bodies? Can we really birth instinctively if we cannot use our bodies freely? If we cannot squat; if our back muscles are weak from too much sitting; and if our babies are not optimally positioned because of our lifestyle and the ways we habitually misuse our bodies – can we then expect birth to be smooth and instinctive?

Physical preparation is a vital and important facet of preparing for instinctive birth, helping us to open to the "specified reactions" of our instincts through, for example, different postures and positions. Janet Balaskas' *Active Birth* exercises,[9] optimal fetal positioning,[10] *The Pink Kit* and/or prenatal yoga, for example, are excellent tools for this. These forms of birth preparation have similarities to bodywork; when we stretch our bodies, we are also stretching our internal beliefs and feelings, because our bodies and our minds are inseparable.

It can be hard, outside the birth room, to realise how deeply we can go into our bodies during birth. For me this was one of the most powerful realisations after I gave birth to my first baby, Emma, and I was very thankful for my yoga practice, which had so beautifully taught me to "yoke" (as the word yoga translates) my body and mind.

Treating our bodies gently in all that we do, talking kindly to our bodies, and navigating, as best we can, the negative attitudes about women's bodies that are so common in our culture – these simple practices will help us to keep faith in our ability to give birth instinctively, sustaining us in pregnancy and during the challenging times of labour.

Going within

During pregnancy we are called to go deeper into our minds, our bodies, and our spirits than ever before. We may find that memories, attitudes, and experiences that were previously outside our awareness will surface. This can be confusing and challenging. Fortunately, these will usually arise gradually during pregnancy, giving us the time we need to contemplate, digest, and process. Taking time for our internal work during pregnancy is important, as it will leave us much clearer for labour and birth.

This internal work can be as simple as writing in a journal, creating time for reflection about our emotional states. Dreams can also be an invaluable resource for our inner life, and our pregnancy dreams may be especially vivid and accurate. I recommend writing down and reflecting on any memorable dreams; you can even elaborate on them with fantasy (making up a story, or "dreaming on" further with the dream) or draw, paint, or sculpture them. A Jungian perspective is to take each dream element, from animate to inanimate objects, and ponder what aspect of your self is represented by each element.

As well as our solitary internal work, we may also need to check in regularly with our partner, if appropriate, to keep in tune and in harmony. A partner can give us valuable support and feedback – and sometimes a very useful reality-check! A close friend, therapist, or midwife can offer similar support or, if we are so lucky, a circle (or workshop) with friends or wise women can give us the space to share and experience our deepest feelings. For example, Rachana and her Women's Mysteries workshops (Melbourne, Australia)[11] provide superb support for exploring the inner work of pregnancy.

I also used artwork in my pregnancy with Zoe, filling five books with huge pastel mandalas (drawings based on a circle). These are now a wonderful record and Zoe can see the pictures that I drew of her in my belly, which are a more personal – and more colourful – record that a photo from an ultrasound scan. It is amazing to compare the drawings I made of my four babies and to see how my simple pictures were often accurate reflections of their nature and development. For example, I found myself drawing

Maia with an elaborate heart early in pregnancy, around the time when her physical heart was developing.

You can read more about this approach in the wonderful book *Birthing from Within,*[12] and there are also some beautiful and inspiring pregnancy journals available. I suggest that you avoid books with factual accounts of your body and baby, and see how it feels to explore, and learn to rely on, your own inner knowing.

Instinct and energy

There are many wise women (and men) who have observed that our relationships with our loved ones are potent factors, and facets, at birth. Ina May Gaskin, for example, believes, "If a woman doesn't look like a Goddess in birth, someone isn't treating her right." Her book, *Spiritual Midwifery,*[13] has many stories about midwives acting to change the birth energy, often between the baby's mother and father, to help the birth process.

Another of Ina May's insights, in terms of birthing energy, is that the energy that got the baby in can help to get the baby out. We can use her wisdom and allow ourselves free expression of emotion, especially loving and sexual feelings, with our partners in labour, if it feels right. As I describe in chapters 2 and 13, "Ecstatic Birth" and "Undisturbed Birth", giving birth and making love both involve the release of large quantities of oxytocin, the hormone of love, and this hormone (and the feel-good things we can do to release it) can certainly pick up a slow or stuck labour.

The other major relationship that can affect birth energy, and our ability to birth instinctively, is the relationship between mothers and daughters, especially if the mother is present at the birth. I have heard women say that they could not give birth until their mother had left the room – and there are others for whom the opposite is true.

Finally, in her book, *Prenatal Yoga and Natural Childbirth,*[14] Jeannine Parvati Baker advises us to choose our helpers carefully because giving birth will not be easy, she believes, unless every person present in the birth room has faith in the ability of the birthing woman.

Trusting our instincts

I experienced another powerful facet of instinctive birth through birthing my fourth baby unassisted, and this is a perspective that I see reflected in many stories of unassisted or free birth. During my labour with Maia, I had an exquisite awareness of her body inside me and of exactly where I was in labour. For me, this was clearly because I had no observers or assistants, and because I trusted my own instincts and body knowledge. Many other women have similar stories about following their instincts and intuition when there was no help available. For example, Laura Shanley's pregnancy dream told her how to birth her footling breech without assistance;[15] and Leilah McCracken's son was stuck at his shoulders for several minutes, but then was born easily with one enormous contraction.[16]

Conversely, women have told me, many years later, that they wish they had acted on their instincts in pregnancy and birth, instead of going along with expert opinion. I conclude that, just as we have been naturally selected for our physical ability to birth, we – and all our foremothers – have been selected for our accurate instincts and intuition in birth.

This makes birth as safe as possible, and also tells us, as carers, that we should listen carefully to women's gut feelings in pregnancy, labour, and birth. This intuitive aspect of birth is easily clouded, especially when we are conditioned to favour information from the outside – medical and technological tests – over our own internal knowledge.

We are also more able to respond to our body's instincts when we fully inhabit our bodies. This can be challenging in our overly intellectual culture; however, the simple realisation that these intuitive capacities exist can bring a huge awakening in our instincts and intuition.

The dance of birth

Birth is also an instinctive act for all mammalian babies. In other words, our babies know how to get themselves born. This is true for babies in all positions, whose active participation in the birth process is amazing to witness. For example, in *Breech Birth Woman Wise*[17] New Zealand midwife and author Maggie Banks includes photos of a breech baby, born to the waist, making cycling movements between his mother's contractions, which bring him down steadily and easily.

My third baby, Jacob, at age two, showed me how he pushed with his legs to "...born myself [in the] water." Some people have called this "the dance of birth", and it reminds us that there are two partners, both instinctively primed for birth, and both moving together in this most exquisite of dances.

We can bear in mind that "birth is as safe as life gets" and there is nothing, whether total instinct or total reliance upon technology, that can guarantee a perfect outcome, a perfect dance, for every mother and baby. Tragedy and grief are also major facets of birth, as we know intuitively. We acknowledge this with our birth rituals, which, like those of all cultures, are designed to contain our natural and appropriate fear of these extraordinary and supernatural processes.

Finally...

Birth is vast and multi-faceted, radiant and mysterious. Birth contains multitudes, and through her we birth our multitudes. We give birth to our hopes and fears, to our ecstasies and our agonies, to our joy and our disappointments. We give birth to our babies, each one perfect and radiant. We give birth through our instincts and we give birth to our instincts. We give birth to our capacity for instinct, which will match us perfectly with our babies who are, and always will be, instinctive creatures.

May we all be blessed through instinctive birth.

A previous version of this article was published as 'A Vision of Birth' in Midwifery Today, *number 68, winter 2003. This version updated March 2005.*

References

1. Garmonsway G. *The Penguin English Dictionary*. 2nd edn. Middlesex: Penguin, 1969, p 390.
2. Odent M. *Birth Reborn*. 2nd edn. London: Souvenir Press, 1994.

3. Common Knowledge Trust. *The Pink Kit; Essential preparations for your birthing body*. Nelson New Zealand: Common Knowledge Trust, 2001.

4. International College of Spiritual Midwifery. Melbourne: www.womenofspirit.asn.au.

5. Naish F, Roberts J. *The Natural Way to Better Babies: Preconception Health Care for Prospective Parents*. Sydney: Random House, 1996.

6. Naish F, Roberts J. *The Natural Way to Better Birth and Bonding*. Sydney: Doubleday, 2000.

7. Naish F, Roberts J. *Healthy Parents, Better Babies: A Couple's Guide to Natural Preconception*. Freedom CA: The Crossing Press, 1990.

8. Kitzinger S. Sheila Kitzinger's letter from Europe: the clock, the bed, the chair, the pool. *Birth* 2003; 30(1):54–6.

9. Balaskas J. *Active Birth: The new approach to giving birth naturally*. Revised edn. Boston: The Harvard Common Press, 1992.

10. Sutton J, Scott P. *Optimal Foetal Positioning*. Tauranga New Zealand: BirthConcepts, 1996.

11. Women's Mysteries 5 day workshops. www.humantransformation.com.au/

12. England P, Horowitz R. *Birthing From Within: An extraordinary guide to childbirth preparation*. Albuquerque NM: Partera Press, 1998.

13. Gaskin IM. *Spiritual Midwifery*. 4th edn. Summertown TN: The Book Publishing Co, 2002.

14. Baker JP. *Prenatal Yoga and Natural Childbirth*. 3rd edn. Berkley: North Atlantic Books, 2001, p 90.

15. Shanley LK. *Unassisted Childbirth*. Westport CT: Bergin & Garvey, 1994.

16. McCracken L. *Resexualizing Childbirth*. Coquitlam BC: Birthlove, 2000.

17. Banks M. *Breech Birth, Woman Wise*. Hamilton New Zealand: Birthspirit Books, 1998.

Healing Birth,
Healing the Earth

BIRTH, she is dying.
This primal and unspeakably powerful initiation, the only road to motherhood for our ancestors, has been stripped of her dignity and purpose in our times. Birth has become a dangerous medical disease to be treated with escalating levels, and types, of technological interventions.

What is worse perhaps is that the ecstasy of Birth – her capacity to take us outside (*ec*) our usual state (*stasis*) – has been forgotten, and we are entering the sacred domain of motherhood post-operatively, even post-traumatically, rather than transformationally.

These deviations from the natural order, whose lore is genetically encoded in our bodies, have enormous repercussions.

We live in a society where new mothers experience unprecedented levels of distress and depression, and where our babies, with their colic, reflux, and sleep problems, are also having their distress medically treated. We live in a society where depression and anxiety are among the largest burdens of disease worldwide, according to the World Health Organization, and children as young as four are being diagnosed with these conditions; and where young people, at the prime of their lives, are choosing in large numbers to opt out of reality, with mind-altering drugs, or to opt out permanently through suicide.

More than this – we have set ourselves as a species on the road to self-destruction through our despoiling of our collective mother, the Earth. The havoc that we wreak through waste and greed has many parallels with our treatment of mothers and babies, and of our primal environment – our mother's womb.

And just as we have pitted ourselves against the Earth, forgetting that we are interdependent, so too have we begun to pit the rights of the baby against the rights of the mother; imagining a separation, a competition that does not and cannot exist.

The wounds of Birth and of the Earth are severe but, as the Goddess Hygieia tells us, "The wound reveals the cure".[1] My belief is that we are suffering in birth from lack of passion; of love; of surrender; and from a misunderstanding of our own power, and I believe that these qualities can provide us with a way of healing birth and, at the same time, healing the Earth.

Passion

We all began our lives in a passionate act. Our human bodies crave the intensity and pleasure that sex brings and many cultures have recognised the capacity for healing that is inherent in the sexual act. Why is sex so powerful? As well as giving us the potential to create new life – the ultimate power – sex involves peak experiences, and peak hormone levels – of love, pleasure, excitement, and tenderness. These hormones (our bodies' chemical messengers) and their actions are exactly the same as those of birth.

In other words – giving birth is, inherently and hormonally, a passionate and sexual act. From the perspective of hormone levels in both mother and baby, we could say that birth is the most passionate experience that we will ever have.

Oxytocin, the hormone of love, builds up during labour, reaching peak levels at the moment of birth and creating loving, altruistic feelings between mother and baby. Endorphins, hormones of pleasure and transcendence, also peak at birth, as well as the fight-or-flight hormones adrenaline and noradrenaline (epinephrine and norepinephrine). These fight-or-flight hormones protect the baby from lack of oxygen in the final stages of birth and ensure that mother and baby are both wide-eyed and excited at first contact. Prolactin, the mothering hormone, helps us to surrender to our babies, giving us the most tender of maternal feelings as our reward.

But these passionate hormones are not just feel-good add-ons. They actually orchestrate the physical processes of birth (and sexual activity) and enhance efficiency, safety and ease for both mother and baby. This hormonal cocktail also rewards birthing mothers with the experience of ecstasy and fulfilment, making us want to give birth again and again. All mammals share virtually the same hormonal crescendo at birth, and this is a necessary pre-requisite for mothering in most species, switching on instinctive maternal behaviour.

Birthing passionately does not necessarily mean birthing painlessly (although this may happen for some women). Giving birth is a huge event, emotionally and physically, and will make demands on the body equivalent to, for example, running a marathon. But when a woman feels confident in her body, well supported, and able to express herself without inhibition, the pain that she may feel can become easily bearable, and just one part of the process. She can then respond instinctively with her own resources, including her most basic and accessible tools: breath, sound, and movement.

The problem in our times is that the passion of birth is neither recognised nor accommodated. Birth has become a dispassionate medical event, usually occurring in a setting that discourages emotional expression. If we are to reclaim our birthing passion, we must give ourselves permission to birth passionately and we must choose our birth setting and birth attendants with this in mind. Birth in these circumstances will be more straightforward, with less need for interventions, helping us to step into new motherhood with confidence and grace.

Passion, to my mind, is an opposite and an antidote for despair and depression. This is clear physiologically and hormonally. If we gave birth, and were born, in passion, how different would our primal emotional imprint be? And what about our brain chemistry, which is being set even as we are born? Some studies have linked exposure to drugs and medical procedures at birth with an increased risk of drug addiction, suicide, and anti-social behaviour in later life, and other commentators have suggested that contemporary problems such as learning disorders and ADHD may also be linked to drugs and interventions at birth.

As a birthing mother I have both witnessed and experienced the enormous passion that can be unleashed at birth, and that can fuel both passionate motherhood and a lifetime's work on behalf of mothers, babies and the Earth, and I ask: "Can we afford, as a species, to be born, and to give birth dispassionately?"

Love

Passion and love are as powerful a combination at birth as they are in sexual activity. And in birth, as in sex, we release oxytocin, the hormone of love, in huge quantities. Here again, our hormones are directing us toward optimal and ecstatic experiences, yet this system is also extremely vulnerable to interference.

For example, a labouring woman's production of oxytocin is drastically reduced by the use of epidural pain relief – this is the reason why epidurals prolong labour. And even when an epidural has worn off, her oxytocin peak, which causes the powerful final contractions that are designed to birth her baby quickly and easily, will still be significantly lessened and she is more likely to have her baby pulled out with forceps as a result.

The drug Syntocinon (Pitocin), which has been called the most abused drug in obstetrics, is also implicated. It is a synthetic form of the hormone oxytocin, and is used for induction and for augmentation (or acceleration) of labour. Large numbers of women giving birth in developed countries receive large doses of this drug in labour for one of these reasons. For example, in Australia this figure approaches 50 percent.

When a labouring woman has Syntocinon administered by drip, for induction or augmentation, her body's oxytocin receptors may lose their sensitivity and ability to respond to this hormone. We know that women in this situation are vulnerable to haemorrhage after birth, and even more Syntocinon becomes necessary to counter that risk.

We do not know, however, what the long-tern consequences of interference with the oxytocin system may be for mothers and babies, and for their ongoing relationship.

I had a very powerful experience of oxytocin as the hormone of love while labouring with my fourth baby, Maia Rose. As the waves of labour strengthened I found myself looking into the eyes of my beloved, telling him "I love you, I love you, I love you…" as each wave of labour washed over me. This ecstatic experience has created more love in my heart, in our relationship, and in our family, and has taught me, in a very physical way, that giving birth is also making love. (See "Maia's Birth", chapter 8.)

Surrender

Surrender is not a popular virtue in the West. In fact, surrender is often seen as a weakness in our culture, where we are instead encouraged to be active and in control of our lives. This very yang, masculine attitude may serve us in some circumstances but we cannot birth our babies through sheer force of will. We need to learn the more subtle – yet equally powerful – path of surrender.

I sense that, for modern women, difficulty with surrender can reflect a lack of confidence in our female bodies. This is not surprising when our society is distrustful of the natural order in general, and women's bodies in particular. This view is further reinforced by the obstetric model, with its long lists of all that can possibly go wrong with our birthing bodies, and its myriad of technological fixes, designed to rescue us from these exaggerated dangers.

Along with this forgetting of the awesome but natural power of our female bodies, we have also lost our birthing patronesses: the goddesses and saints who have, for millennia, guided women through this transition, where the veil between life and death is at its thinnest. Today guidance is available to us, when and if we need it, in the living form of a midwife: a woman who has pledged to be with (*mid*) women (*wif*) in birth. A good midwife can remind us by her presence that we genetically carry the birthing successes of all our foremothers and that we already know how to give birth.

As midwife and author Jeannine Parvati Baker reminds us, giving birth is women's spiritual practice, requiring "…purity in strength, flexibility, health, concentration, surrender and faith."[2] It has also been said that to be consciously present at birth is equivalent to seven years of meditation. When we birth consciously, putting our great rational mind on hold, and allowing our instinctive nature to dominate, we can access the wisdom that all spiritual traditions teach: that the ego is our servant, not our mistress, and that our path to ecstasy and enlightenment involves surrendering our egoistic notions of control. This level of surrender will also serve us well through our many years of motherhood.

When we surrender conscious control, we also allow our deeper innate rhythms to surface: this can be a profound experience for a birthing woman. In allowing her labour to go at its own pace, without hurry or interference, a woman learns to trust her own, and her baby's, natural rhythms. Such trust is another gift; another way that Mother Nature ensures optimal mothering and maximum survival for our young.

In surrendering to birth, we also learn about our role on the Earth: we are neither the rulers nor the architects of creation. Life comes through us, simply and gracefully, when we allow it.

Power

It is easy to say that our problems in birth stem from the excessive power of the medical system and its agents, and a lack of power for the birthing woman. However, a deeper analysis is necessary, I believe, because the time has come to dispel this idea of a power imbalance and to assert our innate authority in birthing.

We live in a culture that prizes, and puts its faith in, technology. We reward those, such as doctors, who are masters of technology and indeed we are fortunate to have their skills available to us when we need them. And even though we may want less technology in birth, we are witnessing more and more litigation against obstetricians, almost all of which blames them for not using enough technology.

Along with technology, we also prize information. In pregnancy and birth, becoming informed is equated with being responsible, both of which are strongly encouraged culturally; yet there is also a price to pay. We may have all of the information in the world, but we cannot predict our experiences in birth. And we diminish our own authority in birthing and in mothering – we disempower ourselves – when we put more faith in information from the outside (tests, scans, others' opinions) than our own internal knowing of our bodies and our babies.

The truth is that our babies are constantly informing us of their needs and desires, and how we can best care for them. This is a physiological reality – the baby's placenta is in constant communication with our bodies, transferring blood and nutrients and generating the placental hormones, which organise our bodies and our psyches for the optimal and specific mothering that this baby requires. In the same way, our cravings, yearnings, dreams, and inclinations in pregnancy can be communications from our babies, showing us the deeper ways of knowing that are richer and more true, even if less numerical or detailed, than information from the outside, such as medical tests.

In fact, from the very beginning, when we first suspect that we are creating new life in our womb, we can use this ancient system and allow our bodies, rather than a pregnancy test, to inform us. Often the truth will unfold gradually, allowing us the space to learn and adapt at our own pace, and giving us opportunities for reflection and dreaming.

When we choose this traditional women's path, the path of all our foremothers, we can both discover and reinforce an inalienable trust and power in ourselves and in our female bodies. This deep faith is the best preparation possible for birth and is also, to my mind, the basis of true responsibility; we are able to respond with our own truth. We also become able to use the medical system, if we choose, without giving away our power.

Beyond this, when we tap into women's ways of knowing we can open channels of communication with our babies, enhancing the psychic powers of communication that Mother Nature intends for mothers of all species. Mothering can become a meditation, a deep mindfulness that is satisfying spiritually as well as physically and emotionally. I believe that this is nature's intent and a possibility for all of us.

How would it be to live in a society where we are all, through giving birth or being born, in possession of our own power and our own deep knowing? Where science and technology are our tools, rather than our masters? How differently would we treat our babies? How differently would we treat each other? How differently would we treat the Earth?

Birth is dying, but, like cells in her body, we each have the power to enliven her and to resurrect her in all her glory. What is needed, I believe, is the collective passion, love, surrender, and power that we pour into the ether as we birth our babies.

And in healing Birth, we are healing ourselves, our babies and the Earth.

A previous version of this article was published in Living Now, *winter 2002, supplement* Women Now. *This version updated March 2005.*

References

1. Baker JP. Hygieia College Mystery School. www.birthkeeper.com
2. Baker JP. *Prenatal Yoga and Natural Childbirth.* 3rd edn. Berkeley CA: North Atlantic Books, 2001.

Lotus Birth ~ a ritual for our times

Lotus birth is the practice of leaving the umbilical cord uncut, so that the baby remains attached to his or her placenta until the cord naturally separates at the umbilicus, exactly as a cut cord does, at three to ten days after birth. This prolonged contact can be seen as a time of transition, allowing the baby to slowly and gently release their attachment to the mother's body.

Although we have no written records of cultures that leave the cord uncut, many traditional peoples hold the placenta in high esteem. For example, Maori people from New Zealand bury the placenta ritually on the ancestral *marae* (meeting place) and the Hmong, a hill tribe from South East Asia, believe that the placenta must be retrieved after death to ensure physical integrity in the next life. A Hmong baby's placenta is buried inside the house of birth.

Lotus birth is a new ritual, having only been described in chimpanzees before 1974 when Clair Lotus Day, pregnant and living in California, began to question the routine cutting of the cord. Her searching led her to an obstetrician who was sympathetic to her wishes and her son Trimurti was born in hospital and taken home with his cord uncut. Lotus birth was named by, and seeded through, Clair to Jeannine Parvati Baker in the US and Shivam

Rachana in Australia, who have both been strong advocates for this gentle practice.

Since 1974, many babies have been born this way, including babies born at home and in hospital, on land and in water, and even by caesarean section. Lotus birth is a beautiful and logical extension of natural childbirth, and invites us to reclaim the so-called third stage of labour for our babies and ourselves, and to honour the placenta, our babies' first source of nourishment.

I was drawn to lotus birth during my second pregnancy through contact with Shivam Rachana, the director of the International College of Spiritual Midwifery[1] near Melbourne, and have experienced lotus birth with my second and subsequent children. Lotus birth made sense to me as I remembered my experiences in hospital obstetrics, and the strange and uncomfortable sensation of cutting through the gristly, fleshy cord that connects baby to placenta and mother. Cutting a cord was, for me, like cutting through a boneless toe, and it felt good to avoid this with my coming baby.

Through the Rachana I spoke with women who had chosen lotus birth for their babies, and experienced a beautiful postnatal time. Some women also described their lotus-born children's self-possession and completeness. Others described it as a challenge, practically and emotionally. Nicholas, my partner, was concerned that it might interfere with the magic of those early days but agreed to go along with my wishes.

Zoe, our second child, was born at home on 10 September 1993. Her placenta was, unusually, an oval shape, which was perfect for the red velvet placenta bag that I had sewn. Soon after the birth, we wrapped her placenta in a cloth nappy, then in the placenta bag, and bundled it up with her in a shawl that enveloped both of them. Every 24 hours, we attended to the placenta by patting it dry, coating it liberally with salt, and dropping a little lavender oil onto it. Emma, aged two, was keen to be involved in the care of her sister's placenta.

As the days passed, Zoe's cord dried from the umbilical end, and became thin and brittle. It developed a convenient 90-degree kink where it threaded through her clothes and so did not rub or irritate her. The placenta also dried and shrivelled due to our salt treatment, developing a meaty smell that interested our cat!

Zoe's cord separated on the sixth day without any fuss. Other babies have cried inconsolably or held their cord tightly before separation. We planted her placenta under a mandarin tree on her first birthday, which our dear friend and neighbour Annie later dug up and put in a pot in her yard when we moved interstate. She told us later that the mandarins from the tree were the sweetest she had ever tasted.

Our third child, Jacob Patrick, was born at home on 25 September 1995, into water (see chapter 6). Jacob and I stayed in the water for some time after the birth, so we floated his placenta in a plastic ice-cream tub (with the lid on, and a corner cut out for the cord) while I nursed him. This time, we put his placenta in a sieve to drain for the first day. I neither dressed nor carried Jacob at this time, but stayed physically in touch with him in a still space while Nicholas cared for Emma (four) and Zoe (two). His cord separated in just under four days, and I felt that he drank deeply of the still-ness of that time.

His short "breaking forth" time was perfect, because my parents arrived from New Zealand the following day to help with our household. Jacob later chose a Jacaranda tree under which to bury his placenta at our new home in Queensland.

My fourth baby, Maia Rose, was born in Brisbane, where lotus birth is still very new, on 26 July 2000. We had a beautiful do-it-yourself birth at home (see chapter 8), and my intuition told me that her breaking forth time would be short. I decided not to treat her placenta at all, but kept it in a sieve over a bowl in the daytime and in our red velvet placenta bag at night.

Maia's cord separated in just under three days and, although it was a cool time of year, it did become friable and rather smelly. (Salt treatment would have prevented this.) Her placenta has been buried in our garden, with a rose bush planted on top. I broke off a piece of her dried cord, which had some amazing and beautiful twists, to keep for her.

My older children have blessed me with stories of their experiences in pregnancy and birth, and have been unanimously in favour of not cutting the cord, especially Emma, who remembered the unpleasant feeling of having her cord cut (after it had stopped pulsating), which she describes as being "painful in my heart". Zoe, at five years of age, described being attached to a "love-heart thing" in my womb and told me "When I was born, the cord went off the love-heart thing and onto there [her placenta] and then I came out." Perhaps she remembers her placenta in utero as the source of nourishment and love.

Lotus birth has been, for us, an exquisite ritual that has enhanced the magic of the early postnatal days. I notice an integrity and self-possession with my lotus-born children, and I believe that lovingness, cohesion, attunement to Mother Nature, and trust and respect for the natural order have all been imprinted on our family by our honouring of the placenta, the Tree of Life.

A previous version of this article was published in Lotus Birth *(Rachana S (Ed), Yarra Glen, Australia: Greenwood Press, 2000). This version updated March 2005.*

References

1. Rachana S. International College of Spiritual Midwifery. www.womenofspirit.asn.au/lotus.html

Jacob's Waterbirth ~
a gentle start

WATER – it's the first medium of life, and where we all began. When we are pregnant, our bodies are the pool in which our babies float; perhaps this is why water holds a particular attraction for women in pregnancy, labour, and birth.

There are stories of babies being born into water from all over the globe, and recorded as far back as ancient Egyptian times. However, it is only with the advent of modern plumbing that warm water has become an accessible resource for modern women during labour and birth.

Waterbirth as we know it was pioneered by Russian Igor Tcharkovsky in the 1960s, and developed by Michel Odent in his natural birth clinic in Pithiviers, France, from 1977. Odent noticed how helpful water could be, especially when labour was slow or painful, and that women using the birthing pools had little need for pain relieving drugs. At first, births that took place in the water were unplanned, but Odent trusted the labouring mother's instincts and soon accumulated an experience and understanding of waterbirth that is still unparalleled.[1]

Janet Balaskas, the founder of the Active Birth movement, was also very influential in promoting waterbirth,[2] and her 1992 video "Water and Birth" remains a classic. The first waterborn baby in

Australia was born in a converted concrete pipe that was lifted by crane into a home in South Melbourne in 1983.

Since then, the use of water in labour has become more widespread, with purpose-built tubs being used in many hospitals in the UK, parts of Europe, North America, and New Zealand. In Australia there is still much fear and conservatism around the use of water; tubs are available in some hospitals but hospital policy may not permit their full use, and women may be asked to get out when their baby's birth is imminent.

Some of this reluctance is due to hospital staff's lack of experience and expertise in this area. There has also been a worldwide lack of research on the effects of water on mother and baby. However, the First International Water Birth Conference, held in the UK in 1995, heard experiences and evidence from over 19,000 underwater births, with participants reporting excellent safety and satisfaction outcomes.

In particular, no baby had drowned or aspirated water after a carefully supervised waterbirth, and there was no increased risk of infection for mother or baby. Waterborn babies were generally in good condition, although it was noted that babies' wellbeing could be compromised if a woman labouring in water became overheated. One recommendation was that pool temperature should be below 35 °C (95 °F) in the first stage of labour, and 35 to 37 °C (95 to 98.5 °F) at the time of birth. The labouring woman's temperature should be checked regularly.[3]

Women often experienced rapid progress after entering the water, especially if they entered the pool when labour was well established. They also had little need for intervention or pain relief; had fewer episiotomies or serious tears; and were more satisfied with their experience than mothers birthing on land.

UK consumer activist and author Beverley Beech points out that the staff who are most opposed to the use of water, because of the theoretical risks, may be the first to suggest other labour interventions such as epidural pain relief and routine electronic monitoring, which have been shown to pose real risks for mothers and babies.

Jacob's birth

I was drawn to water during my first two pregnancies, but only seriously considered using a tub in labour for Jacob's birth – my third at home. I wanted my older children Emma (then four) and Zoe (two) to be present for the labour and birth, along with a good friend to care for them: add in the doctor, the midwife and Nicholas, my partner, and the room was very full. I figured that using a birth pool would allow me some private space, and help me to be less concerned about my surroundings, especially if I laboured in the daytime.

The tub I hired from my midwife had been especially made from hollow metal pipes (actually, car exhaust pipes) that fitted together, with a liner that was laced over the frame. It was quick to set up and not too high so that I could step into the pool relatively easily. We had a practice run to see how many tanks of hot water would be needed to fill it and how long it would take, allowing for time for the hot water tank to reheat (three tanks, and about four hours). During the practice run I managed to cook the waterbed heater that kept the tub warm onto a piece of foam, and I had to buy a new heater! The tub, set up and ready to be filled, kept vigil in our back room as I went one, then two, then three weeks past my original expected date.

Labour started for me at one in the morning and I woke Nicholas to fill the tub around two-thirty. This labour was very slow and gentle from the start and I spent time both in and out of the water. I found that I couldn't sway my hips as well in the tub – at least not without causing a tidal wave – but I certainly relished the water as I rested between contractions. Other women have found that the water gives them an increased mobility that encourages movement. Zoe, who was naked from early on, spent much of early labour trying to get in with me and then contented herself with floating her dollies in the water.

We had the tub in our family room, and Nicholas had thoughtfully grown some beautiful cinerarias in the adjoining garden, which I could see through the window. My task in this labour was to slow down and go with the gentle pace. Getting out and walking

46

around didn't speed labour up for me, as it does for some women after a few hours in the tub.

When the contractions became strong, later in the morning, I found the water soothing and supporting. I had a feeling that this baby would be born in the water but it was important to me that I was not fixed on this idea. I remembered how critical it had been to me to have my feet on the earth, and allow gravity to help me give birth to my second baby Zoe, who was born posterior (face up). In most centres, around two-thirds of women who labour in the water feel the need to get out of the tub to deliver their babies.

At transition, before the urge to push was strong, I felt the reality of this baby; that I would soon be holding him in my arms. I felt a wave of fear followed by a strong connection and commitment. Michel Odent calls this "physiological fear", as this emotion often parallels the release of the fight-or-flight hormones that give us the power to push our babies out in the second stage of labour.[4] As my baby's head came lower, we saw a mass of white in the water; the soft creamy vernix that covered his skin was floating out as I pushed.

I was kneeling, supported by the side of the tub, as he was born. It was around midday. Chris, my midwife, caught him in the water and passed him to me. In contrast to other waterborn babies he cried quickly and vigorously. In the exhilaration of the moment we didn't think to check his sex and we had another wave of joy when we discovered, some minutes later, that we had a son.

I stood up out of the water to deliver the placenta in ease and comfort. Odent advises this, and points out that allowing water to enter the uterus (and placental site after the placenta is birthed) could theoretically be risky.[5] There have been no problems reported worldwide, so far; however, some centres routinely advise women to leave the water after delivery. This may also help the midwife to assess the new mother's blood loss, which can be difficult in a pool.

We chose not to cut the cord (a practice known as lotus birth), and so we floated Jacob's placenta in an ice-cream tub until I was ready to get out, about an hour after the birth. Before this, Emma and Zoe climbed in and said hello to their new brother. After the birth, we siphoned the water onto the garden, which made cleaning up very easy.

Water was a wonderful resource for Jacob's birth, giving me privacy in labour and soothing me in birth. Water immersion in labour is, for many women, an excellent alternative to conventional forms of pain relief.[6] Waterbirth provides a safe, satisfying and gentle start for mother and baby.

A previous version of this article was published in Australia's Parents Pregnancy *magazine, winter 1999. This version updated March 2005.*

References

1. Odent M. *Birth Reborn*. 2nd edn. London: Souvenir Press, 1994.
2. Balaskas J, Gordon Y. *Waterbirth; the concise guide to using water during pregnancy, birth and infancy*. London: Thorsons, 1992.
3. Beech B. *Water Birth Unplugged – Proceedings of the First International Waterbirth Conference*. Cheshire: Books for Midwives Press, 1996.
4. Odent M. The fetus ejection reflex. *The Nature of Birth and Breastfeeding*. Sydney: Ace Graphics, 1992:29–43.
5. Odent M. Birth under water. *Lancet* 1983; 2(8365-66):1476–7.
6. Cluett ER, et al. Immersion in water in pregnancy, labour and birth. *Cochrane Database Syst Rev* 2004(2):CD000111.

Emma's Birth ~
sweet and oceanic

G IVING birth to Emma, my firstborn, was a pivotal experience
in my life. Not only did she initiate me into motherhood; she
also taught me how immense and exciting birth can be, igniting an
enduring passion for birth and mothering.

Emma was conceived in March 1990, a few months after
Nicholas, my beloved, and I were married. This was our exact intention. I was challenged by nausea right through my pregnancy
– in retrospect I think that my busy working life was a major factor
– but it didn't stop me from relishing my pregnancy and the amazing changes that my body was going through. I was also nourished
by my ongoing yoga practice, and I read every book I could find
by Sheila Kitzinger, whose gentle approach to birth was inspiring
and easy to absorb.

We chose to give birth at home, and found a midwife and
doctor to help us without difficulty. I had attended many women
in hospital during my training as a GP (family physician), and
had also been privileged to support two friends giving birth at
home, and I had seen a huge difference in the quality of experience
between hospital and home birth. Also, Nicholas's sister Sue (who
features in the story) was a homebirth midwife, and we were lucky
to be influenced by her wisdom and experiences.

Another major influence for me was my on-going commitment to Jungian psychotherapy, where I had the opportunity to explore, at a deep level, my attitudes towards mothering; my early experiences of being mothered; and my relationship with my own mother. Working with my therapist on these issues during my pregnancy, often through dreams, brought me to a place of ease and helped me to make the transition to motherhood smoothly and gracefully.

I was certain of the time of Emma's conception and knew, without an ultrasound scan, that she was due in early December. In late October we were surprised to discover that our baby was already deeply engaged – her head was very low in my pelvis – and we wondered if we might have an early birth. I finished work in early November, expecting to have a month of resting and nesting... but this was not to be.

The weekend that Emma was born, around four weeks before her due date, Nicholas's sister Sue (the midwife) was staying in Melbourne, where we lived. (She was en route from her home in New Zealand to Hobart, an hour south by plane, where John, their father, was ill with cancer.) On that Sunday morning I was enjoying a leisurely back-yard chat with Sue about birth. She told me that, in her experience, having a lot of support people at the birth could make the labour slower. This was important information; I already had four friends, plus my sister from New Zealand, enlisted as support people, although with the proviso that I might not call them all. Around the same time I began to notice that my usual pattern of mild tightenings was more pronounced, and that I had a little red discharge. In the afternoon, as we drove Sue across town to her friend's place, I timed my contractions – they were regularly ten minutes apart and on arrival I had a more obvious show of blood.

Sue suggested that we abandon our plan for a walk on the beach and have a quiet night instead. Back home I settled myself on the sofa, discovering that whenever I walked about the contractions became stronger. Nicholas cooked me a delicious plate of scrambled eggs and we talked about calling Chris, our midwife. I was reluctant – in denial, really – but eventually it became clear that we needed to talk to her. She came around about ten pm, examined me, and told me I was in early labour. Even though it was obvious to everyone else, I was still shocked to hear this. She advised us to have an early night and call her in the morning, when she expected labour to get going properly.

At ten-thirty Nicholas and I were lying in bed together, coming to terms with this new development. I still had baby clothes to wash and sort, and hadn't put the second coat of paint in the spare room… but here was our baby, eager to come. So, as I lay down on the bed, Nicholas sorted the clothes and we realised that nothing else mattered. Our task was to accept this time, this labour, in the present moment.

With this surrender, labour really began for me. At first I found that moving around during contractions was most helpful; hanging off the wardrobe door felt good too!

I used the clock to help me in early labour, discovering that the most challenging part of my contractions lasted only about half a minute; after this, my body would come down off the wave, and I used my yoga training for deep relaxation in between. At the peak, breathing, and later, sound were my allies. As labour strengthened, I rocked and circled with my pelvis, moaning and moving in synchrony.

It was a sweet and intimate space; the house was dark and quiet and, although I didn't want Nicholas to touch me (I found it too distracting), I felt held by his love and presence. There was an oceanic feeling; I felt like I was riding the waves, challenged but exhilarated as I came down each time. At one point Nicholas had tears in his eyes: "It's hard to see you in so much pain," he said. "I'm fine," I replied, "I get a good break in between, and I can really relax."

After a few hours, I said, "We need to call Chris." Nicholas was reluctant: "We are having such a beautiful time with the two of us…" I agreed, but my instinct was still to call her.

He also called Sue, again rather reluctantly but I was sure that I wanted her. In the half hour or so that it took for Chris to arrive, I began to feel a catch in my throat and a mild urge to push with each wave. Nicholas began to move the furniture around, as we had planned, putting our bed into the lounge, which could be easily heated for the birth.

A little after two in the morning, Chris walked down the corridor and Nicholas said, "She's pushing." Chris turned around and went back out to get her birth equipment! By this time I was on all fours on the bed. I knew that my baby would be born soon, and I held some fears. She was early and little: would it be all right? I still remember the reassurance that I felt as I looked into Chris's eyes: I trusted her and knew that everything would be OK.

The pushing was the least enjoyable part of this labour for me – the rock-hard feeling of her head in my vagina, which I wanted to hold against – but every fibre of my body was pushing and pushing with each wave. Like the ocean, my body's instincts were immense and unstoppable.

My baby's watery sac was bulging and I agreed for Chris to break it. Soon after, she suggested that I roll onto my side, which felt good. I wanted things to be fast and they were. Within a few pushes, her head was born – face-up (posterior) to our surprise. Nicholas took a few amazing photos as her body was born. At the same time, Peter Lucas, our doctor, arrived, which was wonderful timing. It was two-fifty am. Chris caught her and put her on my belly, warm and wet. We discovered her sex straight away: "Oh, Emma!" I said. She was tiny and scrawny, like a little bald rabbit. We covered her – the hat we had was several sizes too big – and I held her tenderly. After five or ten minutes, her cord had stopped pulsating and Chris clamped and cut it. Her placenta came easily, 12 minutes after her birth and just before Sue arrived.

I was elated, amazed, and a bit shocked; it had been so fast and unexpected. We made phone calls a few hours later, waking my mother in New Zealand, who said sleepily: "That's nice dear." When I rang her back later that day, she told us she hadn't believed me! Although small – in fact, at 5 lb 1 oz (2,250 g), the smallest baby that either Chris or Peter had attended at home – Emma was alert and fed well.

In the days that followed we lavished our special care on her, checking her temperature regularly and dutifully recording her feeding and eliminating patterns. Her first pee, 12 or so hours after birth, was especially important as it indicated that she was being well fed from my early milk and didn't need supplementary feeding. Later she became moderately jaundiced and we used home phototherapy – a few minutes in the sun, and sleeping her under the window.

Sue provided wonderful support and breastfeeding help, and Chris or Peter visited us twice daily for a week. Also friends (and the birth supporters whom we hadn't called) brought us meals and did our shopping. Emma and I stayed cocooned at home, venturing tentatively out to the corner store a week later with her snuggled in the front carrier. The shopkeeper said, "I thought you had a doll in there!" Nicholas had two weeks off work, and we had a peaceful and nourishing new-family baby moon.

When Emma was three weeks old my sister Louise arrived as planned (for the birth), giving us lots of help and support. She was luckily staying when Nicholas was suddenly called to be with his dying father, and later helped me to fly over to Tasmania for the funeral. It was a blessing for Betty, Nicholas' mother, to have her newest grandchild in her arms and there was a rightness to it for us too. As we had written in our wedding ceremony, we were "…part of the endless cycle of birth and death which, with its joys and sorrows, involves all of us."

I have many things to be grateful for in Emma's birth. I especially appreciate my carers – midwife extraordinaire Christine Shanahan and the wonderful Dr Peter Lucas – who trusted that, early as we were, birth and baby would still be safe at home. I know, from my training and experiences in hospital obstetrics, how differently we would have fared in hospital.

I am grateful also for the help and support of friends and family, who formed an outer circle which held us at this time. I am thankful too for the synchronicity that put Emma's birth several weeks ahead of Nicholas' father's death, and that gave me my sister's support at that difficult time. Finally, my deepest gratitude goes to Emma herself who, in her soul's wisdom, chose us as her parents and gave us a sweet and oceanic birth that set us joyfully on the path to parenting.

Posted at www.birthlove.com – *This version updated March 2005.*

Maia's Birth ~
a family celebration

Faith in a creative, fulfilling, desired end – sustained faith –
literally draws from the [Universe] all the necessary ingredients, all of the details, and then inserts into [physical life] the
impulses, dreams, chance meetings, motivations or whatever
is necessary so that the desired end falls into place as a completed pattern.[1]

THE night that Maia, my fourth baby, was born, I was cooking
soup for dinner. I leaned over in the pantry for ingredients
and – pop! – floods of clear fluid, and the smell of babies and birth.

Two photos of our family at dinner are the only pictures that
we have from Maia's birth. Each of us wears the expression of
that night's experiences. I look like I am in a state of total bliss.
My beloved, Nicholas, looks proud. Nine-year-old Emma looks
excited; four-year-old Jacob looks uncertain; and six-year-old Zoe
radiates blessings.

Maia's birth was to be witnessed only by the family. I had a
strong feeling from the start that this was what my baby wanted.
Nicholas had not been entirely comfortable with this option; like
myself, he was trained in GP (family physician) obstetrics, and was
very aware of the possible complications and of his responsibilities. However, toward the end of the pregnancy he accepted my
wishes, and we stopped arguing about medical versus alternative

responses. He simply prepared his medical kit – IV fluids and Syntocinon (Pitocin) in case of bleeding – and I prepared my box of homeopathics and herbs for my baby and myself.

Along with the decision to give birth without assistance, I committed myself to being optimally prepared on every level. My body was well nourished and I practised yoga and meditation daily. I had regular massage, osteopathic and cranio-sacral treatments, and later in my pregnancy shiatsu, which revitalised and balanced my body wonderfully. In my daily yoga practice I worked with pain, stretching into tight and painful areas and finding the bliss at the centre. I wondered how it would be in this labour – could I find the ecstasy at the heart of giving birth?

I opted against medical care or tests – even blood pressure tests – in this pregnancy. I trusted my body and my baby to tell me, through feelings, dreams, and impulses, what was needed. Through my meditation I developed a series of affirmations, one for each level of my body, which I used in the last months. In the final weeks, it was only the last affirmation that I needed: I totally surrender and trust.

That night, as my labour deepened, I moved into our bathroom where I had my trusty yoga mat on the floor to protect me from the cold tiles. My expansions (not contractions) were very close together. I couldn't even get back to our adjoining bedroom to read the birth blessings sent to me by my women's circle in Melbourne, or to gaze at the birthing mandalas (pictures based on a circle) which the children had coloured so exquisitely in my pregnancy. No time either for music, dancing, essential oils, or water. As my friend Davini wished for me, this birth was to be "simple and present".

By this time I was standing, moaning and circling my pelvis with each expansion. Then a new space opened up for me, and for the remainder of my labour I was looking into the eyes of my beloved, telling him: "I love you, I love you, I love you, I love you…" peaking and subsiding with each wave.

After an hour or so, I felt a familiar catch in my throat – a feeling that the urge to push was close. "This baby will be born soon," I said. Nicholas filled the tub and woke Emma and Zoe. As he left again to wake Jacob I had a sudden desire for water. I jumped into the bathtub, finding a beautiful position in the triangle of the tub; upright and kneeling with my feet supported on the sides as I pushed.

I felt every centimetre of my baby descending, and I could hold the growing pressure in my vagina without contracting against it. In this way, progress was very quick; two or three pushes, and not even a strong stretching feeling. I said, "I'm crowning." One more push and, "Here's the head." Yet strangely I had no feeling of my push finishing easily at the baby's neck.

We were in candlelight and I was tucked into the darkest corner of the bathtub. Nicholas had a torch ready and he shone it into the water to check the baby. "It's a foot!" he said. I turned, baby still half in my body, and saw a left leg waving in the water. Nicholas leant down – I still don't know how he did it without getting wet – and freed the other leg, which was straight against her belly, held only by the foot.[2]

I asked Nicholas to feel the cord – she was born past her umbilicus by now. "It's not pulsating," he said. We both knew what this meant; our baby would need to be born quickly, as the cord was being compressed between her head and my pelvic bones, cutting off her blood supply. "I'll stand up," was my instinctive response.

Standing with ease, I leaned forward, my hands supporting her slippery little legs and bottom. Without waiting for the next wave, I pushed. Out came her chest, arms spilling out, cord tumbling and tangled, then finally, with one push, her head.

I scooped her up into my arms, to the warmth of my heart. She was like a little bundle of kelp: floppy, blue, and not breathing. (The children said later: "We thought she was a dead baby.") "We love you, baby, we love you!" they cried, calling her in. After 20 or 30 seconds – it seemed longer, but Nicholas was watching her closely – she opened one eye, squeaked, and took a breath, pinking up straight away.

From blue kelp to pink flesh, here was our little breech mermaid, born tail in the water and top out! Emma and Zoe both saw deep blue and pink – her colours – surrounding her at birth, and Jacob saw "Blue, pink, purple, yellow, and orange". Emma had the important job of recording the time of birth – 10:48 pm, 26 July 2000.

Nicholas helped me out of the tub and back to the bedroom and I lay on the bed, skin to naked newborn skin, all of us in the purest bliss. The children were very keen to know her sex but Nicholas and I needed a bit of time to recover, which we did with joyous laughter. After a few minutes, we pulled back the towel to see that our baby was, as we had guessed, our own girl – Maia Rose!

I put her to my breast – her eyes were open now – and she suckled straight away. Zoe went to get our friend Suzanne, who was sleeping over with her two children. She had heard the whole process from the other end of the house, including our laughter, which told her that all was well. She helped with the children and with cleaning up, and prepared us a beautiful plate of fruit, along with the juice that I hadn't had time to drink in labour. I sat up after half an hour or so – it was getting a bit uncomfortable – and squatted to deliver Maia's placenta.

We didn't cut Maia's cord, as we had chosen lotus birth (as we had for Zoe and Jacob) where baby, cord, and placenta remain whole and attached until natural separation. My perineum was totally unscathed – I have been blessed this way with all of my births – and I bled barely at all. My body felt amazing.

"Perfect!" said Nicholas: "An evening birth, then a full night's sleep." Well, almost!

In the days that followed, I was respectful of the enormous opening that my body had been through, and I stayed in bed, in a quiet space, with my baby. Maia's cord came away, without any fuss, on her third evening. It was seven days before I even left the bedroom and I didn't go past the letterbox or in a car for a full six weeks. Nicholas had arranged one month off work to care for our household, which he did beautifully. As well as this, friends and neighbours brought meals and flowers, and gave practical help. We were fully nourished and our community shared in the magic of birth and baby.

Maia's birth blessed our household for this time and beyond. The love that I had felt pouring through my body as I birthed her continued to radiate and fill us all; we were truly "in love" for weeks afterwards.

As Maia has grown, I have seen, as with my other children, the imprint of her character on her birth. At four, she is a strong, lively girl: passionate, energetic, and loving. Her birth, too, was strong and passionate, and she was born in the sun-sign Leo; sign of drama, courage, and love.

Maia's birth continues to be a source of gratitude, inspiration, and nourishment for me in all facets of my life. Her birth was a major opening that has transformed me, making me the mother that Maia needs me to be, as well as deepening my understanding of, and commitment to, gentle and instinctive birth.

A previous version of this article was published in Midwifery Today Birthkit, *winter 2001. An expanded version is posted at* www.sarahjbuckley.com

References

1. Roberts J. *The God of Jane: A psychic manifesto.* Englewood Cliffs NJ: Prentice-Hall, 1981. Quoted in Shanley LK. *Unassisted Childbirth.* Westport CT: Bergin & Garvey, 1994.
2. This means that Maia was probably frank breech, with straight legs, in my belly.

Homebirth in Australia ~ the personal and the political

WHEN I became pregnant with my first child in 1990 my partner Nicholas and I, both GPs (family physicians), made a rather unusual decision. We decided to have our baby at home.

This was perhaps even more unexpected for me: my father was qualified as a specialist obstetrician (Ob/Gyn) and my childhood had been dominated by his frequent calls to the maternity wing of our local hospital in regional New Zealand.

My paternal grandfather, 'Buck' Buckley, had also attended birthing women, and his skills with rotation forceps, in the pre-caesarean days, had been legendary. Buck had attended labouring women in the country on horseback, and we have a famous family story about his wife (my paternal grandmother) shocking my maternal grandmother by not waiting up for him when he was away at a birth. He came home two days later! My mother was a nurse, and two of my three siblings also worked in the medical area.

On the other side, Nicholas's sister worked as a homebirth midwife in New Zealand, and we had been heavily influenced by her beliefs and experiences. We had also supported two friends giving birth at home (one in New Zealand; one after we moved to Australia) and we observed that their experiences were richer and more satisfying than those of the women whom we had attended during our six-month training in GP (family medicine) obstetrics, a few years earlier. (We had been fortunate, though, training in the same hospital where I was born and where my father still worked – most of the women birthed without major intervention, and the only epidural I saw was administered to the chief midwife, who was attended by the chief obstetrician).

Even though we chose homebirth from our hearts, we had a lot of questions for our carers. For example, could they respond to emergencies such as haemorrhage? Could they stitch a tear at home? What if our baby was not breathing at birth? All these possibilities were fresh in our minds from our training and we decided to have a doctor attend because we felt that his extra skills could, in some situations, avert a transfer to hospital. I wasn't hospital-phobic, but I knew that, being a doctor myself, I would be treated differently in hospital. Some of my medical friends had been badly neglected, especially after the birth – perhaps the staff were embarrassed or expected them to know everything already. I knew that my medical and obstetric knowledge was, at best, a minor advantage, and I asked my midwife to treat me the same as her other first-baby clients.

I thoroughly enjoyed this first pregnancy, despite constant nausea – perhaps heightened by working two jobs and not resting enough – and I finished work looking forward to a month of resting and nesting. However, our baby had different ideas and Emma was born three days later, after a short, intimate, and amazingly easy labour. (See "Emma's Birth", chapter 7.) I was so pleased to have the support of both my midwife (who arrived as I was starting to push) and doctor (who walked in as she was emerging), because she was small as well as early, and required our devoted and special care in the early weeks. I knew also that, had I birthed in hospital, both Emma and myself would have been treated as high risk, and she would have spent many hours under the lights for jaundice. At home she lived in our arms, and enjoyed home phototherapy in the sun on our front porch.

After the exhilaration of Emma's birth, we had no doubts about homebirth for our second and third children, Zoe and Jacob. Again we chose Christine Shanahan as our midwife and Dr Peter

Lucas, with whom we had become better acquainted in the years since Emma was born.

Giving birth to Zoe and Jacob, born barely two years apart, brought me new realisations. Intellectually I could compare my experiences at home with standard hospital practices, and I knew that what were minor problems at home would have created major worries and conflicts in hospital – an anterior lip (a front rim of the cervix that was slow to lift) with Zoe, where (very loud) sound was my ally; and being three weeks "overdue" with Jacob.

On an emotional level, I appreciated the space and support that I had for each journey to new motherhood. This journey was particularly challenging for me with Zoe, but birthing her without drugs or interventions kept my issues simple and focused, rather than overlaid with birthing trauma, as they could have been in hospital. I was also blessed, at this time, to find a beautiful women's circle, with Shivam Rachana and her Women's Mysteries workshops, in which to explore my path as woman and mother. Through this work, I have come to realise that birth, and being born, is not just an isolated event. Birth sets a blueprint for our lives, and gentle birth makes gentle people, which creates a gentle society.

In these years, I also began my involvement in birth politics, forming a lobby group when Dr Peter Lucas was called before the medical board and his registration was threatened. This was no co-incidence – he was the only doctor attending homebirths in Melbourne, a city of three million people. When he was suspended from practice for four months, I stepped into both his family and homebirth practices, bringing Zoe, then four months old, to both clinic and births. Fortunately she was a very relaxed baby, and came along for the ride, but I was very relieved when Peter came back from his compulsory holiday! After this, I continued to work at his clinic, bringing Zoe (and later Jacob) to work with me. I enjoyed the homebirth-minded clientele, and Peter enjoyed my support in what was a difficult climate for him as a homebirth doctor.

Just before Jacob turned two we moved from Melbourne to Brisbane, 2,000 km north. With three children, my enthusiasm for family medicine had waned, and this move – for Nicholas, a new job as associate professor in developmental disability – gave me a reason to take a break from medicine. But not, of course, from birth: I became involved with the local homebirth group, the Home Midwifery Association, and I began to write about pregnancy, birth, and parenting for the local newspaper as well as for a national parenting magazine. I certainly did my share of "nak" (nursing at keyboard) and loved discovering the worldwide web. Writing had always been a joy to me, and it has been wonderful, although challenging at times, to be able to do all my writing and research from home.

My fourth baby, Maia Rose, was born in Brisbane in 2000, and this time I chose to have no midwifery attendant. This was a very personal decision, which has deepened my passion for birth and my trust in our female bodies. (See "Maia's Birth", chapter 8.) With this experience, I have felt the awakening power of birth, more potent for me than any spiritual or shamanic practice, and realised how much we have given away through accepting medicalised birth. Maia's birth continues to inspire me in my writing, and has taught me, at a cellular level, that birth is about love and ecstasy.

I have the deepest gratitude that we made that primary decision, and chose homebirth for our first baby. I see how a medicalised birth would have been a transgression on the soul of our new family, and I feel grateful to have avoided it each time. For me, mothering is a big enough job without birth trauma in the family. Homebirth is rare and endangered in our culture, as outlined below – yet I see that the preservation of homebirth is vital to all of us. Homebirth mothers, families, and attendants hold the experience of birth as a sacred journey, and the knowing that birth has the power to awaken and heal.

Political perspectives

When I lived in New Zealand (NZ), up until 1987, homebirth was uncommon but not unknown; around one percent of births overall. In the small NZ city where I did my GP (family physician) training, there were at least three doctors attending homebirths.

Australia, as I came to realise, is more conservative in birth. Not only is the homebirth rate lower but, in every state, homebirth midwives are unsupported (or even harassed) by the system and there are still only a handful of doctors Australia-wide who openly support or attend homebirths. Independent midwives – around 80 Australia-wide – have been further threatened in their viability by the withdrawal from the market of the company who provided their indemnity insurance, leaving them personally vulnerable to litigation.

Another impediment for Australian families considering homebirth is the cost (around A$2,500), which is borne entirely by the birthing family. Health insurance is optional in Australia (we have a public hospital system that is free to all) and a few insurance companies will reimburse private midwifery costs, but the financial benefit is marginal. In contrast, all women who choose hospital birth, even in the private sector, have at least some government reimbursement through Medicare, the Australian national healthcare system. Homebirth is available free to women in NZ and the UK and is covered by some health care providers in the US. (See "Choosing Homebirth", chapter 18.)

In Australia, as in many countries, there is only one kind of officially recognised midwife; one who has trained as a nurse, then as a midwife and who is registered by one of the state nursing councils – equivalent to the US certified nurse-midwife (CNM) and the UK registered midwife. In most states, there is legislation forbidding anyone but a registered midwife from attending a woman in childbirth, although the actual wording and its interpretation vary. This has shifted in the last few years, as our new "direct entry" midwives have graduated. These midwives have studied solely midwifery for four years, and include many with a real calling to be "with women" (the original meaning of the word *midwife*) in birth. There are also lay (traditional or apprentice-trained) midwives in every state, with most practising underground, even though national homebirth figures, collected from 1985–90, attest to the safety of their practices.

Even our registered midwives are poorly supported when they work independently of the hospital system. Here in Queensland, the nurses' council has investigated almost all of our registered homebirth midwives, with some of our most experienced midwives being taken out of practice. Some of these investigations have centred around the midwives' support for informed choice and for "high-risk" women who choose homebirths; for example women with breech babies and previous caesareans, whose only other choice is a caesarean in hospital.

The situation for homebirth and genuine midwifery in Australia is obviously dire, but this adversity has also served us. All around Australia, consumer groups have become active and organised, and are now pushing for implementation of the National Maternity Action Plan (NMAP)[1], which calls for continuity of care with a community-based midwife as a choice for all pregnant women Australia-wide, whether birthing in home or hospital. There is a popular model for community midwifery in one state, Western Australia, which has been running successfully for over seven years.

Birth and her sequelae – breastfeeding and mothering – have occupied me intensely for more than 14 years. My passion has grown (so much that I am on the computer half of the day, as my children remind me!) and I feel that positive change is inevitable. There has been a resurgence of the feminine at every level of society, and I believe the current medical backlash in birth is actually reflecting the death throes of an outmoded way of thinking and behaving.

Men and women, mothers and babies, midwives and doctors – we are all awakening together.

First published in Midwifery Today, *issue 66, summer 2003. This version updated March 2005. (For more about homebirth, see chapter 18, "Choosing Homebirth".)*

References

1. National Maternity Action Plan posted at
    http://www.maternitycoalition.org.au/nmap.html

Gentle Birth ~ the Evidence

In Praise of Normal Birth

I N western cultures, normal birth has been in steep decline in recent years.

Women who give birth normally – that is, without surgical intervention, use of instruments, induction, epidural or general anaesthetic – are now in the minority in the UK[1] (where these figures are collected) and caesarean rates are upwards of 25 percent in many developed countries, including here in Australia.[2] In some places, pregnant women are said to be abandoning vaginal birth in favor of planned caesareans. Of those women who do give birth vaginally, very few experience a normal birth. For example, an increasing number of women are choosing epidural pain relief, which, according to the World Health Organization, will transform their labour from a physiological event to a medical procedure.[3]

The validity of normal birth is also under attack from some quarters of the medical profession. In 2004 two UK obstetricians opined, in *The Observer*, that natural birth was riskier than drink driving.[4] Recent articles in major journals have offered support for a randomised controlled trial of vaginal birth versus elective caesarean for low-risk women,[5-7] and a 2002 Canadian conference was dedicated to the theme "Choosing Delivery by Cesarean: Has its Time Come?" And while many obstetricians are happy to agree to a medically unnecessary caesarean, with well-documented risks,[8] there are few doctors worldwide who will support a woman if she wishes to give birth without medical intervention.

As a doctor trained in GP (family physician) obstetrics, and the mother of four children, all born without medical intervention, I know that birth can be inconvenient, painful, messy, and challenging. I also know that giving birth can be a source of great pleasure, and that the rewards of normal birth are long-lasting. The following is a representative, but not comprehensive, list of the rewards that normal birth continues to offer to twenty-first century mothers and babies.

First, a woman who has given birth under her own steam gains an immense sense of personal accomplishment. Many women, myself included, feel, "If I can do this, I can do anything." I believe that these feelings are part of our evolutionary blueprint for birth, giving a new mother the confidence that she needs to care for her baby. This euphoria is reinforced by a cocktail of hormones, including oxytocin, beta-endorphin, noradrenaline and prolactin, which all peak most dramatically after a normal birth.[9]

Conversely, research shows that medical interventions will interfere with the hormonal orchestration of birth, and will reduce the postnatal levels of these euphoric hormones. For example, women who give birth with an epidural have lower postnatal peaks of oxytocin,[10] beta-endorphin,[11] and noradrenaline,[12] than women who give birth normally; both animal[13] and human research[14, 15] suggest that this may have an impact on early mothering.

Second, normal birth gives an ideal start to the mother–baby relationship. When a mother has received no pain killers, her baby will be naturally alert and will display the full range of early breastfeeding and attachment behaviours, such as breast massage and early suckling.[16] The mother will also be alert, and able to hold her baby immediately. The early days with my own babies have been easy and pleasurable, partly because we have been free from the need to recover from drugs or procedures used during labour and birth.

Third, we know that early events can affect our offspring lifelong; I believe that this applies to the way that babies are born. In my experience, babies given a gentle start are generally calm and easy to mother throughout infancy. Conversely, research has suggested that babies exposed to higher levels of epidural drugs are less alert on the first day of life, and more irritable and difficult to settle throughout the first six weeks,[17] which is the limit of studies to date. As Murray et al. highlight, first encounters with a disorganised baby can shape long-term maternal expectations and mother–baby interactions.[14]

Primate studies have also suggested that offspring exposed to analgesic drugs (opiates, epidurals) in labour may display abnormal neurobehavioural (brain-behaviour) maturation in infancy.[18] Such studies remind us that we need to look long-term to ensure that, as the Cochrane database researchers state, "...any interference with the natural process of pregnancy and childbirth should also be shown to do more good than harm."[19]

Finally, neither normal birth nor medicalised birth can guarantee a good outcome. I have chosen one set of risks and rewards because I believe that normal birth has evolved, over millennia, for long-term reproductive success. The drugs and procedures of medicalised birth are, in contrast, very new and their long-term implications are poorly understood.

I also see parallels between our current enthusiasm for intervention in birth, and the enthusiasm with which the medical profession, to its shame, has promoted breastmilk substitutes. Both involve an assumption that we can improve on nature, but neither has been based on an understanding of the complex physiology, endocrinology, and psychology of these highly evolved processes, nor of the long-term implications of such interference.

Just as we are now discovering the comprehensive benefits of breastfeeding, so may we, in the coming years, come to appreciate the biological intricacy, and the evolutionary wisdom, of normal birth.

Submitted to British Medical Journal *October 2004; unpublished.*

References

1. Department of Health. *NHS maternity statistics, England: 2003–4.* London: DoH, 2005.
2. Laws P, Sullivan E. *Australia's mothers and babies 2002.* Sydney: AIHW National Perinatal Statistics Unit, 2004.

3. World Health Organization. *Care in Normal Birth: a Practical Guide. Report of a Technical Working Group.* Geneva: World Health Organization, 1996.

4. Fisk N, Patterson Brown S. The safest method of birth is by caesarean. *The Observer* 2004 Sunday 2 May; 18.

5. Hannah ME. Planned elective cesarean section: a reasonable choice for some women? *Can Med Assoc J* 2004; 170(5):813–4.

6. Robson S, Ellwood D. Should obstetricians support a 'term cephalic trial'? *Aust N Z J Obstet Gynaecol* 2003; 43(5):341–3.

7. Ecker JL. Once a pregnancy, always a cesarean? Rationale and feasibility of a randomized controlled trial. *Am J Obstet Gynecol* 2004; 190(2):314–8.

8. National Institute for Clinical Excellence. *Caesarean Section Clinical Guidelines.* London: National Collaborating Centre for Women's and Children's Health, 2004.

9. Buckley SJ. Undisturbed Birth: Nature's Blueprint for Ease and Ecstasy. *Journal of Prenatal and Perinatal Psychology and Health* 2003; 17(4):261–288. See also Chapter 13.

10. Goodfellow CF, et al. Oxytocin deficiency at delivery with epidural analgesia. *Br J Obstet Gynaecol* 1983; 90(3):214–9.

11. Bacigalupo G, et al. Quantitative relationships between pain intensities during labor and beta-endorphin and cortisol concentrations in plasma. Decline of the hormone concentrations in the early postpartum period. *J Perinat Med* 1990; 18(4):289–96.

12. Jones CR, et al. Plasma catecholamines and modes of delivery: the relation between catecholamine levels and in-vitro platelet aggregation and adrenoreceptor radioligand binding characteristics. *Br J Obstet Gynaecol* 1985; 92(6):593–9.

13. Krehbiel D, et al. Peridural anesthesia disturbs maternal behavior in primiparous and multiparous parturient ewes. *Physiol Behav* 1987; 40(4):463–72.

14. Murray AD, et al. Effects of epidural anesthesia on newborns and their mothers. *Child Dev* 1981; 52(1):71–82.

15. Sepkoski CM, et al. The effects of maternal epidural anesthesia on neonatal behavior during the first month. *Dev Med Child Neurol* 1992; 34(12):1072–80.

16. Ransjo-Arvidson AB, et al. Maternal analgesia during labor disturbs newborn behavior: effects on breastfeeding, temperature, and crying. *Birth* 2001; 28(1):5–12.

17. Rosenblatt DB, et al. The influence of maternal analgesia on neonatal behaviour: II. Epidural bupivacaine. *Br J Obstet Gynaecol* 1981; 88(4):407–13.

18. Golub MS. Labor analgesia and infant brain development. *Pharmacol Biochem Behav* 1996; 55(4):619–28.

19. Enkin M, et al. *Effective Care in Pregnancy and Childbirth.* 3rd edn. Oxford: Oxford University Press, 2000, p 486.

Prenatal Diagnosis ~ technological triumph or Pandora's box?

YOU'VE never received bad news from the doctor's surgery before, and this was even worse because it was about your unborn baby. Your doctor was kind and gentle, and there must have been a lot of talking, as you were in there for over 30 minutes, but all you can remember is a creeping numbness, a fog that thickened around you, and the words "blood test", "high risk" and "Down syndrome."

That evening you try to retrieve some detail for your partner, but today is still foggy, and you have little memory of the pre-test counselling that the doctor said she gave you before the test. The number one in 300 comes to mind, but this doesn't make sense: how can there be all this worry over such a small number?

Eventually you find the brochure in your bag. Your doctor called it invasive testing, and said it was the next step, if you want to take it. Here it is called amniocentesis, which means taking a sample of your baby's waters. "Poor baby," you tell your belly as you absorb the information, "the test might kill you, or else you might have Down syndrome. Then we would have to choose whether or not to get rid of you."

That night you dream of a field of babies: perfect pink chubby babies, skinny grey babies with horrible deformities, Chinese babies, African babies, Romanian babies, and they all want to come home with you. In the morning you can hardly remember how it felt to simply enjoy your pregnancy. Your belly has become a heavy weight that you find yourself supporting as you go through that difficult day.

Welcome to the brave new world of prenatal diagnosis, where we are given information that is unprecedented in human history, and choices that can be as painful as they are complex.

Prenatal diagnosis – the detection of abnormalities of babies still in the womb – is driven by the increasing expertise of medical technology but it is clearly sanctioned by our society; the majority of people in Australia support abortion when there is a major abnormality[1] and legislation has been passed to enable this in most developed countries. It seems that we have decided, collectively as well as individually, that we want to avoid the difficulties of raising children with disabilities and especially, in our society, with intellectual disabilities.

However, for prenatal diagnosis to contribute to this end, some of us must choose to terminate our wanted pregnancies.

Pandora's box

Prenatal diagnosis can open a veritable Pandora's box for the woman and her family, and also raises wider, profound ethical and philosophical questions. For example, how can we call ourselves a tolerant and inclusive society – a society that celebrates difference – when we have an entire industry directed towards eradicating babies who have obvious differences? And our values are portrayed very starkly when we specifically target babies with Down syndrome; a condition that is not usually fatal, but is associated with intellectual disability and with characteristic physical features that our society does not recognise as beautiful.

Some of the personal impact of prenatal testing is illustrated in the story above. Whether this baby is affected (a one-in-300 chance, in this scenario) and aborted; is affected and kept (perhaps one in ten affected babies[2]); miscarries as a result of the procedure (about a one-in-100 chance with amniocentesis) or is unaffected (299 chances out of 300 before amniocentesis) – the mother has been through a difficult process.

Most women who opt for these tests are unaware that they are entering an emotional minefield, with consequences that may last for years. Many are also unaware that the tests that they are accepting will not detect all, or even most, abnormalities in their unborn babies.

Recent Australian research also shows that the majority of pregnant women are not well informed before or after they undergo tests for prenatal diagnosis.[3, 4] A UK survey has suggested that health professionals involved in antenatal care are not well informed,[5] and Australian[6] and Canadian health professionals[7] have also been shown to have a variable knowledge of these complicated issues. A US survey found that more than one-third of primary care physicians admitted to being biased when counselling women with a prenatal diagnosis of Down syndrome.[8]

Screening versus diagnostic tests

Our mother-to-be has accepted a screening test for her baby. Like one in 20 of the women who opt for second trimester maternal serum screening (STMSS) – a blood test at 15 to 18 weeks – she received a positive screening result, with all the anxiety that accompanies this news.

However, only around one in 50 women who test positive will actually have an affected baby; the remaining 49 have had what is called "false positive" results. As well as this, with a detection rate of 60 to 70 percent, STMSS will fail to detect around one in three babies with Down syndrome. Detection rates for spina bifida, the other major condition that may be discovered with STMSS, are around 70 percent, which means that, similarly, one in three affected babies will not be detected with this test.[9]

Why is this widely used test so inaccurate? The major reason is that it is not a *diagnostic test* – that is, it can't give a definite diagnosis for the baby. It is a prenatal *screening test*, designed to give an indication of risk so that the next step – a diagnostic (and invasive) test of the baby's cells by amniocentesis or chorionic villus sampling (CVS, see below) – can be targeted to women who are more likely to be carrying an affected baby.

Limiting these diagnostic tests is desirable because they carry their own risks, especially of causing a miscarriage. Termination can also be risky for the mother, especially after three months because it involves either inducing labour with drugs or the more difficult "dilate and evacuate" procedure.

These prenatal screening tests have been promoted as a "no-risk" test to women (especially younger women) who may not consider themselves likely to have a baby with Down syndrome, and may not consider invasive testing, because of the risk of miscarriage. For example, women aged under 35 have a generally low chance of giving birth to an affected baby, but, because the majority of babies are born to these younger women, they will also give birth to the most babies with Down syndrome.

Screening tests can tell an individual woman whether she has a higher-than-average chance of carrying an affected baby, and she can be offered a diagnostic test when her risk is over one in 250 to 300. This is approximately double the normal risk, as approximately one in 600 women overall carry a baby with Down syndrome. In this way, screening tests increase the overall numbers of Down syndrome babies detected and aborted because around 70 percent of Down Syndrome babies are born to women under 35.

Several studies have found that serum-screening tests are more likely to be false positive in specific situations. Researchers have found, for example, that women who are vegetarian,[10] smokers,[11] from different ethnic groups,[12] and/or who have had a false positive result in a previous pregnancy,[13] require adjustment of their serum markers to avoid an excess of false positive results. Mothers who carry a female baby are also more likely to receive a false positive test result.[14]

Overall, however, the most common reason for inaccurate test results, including false positives, is an error in dating the pregnancy. Accurate dating is important, because levels of the hormones that are tested depend on the age (gestation) of the baby. Between 20 and 40 percent of women with screen-positive results will be found to have normal levels when their pregnancy is more accurately dated by ultrasound scan.[15]

There are two other screening tests that are increasingly used to detect babies with Down syndrome. The first is an earlier blood test, performed at around 10 weeks and known as first trimester maternal serum screening (FTMSS). FTMSS analyses different components of the mother's blood and has, in some studies, given as accurate results as STMSS, although it cannot detect defects like spina bifida.

The second early prenatal screening test is a specialised ultrasound, which measures the thickness of the skin fold at the back of the baby's neck at 10 to 13 weeks. This is known as known nuchal translucency (NT) testing. Babies with Down syndrome (and several other less common abnormalities) are likely to have a thicker skin fold at the back of the neck (nuchal fold) at this particular time in pregnancy. As with all screening tests, most babies who test positive on NT will actually be normal.

Early detection, early relief?

These new, early tests are believed to benefit women because the whole process (screening, diagnosis, and possibly termination) can then take place at an earlier stage of pregnancy, perhaps even before the woman has shared her news. CVS, as a diagnostic test, can be performed from ten weeks, and a termination, if chosen, can also be done at this earlier stage of pregnancy.

However, because of the complexity of these procedures and the time needed to make these major decisions, many women who have had a FTMSS do not actually have a termination until after 16 weeks.[16]

The complexity of prenatal screening is increasing, because researchers are looking at different combinations of FTMSS, STMSS and NT. Currently the best figures for detection of Down syndrome are produced through two-step integrated testing (IT), which detects over 90 percent of affected babies with a false-positive rate of 2.6 percent.[17] Integrated testing involves FTMSS at ten weeks, NT at 10 to 12 weeks, then the 14-week STMSS. When all these results are back (a long wait), the woman will receive her risk estimate and she can then decide whether she wants to proceed with amniocentesis.

The UK Government has pledged to make this test available, funded by the National Health Service, to all UK women in 2007,[18] and it is very possible that Australia may follow suit. The recent joint statement by the Royal Australian and New Zealand College of Obstetrics and Gynaecologists and the Human Genetics Society of Australasia also notes the higher detection rates with combination tests, but currently recommends that women are counselled individually about the most appropriate test or tests.[19] In the US, the Preventive Services Taskforce currently recommends STMSS for all low-risk pregnant women who have access to counselling, and invasive testing for women over 35 or at high-risk of carrying a baby with Down syndrome.[20]

These complex and prolonged testing regimes are argued to be cost-effective, based on the premise that money will be saved through aborting babies with Down syndrome, who are estimated to cost an extra US$677,000 (adjusted to 2002 figures) for life-long care.[2, 21] In the US, it is said to be cost-effective to spend more than US$2.5 billion annually to detect and abort around 7,500 babies with Down syndrome by offering FTMSS and NT to all pregnant women.[22] In the UK, where this testing is funded by the state, Alfirevic and Nielson ask:

> What is the importance of establishing top quality Down's syndrome screening programmes, relative to other priorities in the maternity services – notably tackling inequalities and ensuring that all women in labour have enough midwives to meet their needs? [23]

Ultrasound and nuchal translucency

Nuchal translucency (NT), as noted above, measures the thickness of the skin fold at the back of the baby's neck at 10 to 13 weeks. NT is a very specific test, and requires a trained operator and dedicated equipment, including a sophisticated computer programme to analyse the data, which includes the mother's age and the baby's exact gestation.

Like the serum screening tests, NT gives an estimate of risk of Down syndrome rather than a definite diagnosis. NT detects around 60 to 70 percent of babies with Down syndrome, with a five percent false positive rate. An increased NT measurement may also indicate other less common abnormalities such as trisomy 18 (Edwards syndrome), trisomy 13, and heart defects. However, because NT is performed while the baby is still small and undeveloped, NT cannot be expected to diagnose abnormalities of the body, gut, kidneys, heart, and spinal cord, and an 18 to 20-week scan would still be necessary for this reason.

NT uses ultrasound, which has not, I believe, been adequately shown to be safe for our offspring long-term. Recent research, which compared multiple scans with single scans in pregnancy and followed the offspring until eight years of age, has produced some reassurance, but, as the researchers state, "...our results do not lessen our need to undertake further studies of potential bio-effects of prenatal ultrasound scans."[24] Ultrasound machine output intensities continue to increase, even since this study was conducted, and questions about non-right handedness associated with ultrasound exposure have not been resolved. (For more information on ultrasound, see chapter 12.)

Diagnostic and invasive testing: amniocentesis and chorionic villus sampling (CVS)

Amniocentesis and CVS are invasive tests because they involve invading the pregnant mother's womb to take a sample of her baby's amniotic fluid and developing placenta (respectively) to test for genetic abnormalities. Because of this, both tests carry risks to the baby and, to a lesser extent, to the mother.

Amniocentesis is usually performed at 15 to 16 weeks. In amniocentesis, around one to two tablespoons (15–30 mL, ½–1 ounce) of the baby's amniotic fluid is taken with a needle under ultrasound guidance and the baby's cells, which are floating in the fluid, are removed and grown in the lab. The baby's chromosomes, which are part of the core (nucleus) of the cell, are tested for abnormalities, including Down syndrome.

Results are usually available in about two weeks, although new gene technologies (still too expensive for routine use) can reduce the waiting time to a few days. Amniotic fluid can also be tested for alpha feto-protein (AFP), which indicates neural tube defects (NTDs) in the baby's brain and spinal cord, including spina bifida. AFP is a simpler test, and results are usually available within a day or two. If AFP levels are high, a detailed ultrasound is recommended to give more information.

Amniocentesis is recognised to cause miscarriage in between one in 50 and one in 200 pregnant women overall, and this miscarriage can occur up to three weeks, or even later, after the procedure. In one study involving women under 35, the majority of procedure-related miscarriages occurred after 28 weeks.[25]

More experienced operators tend to have lower miscarriage rates. One large study indicated that the risk of miscarriage might be higher among older women, among women who have experienced bleeding in the pregnancy, and among women who have had more than three previous early miscarriages or abortions and/or a late miscarriage or abortion.[26] In this study, women over 40 had a risk of miscarriage after amniocentesis of around five percent, while those over 40 who had also experienced bleeding had a 10 percent chance of miscarriage. Women over 40 with previous miscarriages or abortions, as above, had a 20 percent chance of miscarriage after the procedure.

It is noteworthy that, with STMSS and follow-up amniocentesis, approximately one normal baby will miscarry for every one to two aborted babies who would have otherwise been born with Down syndrome.[2]

Leakage of the amniotic fluid through the vagina (even though amniocentesis is performed through the mother's abdomen) will occur for about one in 100 women. Although it is rare, the amniocentesis needle can scrape or even penetrate the baby, and the sequelae of this, which may be severe, may not be detected before birth.[27]

Studies have suggested that newborn babies who have been exposed to amniocentesis and CVS may have impaired lung growth and development,[28, 29] and that babies born after early amniocentesis (10 to 13 weeks) are more likely to have breathing difficulties and to require intensive care treatment after birth.[30] A large European study has found that amniocentesis for prenatal diagnosis may increase the risk of premature birth,[31] and the good quality medical evidence concludes that amniocentesis may also cause very low birth weight in around one in 200 babies.[32] Ironically, prematurity and very low birth weight are major risk factors for physical and intellectual impairment, including cerebral palsy.

Amniocentesis is also invasive for the mother, involving penetration of her uterus. Possible complications include infection of the baby and fluid (chorioamnionitis), which will usually cause miscarriage. More severe infections can cause septic shock and serious illness, which can, very rarely, be fatal.[33]

CVS involves taking a sample of the baby's developing placenta under ultrasound guidance, either via the mother's abdomen or vagina, at around 11 to 12 weeks. CVS is a newer test and has extra risks, compared to amniocentesis. First the miscarriage rate from the procedure is higher – between one in 25 and one in 100 overall.[34, 35] Difficulties with the procedure and/or with lab analysis are more common with CVS than with amniocentesis, occurring between 2.2 and 10 percent of procedures[9] and a repeat CVS (or amniocentesis at a later time) may be necessary. Repeated testing increases the risk of miscarriage.

It is also possible that the cells removed by CVS are reported as normal when the baby actually has an unusual (and usually milder) mosaic form of Down syndrome. Alternatively, the baby may be unaffected yet have mosaic cells on CVS. Mosaicism affects around one percent of CVS test results.[9]

CVS was designed so that women could have this diagnostic test early in pregnancy, when a termination, if chosen, is more straightforward. However, the disadvantage of this earlier diagnosis is that some affected babies would have naturally miscarried within a few weeks. This is especially true for Down syndrome babies, for whom one in four (25 percent) will miscarry between 10 and 14 weeks, and another one in four (23 percent) will miscarry before the end of pregnancy.[2] Research has recently suggested that those Down syndrome babies who are detected prenatally may miscarry at a higher rate (50 percent overall) than Down syndrome babies who are not detected on prenatal screening.[36]

CVS may also cause damage to the baby. Early studies have suggested that babies exposed to CVS before 10 weeks may have a small but increased risk of limb deformities (CVS is now performed at 11 to 12 weeks), and other studies have noted increased numbers of CVS babies with clubfoot and malformations of the jaw and gut, as well as haemangiomas (strawberry birth marks).[37]

One small study has reported an increased risk of high blood pressure and pre-eclampsia (toxemia) later in the pregnancy when the baby's placenta has been penetrated with CVS (which is a necessary part of the procedure) or amniocentesis.[38] Mothers who have an Rh-negative blood group should receive anti-D after amniocentesis or CVS to prevent blood incompatibility problems in future pregnancies.

Another irony of both amniocentesis and CVS is that both procedures involve ultrasound, giving the mother the opportunity to see her baby, yet at the same time she is expected to consider abortion. As one mother shared, "I was simply able to see her, reinforcing the love that they told me was for the wrong baby."[39]

Brave new world

Against these very quantitative analyses, Elkins and Brown argue:

> ...individuals with Down syndrome have come to be recognised, over the last three decades, as bringing a valuable quality of life into our society. They are well known for the joy and love they bring to their families. They remind us that the definitions of normalcy are artificial and fragile... In short, individuals with Down syndrome teach the rest of us how to cope, to grow, to overcome and to understand humility, gratitude and joy.[40]

In the research and published material about prenatal diagnosis, the perspectives of those affected by conditions such as Down syndrome have rarely been considered. Most of the prenatal diagnosis information leaflets, designed to help prospective parents decide about testing, paint a very negative and outdated view of Down syndrome.[41, 42]

Alderson examines our presumptions about the value and quality of life with Down syndrome through her interviews with five affected adults.[43] Her interviewees show insight and enjoyment of life; sensitivity to social prejudice; and painful awareness of the issues around testing and selective abortion for Down syndrome babies. There is more excellent and realistic literature written by parents, carers and individuals with Down syndrome, some posted on the Internet, such as Kingsley and Levitz;[44] and Slater.[45]

A recent paper suggests deeper ethical issues for us all to consider. Reynolds sent a questionnaire comprising 19 clinical scenarios, including prenatal testing for Down syndrome (which was not identified as such), to 40 randomly chosen UK research ethics committees.[46] More than half of the respondents expressed the opinion that prenatal screening for a condition with the clinical features of Down syndrome was unethical. When it was disclosed that confirmatory testing could cause miscarriage in normal babies, only 14 percent remained in favour of screening.

Diagnosis and counselling

After so many decisions and tests, you might hope that the results from amniocentesis or CVS would be clear and the decision, whatever it is, would be straightforward. Unfortunately, this is often not the case. For all the babies with a straight diagnosis of Down syndrome, there are as many again with other chromosomal abnormalities, many of which carry an uncertain outcome.

For example, around one third of abnormalities reported involve the sex chromosomes, which can give subtle or unknown levels of abnormality.[9] Rothman, who conducted extensive interviews with women who had experienced prenatal diagnosis, notes that parents can be incapacitated by ambiguous diagnoses.[47] Other research shows that many women will choose to terminate their pregnancy, rather than live with such uncertainty.[48]

New gene technologies such as FISH, mentioned above in relation to quicker testing times, are less likely to give ambiguous diagnoses, as they test for a narrow and specific range of conditions; such tests will not, for example, detect sex chromosomes abnormalities, but are equally accurate in testing for Down syndrome. It may be preferable to choose these methods, if available, for the analysis of cells obtained by CVS or amniocentesis.

Obviously there is a great need for high-quality counselling both before and after testing. Specialised genetic counsellors are the appropriate professionals, and a counselling session – ideally provided to all women considering testing – is recommended for those with positive screening or diagnostic tests.

Genetic counsellors are, however, a part of the industry of prenatal diagnosis, whose purpose is to reduce the number of live-born babies with Down syndrome. This may make it difficult for them to provide impartial information. One analysis of all the written information provided by carers and counsellors in the UK showed very little information about, and a negative attitude towards, people with Down syndrome. This complaint is echoed in a survey of 141 US mothers who chose to continue their affected pregnancy.[49] Thornton notes, "High uptake of prenatal blood tests suggests compliant behaviour and need for more information."[50]

Termination after prenatal diagnosis

Prenatal diagnosis, and the industry that supports it, is based on the premise that the majority of women with affected babies will decide to terminate their pregnancies. Although women may consider this when they are choosing whether to have the screening test, they are unlikely to realise (or to be told) exactly what this entails until they actually confront this situation for themselves.

Early termination, involving a straightforward curette (scraping or suction to remove the lining of the womb and baby), is only possible up to around 14 weeks, which will be hurried if a woman has had her CVS at 11 to 12 weeks and then a two-week wait for results. Later termination may involve induction of labour, which can be as long and difficult as a full-term labour, and the baby may be born alive but unviable. Alternatively, saline may be infused into the amniotic fluid or a lethal injection may be administered to ensure that the baby is stillborn.

In one study, average time from induction to delivery for a mid-pregnancy termination was 18 to 30 hours, depending on the method of induction.[51]

Some centers offer a "dilate and evacuate" termination when the pregnancy is around 14 to 18 weeks, which involves a general anaesthetic for the mother, while the surgeon extracts the unborn baby (fetus) in pieces.

If termination is considered after amniocentesis at 15 to 16 weeks plus two weeks for results, not only will the mother be feeling her baby moving, but, by 20 weeks, the baby is only a few weeks away from the time when it could survive with intensive care – around 24 weeks. Furthermore, babies born after 20 to 24 weeks may require death certification, naming, and a funeral, depending on legislation in the place of birth.

Early termination has been the goal of prenatal diagnosis programs, with the presumption that it will be less traumatic for the mother. However, while termination for fetal abnormality in the first trimester is medically less complicated than later in pregnancy, there is little evidence that the distress for the woman is any less.[52] Some women interviewed by Rothman felt that seeing the baby afterwards, which is only possible after a late termination involving an induced labour, was (or would have been) helpful in their grieving process.[47]

One post-mortem survey found an error in one baby out of 128 diagnosed by amniocentesis or CVS, and three normal babies among 215 aborted because of abnormal ultrasound results.[53] And while termination is regarded as the end of the process of prenatal diagnosis, UK research shows that at least a quarter of women who undergo later termination are significantly distressed two years later.[54]

Eve's apple: the consequences of knowing

Pregnant women are the target, and supposed beneficiaries, of this large and increasingly complex industry, yet there is surprisingly little written about their experiences and opinions. Technological obstetrics makes the assumption that more knowledge is better, but, like Eve's apple, the knowledge that we gain through prenatal diagnosis can cast us from our pregnant paradise, with major and long-lasting sequelae for mother, baby, and family.

Research suggests that most women around the world have a difficult time making sense of this complex area, especially the crucial distinction between screening and diagnostic tests. Perhaps this reflects the difference between our intellectual understanding of, and our emotional reaction to, a positive screening test.

For example, Santalahti reports the experiences of a 34-year-old health professional:

> ...her first thought on learning her positive result was "disaster." That evening she was unable to sleep, and felt like crying desperately. The next day she described herself as being "out of control". Simply having technological information did not prevent a strong emotional reaction.[55]

Another woman in her second pregnancy

> ...described the four weeks of waiting as the most difficult of her life. She was nervous, tearful and hypersensitive, and she decided to abort the fetus if it was abnormal... serum screening had struck her down... she could not believe in a healthy baby before she held it in her arms.[56]

Other women have described their reactions to a positive screening result:

> I was totally shattered, frightened out of my wits.[57]

And

> I said to the midwife who told me the results: it's all gone wrong, its all gone wrong. I don't want to know about it anymore.[57]

Many mothers still remain anxious even when the results are reported as normal. One mother, who said that she had been "totally reassured" by a normal amniocentesis result, asked for a paediatrician to check her baby for Down syndrome immediately after the birth.[39]

For the women whose babies are found to be abnormal, the decision becomes, as Rothman calls it, "the tragedy of her choice"[47] – to terminate a wanted pregnancy or to continue with the knowledge that her baby will be affected, and with the possibility of a stillbirth or a child with a life-long disability. Research indicates that maternal grief may be the same, whether a baby with a lethal abnormality is aborted or stillborn.[58, 59]

One has to wonder at the sequelae for the ongoing mother–baby relationship, when mothers have experienced this degree of "false positive" stress over the wellbeing of their baby. Ordinarily, such anxiety would mobilise a mother's protective instincts, and she would draw closer to her baby. However, this protective instinct is difficult to express when the mother is also considering abortion, and she is likely to protect herself through emotionally distancing from her baby and her pregnancy – to "not want to know about it anymore" as the woman above states – at least until reassuring results are received.

Some women report that this distancing has affected their relationship with their children long after birth, and this anxiety and/or detachment, based on fear of abnormalities, can recur in subsequent pregnancies.[60] As midwife Anne Frye comments, "Nature never intended that parents would have such information, pregnancy as a time of unconditional attachment is severely disrupted by the technology available today."[61]

This difficult emotional situation, which pulls women in two directions, is echoed in the literature of prenatal diagnosis, which refers, for example, to "therapeutic termination" of babies with abnormalities, as though the abortion is curing an illness, rather than enacting a socially sanctioned form of eugenics.

When parents make the decision to terminate, often they describe it as being in their abnormal baby's best interests, which may be true in a society that is so bent on eradicating individuals with conditions such as Down syndrome. As one woman said "I didn't want to give up my baby, yet I had to because I knew what the future held for all of us if I kept her."[39]

Ironically, the stress that prenatal screening and diagnosis generates may create further risks to mother and baby. Research into the long-term effects of pregnancy stress concludes

> ...pregnant women with high stress and anxiety levels are at increased risk for spontaneous abortion and pre-term labour and for having a malformed or growth-retarded baby...[62]

According to these authors (and the many papers that they review) offspring whose mothers were stressed in pregnancy may have delayed development, with alterations in brain and hormone systems, as well as increased susceptibility to stress life-long. Even more worryingly,

> Huizink[63] has demonstrated that maternal stress in the first half of pregnancy is an important predictor of problematic infant behaviour. This was found especially for pregnancy-specific anxieties such as fear of the baby's health and fear of (pain during) delivery.[64]

One also wonders about the effects of prenatal diagnosis on the child themselves. Are we, at some level, accepting the view that our children are commodities that we can subject to a quality control test and reject if faulty? How will our children feel if they discover that our acceptance of them was so conditional? How will these experiences affect our subsequent role and expectations as parents?

Prenatal diagnosis is also said to benefit women through forewarning of their baby's abnormality. This may be true for some women,[65] but others may resent their loss of enjoyment of pregnancy. Discovering the baby's problems during pregnancy is also a very different experience to discovering this at birth, when Mother Nature hormonally primes new mothers to fall in love with their babies. Some parents have also appreciated the opportunity to recognise their baby's disability themselves, even days after the birth.[66]

This chapter has focused mainly on the experience of women whose screening result is positive, especially false positive. However, the promise of prenatal diagnosis – to prevent the birth of babies with abnormalities – also has an influence on those who receive a "false negative result" – that is, their test is normal but they give birth to an affected baby.

In one study, parents of Down syndrome babies who had been misdiagnosed as normal had more problems adjusting, including more feelings of stress, blame, and anxiety, than those who did not have a test.[67] Such parents are increasingly litigating for "wrongful birth", with a number of cases in many countries in recent years. Such litigation further pressures both carers, for whom non-direct counselling is already challenging,[68] and their clients towards routine testing.

A further irony is that most women choose to have prenatal screening in order to receive reassurance that their baby is healthy. Yet, for all the stress, time, and money that are consumed by the prenatal diagnosis industry, neither these, nor any other pregnancy tests currently in use, can tell us with certainty that our babies are normal and healthy. Major conditions such as cerebral palsy and autism cannot be detected by any existing method, and physical abnormalities involving the heart and kidney, some of which are severely disabling, are also unlikely to be picked up through prenatal screening.

The trick of technology

Prenatal diagnosis represents incredible and continuing advances in technology, yet there is a sleight of hand – a trick, perhaps – that is being played on pregnant women. We are told that prenatal diagnosis will increase our choices, but, as these tests become more available, women are feeling that they have less choice to refuse the testing. We are already, through social attitudes, individually responsible for our children's development, and now we are also becoming responsible for producing a healthy baby at birth. As one woman comments,

> I knew it was my responsibility to make sure I was not going to give birth to a handicapped child. But that meant taking the risk of losing a healthy baby. I am responsible for that too.[69]

Finally, as we look more deeply, the parallels between prenatal diagnosis and medicalised childbirth become increasingly obvious. Both industries are centred on high technology, and its superior knowledge, and both consider women's own feelings and instincts about their body and their baby to be of lesser importance.

Women who choose either path are at risk of a cascade of intervention – from induction to caesarean or from screening to abortion – with pressure to conform to medicalised ideas of "the right decision" at each point. As one woman notes, "...once you've got onto the testing trap you have to get to the end."[39]

Where does this end take us, as individuals and as a society? Does prenatal diagnosis represent liberation or the beginning of a slippery slope towards selecting babies on the basis of socially acceptable characteristics? How will the "new genetics" impact prenatal diagnosis, with the huge amount of information that will soon become available about our unborn babies? And does it, as Rothman suggests, make every woman feel that her pregnancy is "tentative" until she receives reassuring news?

The answers to these and other questions are as yet unknown, but what is certain is that this technology will become more sophisticated in the coming years, and our choices more complex. Mother Nature, like many women who are enrolling in these tests, does not know whether to laugh or cry.

First published in byronchild, *Sept 2004, number 11. Also published, in edited form, in* MIDIRS *Midwifery Digest, March 2005, vol 15(1), pp 7–14. This version updated May 2005.*

References

1. Kelly J, Bean C. *Australian Attitudes.* Sydney: Allen and Unwin, 1988.
2. Biggio JR, Jr., et al. An outcomes analysis of five prenatal screening strategies for trisomy 21 in women younger than 35 years. *Am J Obstet Gynecol* 2004; 190(3):721–9.
3. Mulvey S, Wallace EM. Levels of knowledge of Down syndrome and Down syndrome testing in Australian women. *Aust N Z J Obstet Gynaecol* 2001; 41(2):167–9.
4. Rostant K, et al. Survey of the knowledge, attitudes and experiences of Western Australian women in relation to prenatal screening and diagnostic procedures. *Aust N Z J Obstet Gynaecol* 2003; 43(2):134–8.
5. Sadler M. Serum screening for Down's syndrome: how much do health professionals know? *Br J Obstet Gynaecol* 1997; 104(2):176–9.
6. Tyzack K, Wallace EM. Down syndrome screening: what do health professionals know? *Aust N Z J Obstet Gynaecol* 2003; 43(3):217–21.
7. Carroll JC, et al. Ontario Maternal Serum Screening Program: practices, knowledge and opinions of health care providers. *Can Med Assoc J* 1997; 156(6):775–84.
8. Wertz D. Drawing lines: notes for policymakers. In: Parens E, Asch A, eds. *Prenatal testing and Disability Rights.* Washington DC: Georgetown University Press, 2000:44–53.
9. de Crespigny L, Dredge R. *Which Tests for my Unborn Baby? – Ultrasound and other prenatal tests.* 2nd edn. Melbourne: Oxford University Press, 1996.
10. Cheng PJ, et al. Elevated maternal midtrimester serum free beta-human chorionic gonadotropin levels in vegetarian pregnancies that cause increased false-positive Down syndrome screening results. *Am J Obstet Gynecol* 2004; 190(2):442–7.
11. Spencer K, et al. The impact of correcting for smoking status when screening for chromosomal anomalies using maternal serum biochemistry and fetal nuchal translucency thickness in the first trimester of pregnancy. *Prenat Diagn* 2004; 24(3):169–73.

12. Watt HC, et al. Effect of allowing for ethnic group in prenatal screening for Down's syndrome. *Prenat Diagn* 1996; 16(8):691–8.

13. Abdul-Hamid S, et al. Maternal serum screening for trisomy 21 in women with a false positive result in last pregnancy. *J Obstet Gynaecol* 2004; 24(4):374–6.

14. Spong CY, et al. Risk of abnormal triple screen for Down syndrome is significantly higher in patients with female fetuses. *Prenat Diagn* 1999; 19(4):337–9.

15. Wald NJ, et al. Maternal serum screening for Down's syndrome: the effect of routine ultrasound scan determination of gestational age and adjustment for maternal weight. *Br J Obstet Gynaecol* 1992; 99(2):144–9.

16. Wapner R, et al. First-trimester screening for trisomies 21 and 18. *N Engl J Med* 2003; 349(15):1405–13.

17. Wald NJ, et al. SURUSS in perspective. *Br J Obstet Gynaecol* 2004; 111(6):521–31.

18. UK National Screening Programmes Committee Programmes Directorate. Screening for Down's syndrome: Model of best practice (Appendix 3). In: *National Down's Syndrome Screening Programme for England*. Oxford: UK National Screening Programmes Committee Programmes Directorate, 2004 www.nelh.nhs.uk/screening/dssp/Handbook_final.pdf

19. Royal Australian and New Zealand College of Obstetricians and Gynecologists and Human Genetics Society of Australasia, March 2004. Antenatal Screening for Down Syndrome (DS) and other Fetal Aneuploidy. 2004.

20. U.S. Preventive Services Task Force. Screening Congenital Disorders: Screening for Down Syndrome. *Guide to Clinical Preventive Services*. 2nd edn. Rockville MD: Agency for Healthcare Research and Quality, 1996.

21. Centre for Disease Control. Economic Costs of Birth Defects and Cerebral Palsy – United States, 1992. *Morbidity and Mortality Weekly Report* 1995; 44(37):694–9.

22. Cusick W, et al. Combined first-trimester versus second-trimester serum screening for Down syndrome: a cost analysis. *Am J Obstet Gynecol* 2003; 188(3):745–51.

23. Alfirevic Z, Neilson JP. Antenatal screening for Down's syndrome. *Br Med J* 2004; 329(7470):811–2, p 812.

24. Newnham JP, et al. Effects of repeated prenatal ultrasound examinations on childhood outcome up to 8 years of age: follow-up of a randomised controlled trial. *Lancet* 2004; 364(9450):2038–44, p 2043.

25. Antsaklis AJ, et al. False positive serum biochemical screening and subsequent fetal loss in women less than 35 years of age. *Br J Obstet Gynaecol* 2001; 108(6):589–93.

26. Papantoniou NE, et al. Risk factors predisposing to fetal loss following a second trimester amniocentesis. *Br J Obstet Gynaecol* 2001; 108(10):1053–6.

27. Squier M, et al. Five cases of brain injury following amniocentesis in mid-term pregnancy. *Dev Med Child Neurol* 2000; 42(8):554–60.

28. Thompson PJ, et al. Lung function following first-trimester amniocentesis or chorion villus sampling. *Fetal Diagn Ther* 1991; 6(3–4):148–52.

29. Milner AD, et al. The effects of mid-trimester amniocentesis on lung function in the neonatal period. *Eur J Pediatr* 1992; 151(6):458–60.

30. Greenough A, et al. Invasive antenatal procedures and requirement for neonatal intensive care unit admission. *Eur J Pediatr* 1997; 156(7): 550–2.

31. Medda E, et al. Genetic amniocentesis: a risk factor for preterm delivery? *Eur J Obstet Gynecol Reprod Biol* 2003; 110(2):153–8.

32. Enkin M, et al. *Effective Care in Pregnancy and Childbirth*. 3rd edn. Oxford: Oxford University Press, 2000.

33. Elchalal U, et al. Maternal mortality following diagnostic 2nd-trimester amniocentesis. *Fetal Diagn Ther* 2004; 19(2):195–8.

34. Halliday JL, et al. Importance of complete follow-up of spontaneous fetal loss after amniocentesis and chorion villus sampling. *Lancet* 1992; 340(8824):886–90.

35. Harris RA, et al. Cost utility of prenatal diagnosis and the risk-based threshold. *Lancet* 2004; 363(9405):276–82.

36. Leporrier N, et al. Fetuses with Down's Syndrome detected by prenatal screening are more likely to abort spontaneously than fetuses with Down's Syndrome not detected by prenatal screening. *Br J Obstet Gynaecol* 2003; 110(1):18–21.

37. Stoler JM, et al. Malformations reported in chorionic villus sampling exposed children: a review and analytic synthesis of the literature. *Genet Med* 1999; 1(7):315–22.

38. Silver RK, et al. Late first-trimester placental disruption and subsequent gestational hypertension/preeclampsia. *Obstet Gynecol* 2005; 105(3):587–92.

39. Statham H, Green J. Serum screening for Down's syndrome: some women's experiences. *Br Med J* 1993; 307(6897):174–6, p 175.

40. Elkins TE, Brown D. Ethical concerns and future directions in maternal screening for Down syndrome. *Womens Health Issues* 1995; 5(1):15–20, p 17.

41. Elkins TE, Brown D. Ethical concerns and future directions in maternal screening for Down syndrome. *Womens Health Issues* 1995; 5(1):15–20.

42. Asch A. Prenatal diagnosis and selective abortion: a challenge to practice and policy. *Am J Public Health* 1999; 89(11):1649–57.

43. Alderson P. Down's syndrome: cost, quality and value of life. *Soc Sci Med* 2001; 53(5):627–38.

44. Kingsley J, Levitz M. *Count us in: Growing up with Down syndrome*. San Diego: Harcourt Brace & Company, 1994.

45. Slater C. In Praise of Down Syndrome. Based on an article that appeared in Westminster Mencap's Newsletter Feedback, August 1994 and revised 2002, www.altonweb.com/cs/downsyndrome/index.htm?page=praise.html

46. Reynolds TM. Down's syndrome screening is unethical: views of today's research ethics committees. *J Clin Pathol* 2003; 56(4):268–70.

47. Rothman B: *The Tentative Pregnancy. Amniocentesis and the sexual politics of motherhood.* 2nd edn. London: Pandora, 1994.

48. Sagi M, et al. Prenatal diagnosis of sex chromosome aneuploidy: possible reasons for high rates of pregnancy termination. *Prenat Diagn* 2001; 21(6):461–5.

49. Skotko BG. Prenatally diagnosed Down syndrome: mothers who continued their pregnancies evaluate their health care providers. *Am J Obstet Gynecol* 2005; 192(3):670–7.

50. Thornton JG, et al. A randomised trial of three methods of giving information about prenatal testing. *Br Med J* 1995; 311(7013):1127–30.

51. Akoury HA, et al. Randomized controlled trial of misoprostol for second-trimester pregnancy termination associated with fetal malformation. *Am J Obstet Gynecol* 2004; 190(3):755–62.

52. MIDIRS and NHS Centre for Reviews and dissemination. Antenatal Screening for Congenital Abnormalities – Helping Women to Choose. *Informed Choice for Women (brochures).* Bristol: MIDIRS, 1999.

53. Medeira A, et al. Examination of fetuses after induced abortion for fetal abnormality – a follow-up study. *Prenat Diagn* 1994; 14(5):381–5.

54. White-van Mourik MC, et al. The psychosocial sequelae of a second-trimester termination of pregnancy for fetal abnormality. *Prenat Diagn* 1992; 12(3):189–204.

55. Santalahti P, et al. Women's experiences of prenatal serum screening. *Birth* 1996; 23(2):101–7, p 104.

56. Santalahti P, et al. Women's experiences of prenatal serum screening. *Birth* 1996; 23(2):101–7, p 106.

57. Roelofsen EE, et al. Chances and choices. Psycho-social consequences of maternal serum screening. *J Reprod Infant Psychol* 1993; 11(8):41–7, p 43.

58. Salvesen KA, et al. Comparison of long-term psychological responses of women after pregnancy termination due to fetal anomalies and after perinatal loss. *Ultrasound Obstet Gynecol* 1997; 9(2):80–5.

59. Lloyd J, Laurence KM. Response to termination of pregnancy for genetic reasons. *Z Kinderchir* 1983; 38(2):98–9.

60. Brookes A. Women's experience of routine prenatal ultrasound. *Healthsharing Women: The Newsletter of Healthsharing Women's Health Resource Service,* Melbourne 1994/5; 5(3–4):1–5.

61. Frye A. *Holistic Midwifery; A comprehensive textbook for midwives in home-birth practice. Volume 1 Care During Pregnancy.* Portland OR: Labrys Press, 1998, p 759.

62. Mulder EJ, et al. Prenatal maternal stress: effects on pregnancy and the (unborn) child. *Early Hum Dev* 2002; 70(1–2):3–14, p 3.

63. Huizink A. Prenatal stress and its effects on infant development. Academic Thesis, University Utrecht, 2000.

64. Mulder EJ, et al. Prenatal maternal stress: effects on pregnancy and the (unborn) child. *Early Hum Dev* 2002; 70(1–2):3–14, p 12.

65. Beck M. *Expecting Adam: A True Story of Birth, Rebirth, and Everyday Magic*. New York: Berkley Books, 2001.

66. Noble V. *Down is up for Aaron Eagle*. New York: Harper Collins, 1993.

67. Hall S, et al. Psychological consequences for parents of false negative results on prenatal screening for Down's syndrome: retrospective interview study. *Br Med J* 2000; 320(7232):407–12.

68. Williams C, et al. Is nondirectiveness possible within the context of antenatal screening and testing? *Soc Sci Med* 2002; 54(3):339–47.

69. Roelofsen EE, et al. Chances and choices. Psycho-social consequences of maternal serum screening. *J Reprod Infant Psychol* 1993; 11(8):41–7, p 44.

12

Ultrasound Scans ~ cause for concern

WHEN I was pregnant with my first baby in 1990, I decided against having a scan. This was a rather unexpected decision as my partner and I are both doctors and had even done pregnancy scans ourselves – rather ineptly, but sometimes usefully – while training in GP (family physician) obstetrics a few years earlier.

What influenced me most was my feeling that I could lose something important as a mother if I allowed someone to test my baby. I knew that if a minor or uncertain problem showed up, which is not uncommon, I would be obliged to return again and again and that, after a while, I might feel as if my baby belonged to the system and not to me.

In the years since then I have had three more unscanned babies and have read many articles and research papers about ultrasound. Nothing I have read has made me reconsider my decision. Although ultrasound may sometimes be useful when specific problems are suspected, my conclusion is that it is at best ineffective, and at worse dangerous, when used as a screening tool for every pregnant woman and her baby.

History of ultrasound

Ultrasound was developed during World War II to detect enemy submarines, and was later used in the steel industry. In July 1955 Glasgow surgeon Ian Donald borrowed an industrial machine and, using beefsteaks for comparison, began to experiment with the abdominal tumours that he had removed from his patients. He discovered that different tissues gave different patterns of sound wave "echo", leading him to realise that ultrasound offered a revolutionary way to look into the mysterious world of the growing baby.[1]

This new technology spread rapidly into clinical obstetrics. Commercial machines became available in 1963[2] and by the late 1970s ultrasound had become a routine part of obstetric care.[3] Today, ultrasound is seen as safe and effective, and scanning has become a rite of passage for pregnant women in most developed countries. Here in Australia, it is estimated that 99 percent of babies are scanned at least once in pregnancy, usually as a routine prenatal ultrasound (RPU) at four to five months. In the US, where this cost is borne by the insurer or privately, around 70 percent of pregnant women have a scan,[4] and in European countries, it is estimated that 98 percent of pregnant women have an ultrasound, usually once in each trimester (third) of pregnancy.[5]

However, there is growing concern as to its safety and usefulness. UK consumer activist Beverley Beech has called RPU "The biggest uncontrolled experiment in history" [6] and the Cochrane Collaboration – the peak authority in evidence-based medicine – concludes,

> ...no clear benefit in terms of a substantive outcome measure like perinatal mortality [number of babies dying around the time of birth] can yet be discerned to result from the routine use of ultrasound... For those considering its introduction, the benefit of the demonstrated advantages would need to be considered against the theoretical possibility that the use of ultrasound during pregnancy could be hazardous, and the need for additional resources.[7]

The additional resources consumed by routine ultrasound are substantial. In 1997, for example, the Australian Federal Government paid out A$39 million to subsidise pregnancy scans; an enormous expense compared to the A$54 million paid for all other Medicare obstetric costs,[8] and this figure does not include the additional costs paid by the woman herself. In the US, an estimated US$1.2 billion would be spent yearly if every pregnant woman had a single routine scan.

In 1987, UK radiologist HD Meire, who had been performing pregnancy scans for 20 years, commented,

> The casual observer might be forgiven for wondering why the medical profession is now involved in the wholesale examination of pregnant patients with machines emanating vastly different powers of energy which is not proven to be harmless to obtain information which is not proven to be of any clinical value by operators who are not certified as competent to perform the operations.[9]

The situation today is unchanged on every count.

What is ultrasound?

The term "ultrasound" refers to the ultra-high frequency sound waves used for diagnostic scanning: these waves travel at 10 to 20 million cycles per second, compared to 10 to 20 thousand cycles per second for audible sound.[2] Ultrasound waves are emitted by a transducer (the part of the machine that is put onto the body), and a picture of the underlying tissues is built up from the pattern of echo waves that return to the transducer. Hard surfaces such as bone will return a stronger echo than soft tissue or fluids, giving the bony skeleton a white appearance on the screen.

Ordinary scans use pulses of ultrasound that last only a fraction of a second, with the interval between pulses being used by the machine to interpret the echo that returns. In contrast, Doppler techniques, which are used in specialised scans, fetal monitors and hand-held fetal stethoscopes (sonicaids) use continuous waves, giving much higher levels of exposure than pulsed ultrasound. Many women do not realise that the small machines used to monitor their baby's heartbeat are actually using Doppler ultrasound, although with fairly low exposure levels.

More recently ultrasonographers have begun using vaginal ultrasound, where the transducer is placed high in the pregnant woman's vagina, much closer to her developing baby. This is used mostly in early pregnancy, when abdominal scans can give poor pictures. However, with vaginal ultrasound there is little intervening tissue to shield the baby, who is at a vulnerable stage of development, and exposure levels may be high. Having a vaginal ultrasound is not a pleasant procedure for the woman; the term "diagnostic rape" was coined to describe how some women experience this procedure.

Another recent application for ultrasound is the nuchal translucency (NT) test, where the thickness of the skin fold at the back of the baby's head is measured at around three months. A slight increase in the thickness of the nuchal (neck) fold makes a baby more likely, statistically, to have Down syndrome. When the baby's risk is estimated to be over one in 250 to 300, a definitive test (amniocentesis or chorionic villus sampling) is recommended.

Around 19 out of 20 babies diagnosed as high risk by nuchal translucency will not turn out to be affected by Down syndrome, and their mothers will have experienced several weeks of unnecessary anxiety. A nuchal translucency scan does not detect all babies affected by Down syndrome. (See chapter 11 for more about prenatal testing.)

Information gained from ultrasound

Ultrasound is mainly used for two purposes in pregnancy – either to investigate a possible problem at any stage of pregnancy, or as a routine scan at around 18 to 20 weeks.

If there is bleeding in early pregnancy, for example, ultrasound may predict whether miscarriage is inevitable. Later in pregnancy, ultrasound can be used when a baby is not growing, or when a breech baby or twins are suspected. In these cases the information gained from ultrasound can be very useful in decision-making for the woman and her carers. However, the use of routine prenatal ultrasound (RPU) is more controversial, as this involves scanning all pregnant women in the hope of improving the outcome for some mothers and babies.

Routine prenatal ultrasound, also known as a morphology scan, is designed to check the size and integrity of the baby. The timing of routine scans (18 to 20 weeks) is chosen for practical reasons. It offers a reasonably accurate due date – although dating is most accurate at the early stages of pregnancy, when babies vary the least in size – and the baby is big enough to see most of the abnormalities that are detectable on ultrasound. However, at this stage, the expected date of delivery (EDD) is only accurate to a week either side of the given date, and some studies have suggested that an early examination, or calculations based on a woman's menstrual cycle, can be as accurate as RPU.[10, 11]

And while many women are reassured by a normal scan, RPU actually detects only between 17 and 85 percent of the one in 50 babies that have major abnormalities at birth.[12-15] A study from Brisbane, Australia, showed that ultrasound at a major women's hospital missed around 40 percent of abnormalities, with most of these being difficult or impossible to detect.[16] Major causes of intellectual disability such as cerebral palsy and Down syndrome are unlikely to be picked up on a routine scan, as are heart and kidney abnormalities.

When an abnormality is reported, there is a small chance that the finding is a false positive, where the ultrasound diagnosis is wrong and the baby is, in fact, healthy. A UK survey showed that, for one in 200 babies aborted for major abnormalities, the diagnosis on post-mortem was less severe than predicted by ultrasound, and the termination was probably unjustified. In this survey, 2.4 percent of the babies diagnosed with major malformations, but not aborted, had conditions that were significantly over or under-diagnosed.[17] There are also many cases of error with more minor abnormalities, which can cause anxiety and repeated scans, and there are some conditions which have been seen to spontaneously resolve.[18]

As well as false positives, there are also uncertain cases, where the ultrasound findings cannot be easily interpreted, and the outcome for the baby is not known. In one study involving women at high risk, almost 10 percent of scans were uncertain.[19] This can create immense anxiety for the woman and her family, and this worry may not be allayed by the birth of a normal baby. In the same study, mothers with uncertain diagnoses were still anxious three months after the birth of their baby.

These uncertainties include the so-called "soft markers"; conditions that do not cause problems, but which are sometimes linked with more serious diagnoses such as Down syndrome. These include choroid plexus cysts in the brain, echogenic bowel and heart foci, short femur, short humerus and pyelectasis of the kidney. Around one percent of babies, for example, have a choroid plexus cyst but only one in 150 of these babies will have a chromosomal abnormality such as Down syndrome.[20] Some experts have suggested that soft markers should only be disclosed to women at high risk of abnormality.[21]

In some cases of uncertainty, the doubt can be resolved by further tests such as amniocentesis. In this situation, there may be up to two weeks wait for results, during which time a mother has to decide if she would terminate the pregnancy if an abnormality is found. Some mothers who receive reassuring news have felt that this process has interfered with their relationship with their baby.[22]

As well as estimating the EDD and checking for major abnormalities, RPU can also identify a low-lying placenta (placenta praevia), and detect the presence of more than one baby at an early stage of pregnancy. However, 19 out of 20 women who have placenta praevia detected on an early scan will be needlessly worried; the placenta will effectively move up, and not cause problems at the birth. Furthermore, detection of placenta praevia by RPU has not been found to be safer than detection in labour.[18] No improvement in outcome has been shown for multiple pregnancies either;[7] the vast majority of these will be detected before labour, even without RPU.

The American College of Obstetricians, in their guidelines on routine ultrasound in low-risk pregnancy, conclude,

> In a population of women with low-risk pregnancies, neither a reduction in perinatal morbidity [harm to babies around the time of birth] and mortality nor a lower rate of unnecessary interventions can be expected from routine diagnostic ultrasound. Thus ultrasound should be performed for specific indications in low-risk pregnancy.[23]

Biological effects of ultrasound

Ultrasound waves are known to affect tissues in two main ways. First, the sonar beam causes heating of the highlighted area by about one degree Celsius (1.8 °F). This is presumed to be non-significant, based on whole-body heating in pregnancy, which seems to be safe up to 2.5 °C (4.5 °F).[24] Doppler scans, which use continuous waves, can cause more significant heating, especially in the baby's developing brain.[25]

The second recognised effect is cavitation, where the small pockets of gas that exist within mammalian tissue vibrate and then collapse. In this situation

> ... temperatures of many thousands of degrees Celsius in the gas create a wide range of chemical products, some of which are potentially toxic. These violent processes may be produced by micro-second pulses of the kind which are used in medical diagnosis...[24]

The significance of cavitation effects in human tissue remains uncertain.

However, a number of studies have suggested that these effects may be of real concern in living tissues. The first study suggesting problems was a study on cells grown in the lab. Cell abnormalities caused by exposure to ultrasound were seen to persist for several generations.[26] A more recent study involving newborn rats, who are at a similar stage of brain development to humans at four to five months in utero, showed that ultrasound can damage the myelin that covers nerves,[27] indicating that the nervous system may be particularly susceptible to damage from this technology.

Another animal study published in 2001 showed that exposing mice to dosages typical of obstetric ultrasound caused a 22 percent reduction in the rate of cell division, and a doubling of the rate of apoptosis (programmed cell death) in the cells of the small intestine.[28] Other researchers have found that a single ten-minute ultrasound exposure in pregnancy affects the locomotor and learning abilities of mice offspring in adulthood, with a greater effect from longer exposure time.[29]

Experts in this area have expressed concern, especially in relation to exposure of the developing central nervous system, whose tissues are sensitive to damage by physical agents such as heat and ultrasound. Barnett notes that heating of the baby's brain is more likely after the first trimester (three months), as the baby's bone is more developed, and can reflect and concentrate the ultrasound waves.[25] Barnett warns, "When modern sophisticated equipment is used at maximum operating settings for Doppler examinations, the acoustic outputs are sufficient to produce obvious biological effects."[30]

Mole comments:

> If exposure to ultrasound... does cause death of cells, then the practice of ultrasonic imaging at 16 to 18 weeks will cause loss of neurones [brain cells] with little prospect of replacement of lost cells... The vulnerability is not for malformation but for maldevelopment leading to mental impairment caused by overall reduction in the number of functioning neurones in the future cerebral hemispheres.[31]

Recent research has found that ultrasound can induce bleeding in the lung. The American Institute of Ultrasound in Medicine (AIUM) recently concluded,

> There exists abundant peer-reviewed published scientific research that clearly and convincingly documents that ultrasound at commercial diagnostic levels can produce lung damage and focal haemorrhage [bleeding] in a variety of mammalian species... The degree to which this is a clinically significant problem in humans is not known.[32]

Human studies

Studies on humans exposed to ultrasound have shown that possible adverse effects include premature ovulation,[33] miscarriage or preterm labour,[18, 34] low birth weight,[35, 36] poorer condition at birth,[37] perinatal death,[38] dyslexia,[39] delayed speech development,[40] and less right-handedness.[41–44] Non right-handedness (left-handedness and ambidexterity) is a consistent finding in many studies and is, in other circumstances, seen as a marker of damage to the developing brain.[45] One Australian study showed that babies exposed to five or more Doppler ultrasounds were 30 percent more likely to develop intrauterine growth retardation (IUGR) – a condition that ultrasound is often used to detect.[36]

Two long-term randomised controlled trials in Sweden and Norway compared exposed and unexposed (or less exposed) children's development at eight to nine years old, and found no measurable effect on growth, development and learning.[46–51] However, as above, there was more non-right handedness in the offspring.[41, 43, 44] It is difficult to gain reassurance from these trials because, for example, in the Swedish study, 35 percent of the supposedly unexposed group actually had a scan,[41] and in the major branch of the Norwegian trial, scanning time was only three minutes.[44] And, as the authors note, intensities used today are many times higher than in 1979–81.

A more recent randomised trial, comparing outcomes after single and multiple pregnancy (Doppler) scans, has produced some degree of reassurance, finding no differences in the learning and motor functions of offspring followed to eight years old.[52] This study did not, however, include a group of unexposed children so we do not know whether these children's outcomes are actually normal. It is also noteworthy that almost 45 percent of the "single scan" group received two or more scans.[36] The researchers state, "…our results do not lessen our need to undertake further studies of potential bioeffects of prenatal ultrasound scans."[53]

A recent summary of the safety of ultrasound in human studies, published in May 2002 in the prestigious US journal *Epidemiology* suggested:

> Continued research is needed to evaluate the potential adverse effects of ultrasound exposure during pregnancy. These studies should measure the acoustic output, exposure time, number of exposures per subject, and the timing during the pregnancy when exposure(s) occurred.[54]

These authors concluded: "Until long-term effects can be evaluated across generations, caution should be exercised when using this modality during pregnancy."[55]

Ultrasound exposure and dose

As these authors imply, we need to know the exposure involved in all studies of ultrasound but this is not easy to measure because there is a huge range of output, or dose, possible from a single machine. Ultrasound machines can give comparable pictures using a lower, or a 5,000 times higher, output and, because of the complexity of machines, it has been difficult to quantify the output for each examination.[57]

Furthermore, the incredibly fine details that we are now seeing on scans come at the cost of substantial increases in output. Recent changes to US FDA regulations now allow operators to use ultrasound machines at very high outputs, exposing unborn babies to intensities up to eight times higher than previously allowed, provided the output is displayed on the machine.[57]

This new regulation gives operators a worryingly high degree of self-regulation, and its success in protecting unborn babies from harm depends on an appreciation, by each operator, of complex biophysical interactions (which are not well understood) and of the risk–benefit involved in every examination.[58] Such expectations may not be realistic; in Australia, the UK, US, and most other countries, ultrasonography training is voluntary, even for obstetricians, and the skill and experience of operators varies widely. It also seems that few operators are aware of research findings such as those mentioned above.

If you choose to have a scan, I recommend that you copy "My Baby's Ultrasound Exposure Record" and ask the doctor who orders your test, as well as the operator who performs the test, to fill in the details and to sign it. This will give you a record of your baby's exposure and will also raise awareness, in both doctor and technician, of the dosage that is used on your baby.

As the AIUM noted in 2000,

> ... the responsibility of an informed decision concerning possible adverse effects of ultrasound in comparison to desired information will probably become more important over the next few years.[59]

Women's experiences of ultrasound

Women have not been consulted at any stage in the development of this technology, and their experiences and wishes are presumed to coincide with, or be less important than, the medical information that ultrasound provides. For example, supporters of RPU presume that early diagnosis and termination is beneficial to the affected woman and her family. However, the discovery of a major abnormality on RPU can lead to very difficult decision-making.

Some women who agree to have an ultrasound are unaware that they may get information about their baby that they do not want, as they would not contemplate a termination. Other women can feel pressured to have a termination, or at the least feel some emotional distancing, when their baby is diagnosed with a possible abnormality.[22]

Furthermore, there is no evidence that women who have chosen termination for a baby with a lethal abnormality are, in the long term, psychologically better off than women whose babies have died at birth; in fact, there are suggestions that the opposite may be true in some cases.[60] And when termination has been chosen, women are unlikely to share their story with others and can experience considerable guilt and pain from the knowledge that they themselves chose the loss.[61]

When a minor abnormality is found – which may or may not be present at birth, as discussed above – a woman can feel that some of the pleasure has been taken away from her pregnancy. And, as noted in chapter 11, the process of prenatal diagnosis can cause harm to the baby if it generates a high degree of anxiety, and high levels of stress hormones, in the mother, especially in the first half of pregnancy.[62]

Women's experiences with ultrasound, and other tests used for prenatal diagnosis such as amniocentesis, are thoughtfully presented in the book *The Tentative Pregnancy* by Barbara Katz Rothman.[63] The author documents the heartache that women can go through when a difficult diagnosis is made; for some women, this pain can take years to resolve. These issues are further explored in chapter 11, "Prenatal Diagnosis".

My Baby's Ultrasound Exposure Record

The following procedure requires the use of ultrasound:

. . . .

This is necessary to obtain the following information:

. . . .

To my knowledge, there is no current alternative method available to obtain this information that carries less risk to

. . . . (mother's name)

Signature . . . .   Date . . . .
              (doctor or midwife)

The ultrasonographer is asked to specify:

Manufacturer and model of ultrasound equipment . . . .

. . . . Date of last calibration . . . .

Type or combination of types of ultrasound used . . . .

Intensity of exposure (W/cm sq or mW/cm sq) . . . .

Time commenced . . . .   Time Completed . . . .

Duration of exposure . . . .

Name of hospital or clinic . . . .

Carried out by . . . .

Qualifications . . . .   Position . . . .

Signature . . . .   Date . . . .

Adapted with permission from Beech B A L and Robinson J. Ultrasound? Unsound!, Association for Improvements in the Maternity Services, Surbiton, UK.

To my mind, ultrasound also represents yet another way in which the deep internal knowledge that a mother has of her body and her baby is made secondary to technological information that comes from an expert using a machine; thus the cult of the expert is imprinted from the earliest weeks of life.

Furthermore, by treating the baby as a separate being, ultrasound artificially splits mother from baby well before this separation is a physiological or psychic reality. This further emphasises our culture's favouring of individualism over mutuality and sets the scene for possible – but to my mind artificial – conflicts of interest between mother and baby in pregnancy, birth, and parenting.

Conclusions and recommendations

I would urge all pregnant women to think deeply before they choose to have a routine ultrasound. It is not compulsory, despite what some may say, and the risks, benefits, and implications of scanning need to be considered by each mother for herself and her baby, according to their specific situation.

If you choose to have a scan, be clear about the information that you do and do not want to be told. Have your scan done by an operator with a high level of skill and experience (usually this means performing at least 750 scans per year), and say that you want the shortest scan possible. Ask them to fill out "My Baby's Ultrasound Exposure Record", or give you the information, and to sign it.

If an abnormality is found, ask for counselling and a second opinion as soon as practical. And remember that it's your baby, your body, and your choice.

First published in Nexus *magazine, vol 9, no 6, Oct–Nov 2002. This version updated March 2005.*

References

1. Wagner M. Ultrasound: more harm than good? *Midwifery Today Int Midwife* 1999(50):28–30.
2. de Crespigny L, Dredge R. *Which Tests for my Unborn Baby?– Ultrasound and other prenatal tests.* 2nd edn. Melbourne: Oxford University Press, 1996.

3. Oakley A. The history of ultrasonography in obstetrics. *Birth* 1986; 13(1):8–13.

4. Martin J, et al. *Births: Final data for 2002. National vital statistics reports.* Hyattsville MD: National Center for Health Statistics, 2003.

5. Levi S. Routine ultrasound screening of congenital anomalies. An overview of the European experience. *Ann N Y Acad Sci* 1998; 847:86–98.

6. Beech BL. Ultrasound unsound? Talk at Mercy Hospital, Melbourne, April 1993.

7. Neilson JP. Ultrasound for fetal assessment in early pregnancy. *Cochrane Database Syst Rev* 2000(2):CD000182.

8. Senate Community Affairs Reference Group. *Rocking the Cradle: A report into childbirth procedures.* Canberra: Commonwealth of Australia, 1999.

9. Meire HB. The safety of diagnostic ultrasound. *Br J Obstet Gynaecol* 1987; 94(12):1121–2, p 1122.

10. Kieler H, et al. Comparison of ultrasonic measurement of biparietal diameter and last menstrual period as a predictor of day of delivery in women with regular 28 day-cycles. *Acta Obstet Gynecol Scand* 1993; 72(5):347–9.

11. Olsen O, Aaroe Clausen J. Routine ultrasound dating has not been shown to be more accurate than the calendar method. *Br J Obstet Gynaecol* 1997; 104(11):1221–2.

12. Shirley IM, et al. Routine radiographer screening for fetal abnormalities by ultrasound in an unselected low risk population. *Br J Radiol* 1992; 65(775):564–9.

13. Luck CA. Value of routine ultrasound scanning at 19 weeks: a four year study of 8849 deliveries. *Br Med J* 1992; 304(6840):1474–8.

14. Ewigman BG, et al. Effect of prenatal ultrasound screening on perinatal outcome. RADIUS Study Group. *N Engl J Med* 1993; 329(12):821–7.

15. Chitty LS, et al. Effectiveness of routine ultrasonography in detecting fetal structural abnormalities in a low risk population. *Br Med J* 1991; 303(6811):1165–9.

16. Chan F. Limitations of Ultrasound. *Perinatal Society of Australia and New Zealand 1st Annual Congress.* Fremantle, Australia, 1997.

17. Brand IR, et al. Specificity of antenatal ultrasound in the Yorkshire Region: a prospective study of 2261 ultrasound detected anomalies. *Br J Obstet Gynaecol* 1994; 101(5):392–7.

18. Saari-Kemppainen A, et al. Ultrasound screening and perinatal mortality: controlled trial of systematic one-stage screening in pregnancy. The Helsinki Ultrasound Trial. *Lancet* 1990; 336(8712):387–91.

19. Sparling JW, et al. The relationship of obstetric ultrasound to parent and infant behavior. *Obstet Gynecol* 1988; 72(6):902–7.

20. Whittle M. Ultrasonographic "soft markers" of fetal chromosomal defects. *Br Med J* 1997; 314(7085):918.

21. Stewart TL. Screening for aneuploidy: the genetic sonogram. *Obstet Gynecol Clin North Am* 2004; 31(1):21–33.

22. Brookes A. Women's experience of routine prenatal ultrasound. *Healthsharing Women: The Newsletter of Healthsharing Women's Health Resource Service, Melbourne* 1994/5; 5(3–4):1–5.

23. American College of Obstetricians and Gynecologists. ACOG practice patterns. Routine ultrasound in low-risk pregnancy. Number 5, August 1997. *Int J Gynaecol Obstet* 1997; 59(3):273–8.

24. American Institute of Ultrasound in Medicine Bioeffects Committee. Bioeffects considerations for the safety of diagnostic ultrasound. *J Ultrasound Med* 1988; 7(9 Suppl):S1–38.

25. Barnett SB. Intracranial temperature elevation from diagnostic ultrasound. *Ultrasound Med Biol* 2001; 27(7):883–8.

26. Liebeskind D, et al. Diagnostic ultrasound: effects on the DNA and growth patterns of animal cells. *Radiology* 1979; 131(1):177–84.

27. Ellisman MH, et al. Diagnostic levels of ultrasound may disrupt myelination. *Exp Neurol* 1987; 98(1):78–92.

28. Stanton MT, et al. Diagnostic ultrasound induces change within numbers of cryptal mitotic and apoptotic cells in small intestine. *Life Sci* 2001; 68(13):1471–5.

29. Suresh R, et al. Long-term effects of diagnostic ultrasound during fetal period on postnatal development and adult behavior of mouse. *Life Sci* 2002; 71(3):339–50.

30. Barnett SB, Maulik D. Guidelines and recommendations for safe use of Doppler ultrasound in perinatal applications. *J Matern Fetal Med* 2001; 10(2):75–84, p 75.

31. Mole R. Possible hazards of imaging and Doppler ultrasound in obstetrics. *Birth* 1986; 13 Suppl:23–33, p 26.

32. American Institute of Ultrasound in Medicine. Section 4 – bioeffects in tissues with gas bodies. American Institute of Ultrasound in Medicine. *J Ultrasound Med* 2000; 19(2):97–108, 154–68, p 107.

33. Testart J, et al. Premature ovulation after ovarian ultrasonography. *Br J Obstet Gynaecol* 1982; 89(9):694–700.

34. Lorenz RP, et al. Randomized prospective trial comparing ultrasonography and pelvic examination for preterm labor surveillance. *Am J Obstet Gynecol* 1990; 162(6):1603–7; discussion 1607–10.

35. Geerts LT, et al. Routine obstetric ultrasound examinations in South Africa: cost and effect on perinatal outcome – a prospective randomised controlled trial. *Br J Obstet Gynaecol* 1996; 103(6):501–7.

36. Newnham JP, et al. Effects of frequent ultrasound during pregnancy: a randomised controlled trial. *Lancet* 1993; 342(8876):887–91.

37. Newnham JP, et al. Doppler flow velocity waveform analysis in high risk pregnancies: a randomized controlled trial. *Br J Obstet Gynaecol* 1991; 98(10):956–63.

38. Davies JA, et al. Randomised controlled trial of Doppler ultrasound screening of placental perfusion during pregnancy. *Lancet* 1992; 340(8831):1299–303.

39. Stark CR, et al. Short- and long-term risks after exposure to diagnostic ultrasound in utero. *Obstet Gynecol* 1984; 63(2):194–200.

40. Campbell JD, et al. Case-control study of prenatal ultrasonography exposure in children with delayed speech. *Can Med Assoc J* 1993; 149(10):1435–40.

41. Kieler H, et al. Routine ultrasound screening in pregnancy and the children's subsequent handedness. *Early Hum Dev* 1998; 50(2):233–45.

42. Kieler H, et al. Sinistrality – a side-effect of prenatal sonography: a comparative study of young men. *Epidemiology* 2001; 12(6):618–23.

43. Salvesen KA, Eik-Nes SH. Ultrasound during pregnancy and subsequent childhood non-right handedness: a meta-analysis. *Ultrasound Obstet Gynecol* 1999; 13(4):241–6.

44. Salvesen KA, et al. Routine ultrasonography in utero and subsequent handedness and neurological development. *Br Med J* 1993; 307(6897):159–64.

45. Odent M. Where does handedness come from? Handedness from a primal health research perspective. *Primal Health Research* 1998; 6(1):1–6.

46. Kieler H, et al. Routine ultrasound screening in pregnancy and the children's subsequent neurologic development. *Obstet Gynecol* 1998; 91(5 Pt 1):750–6.

47. Kieler H, et al. Routine ultrasound screening in pregnancy and the children's subsequent growth, vision and hearing. *Br J Obstet Gynaecol* 1997; 104(11):1267–72.

48. Salvesen KA, et al. Routine ultrasonography in utero and subsequent growth during childhood. *Ultrasound Obstet Gynecol* 1993; 3(1):6–10.

49. Salvesen KA, et al. Routine ultrasonography in utero and speech development. *Ultrasound Obstet Gynecol* 1994; 4(2):101–3.

50. Salvesen KA, et al. Routine ultrasonography in utero and subsequent vision and hearing at primary school age. *Ultrasound Obstet Gynecol* 1992; 2(4):243–4, 245–7.

51. Salvesen KA, et al. Routine ultrasonography in utero and school performance at age 8–9 years. *Lancet* 1992; 339(8785):85–9.

52. Newnham JP, et al. Effects of repeated prenatal ultrasound examinations on childhood outcome up to 8 years of age: follow-up of a randomised controlled trial. *Lancet* 2004; 364(9450):2038–44.

53. Newnham JP, et al. Effects of repeated prenatal ultrasound examinations on childhood outcome up to 8 years of age: follow-up of a randomised controlled trial. *Lancet* 2004; 364(9450):2038–44, p 2043.

54. Marinac-Dabic D, et al. The safety of prenatal ultrasound exposure in human studies. *Epidemiology* 2002; 13(3 Suppl):S19–22, p S19.

55. Marinac-Dabic D, et al. The safety of prenatal ultrasound exposure in human studies. *Epidemiology* 2002; 13(3 Suppl):S19–22, p S22.

56. Meire HB. The safety of diagnostic ultrasound. *Br J Obstet Gynaecol* 1987; 94(12):1121–2.

57. American Institute of Ultrasound in Medicine. Section 7 – discussion of the mechanical index and other exposure parameters. *J Ultrasound Med* 2000; 19(2):143–8, 154–68.

58. Barnett SB, Maulik D. Guidelines and recommendations for safe use of Doppler ultrasound in perinatal applications. *J Matern Fetal Med* 2001; 10(2):75–84.

59. Fowlkes JB, Holland CK. Mechanical bioeffects from diagnostic ultrasound: AIUM consensus statements. American Institute of Ultrasound in Medicine. *J Ultrasound Med* 2000; 19(2):69–72, p 70.

60. Watkins D. An alternative to termination of pregnancy. *Practitioner* 1989; 233(1472):990, 992.

61. Loach E. The hardest thing I have ever done. *Sunday Herald Sun* 3 August 2004; 8–12.

62. Mulder EJ, et al. Prenatal maternal stress: effects on pregnancy and the (unborn) child. *Early Hum Dev* 2002; 70(1–2):3–14.

63. Rothman B. *The Tentative Pregnancy: Amniocentesis and the sexual politics of motherhood.* 2nd edn. London: Pandora, 1994.

Undisturbed Birth ~
Mother Nature's blueprint for safety, ease, and ecstasy

T HE term "undisturbed birth" came to have great meaning for me when I gave birth to my fourth baby, unassisted (and unexpectedly breech) at home.[1] It describes well this beautiful experience, which awakened me anew to the ecstasy of birth, and I realised that the process of birth can be very simple if we can avoid disturbing it. Comparing this birth to my three previous midwife-assisted home births, and to home and hospital births that I had attended, I saw also how ingrained is our habit of disturbance and that our need to "do something" so often becomes self-fulfilling in the birth room.

I realised that birth is also very complex, and that the process is exquisitely sensitive to outside influences. The parallels between making love and giving birth became very clear to me, not only in terms of passion and love,[2] but also because we need essentially the same conditions for both experiences: to feel private, safe, and unobserved. Yet the conditions that we provide for birthing women are almost diametrically opposed to these; no wonder giving birth is so difficult for most women today.

What disturbs birth?

As I imply, anything that disturbs a labouring woman's sense of safety and privacy will disrupt the birth process. This definition covers most of modern obstetrics, which has created an entire industry around the observation and monitoring of pregnant and birthing women. Some of the techniques used are painful or uncomfortable, most involve some transgression of bodily or social boundaries, and almost all techniques are performed by people who are essentially strangers to the woman herself. All of these factors are disruptive to pregnant and birthing women.

Underlying these procedures is an ingrained distrust of women's bodies, and of the natural processes of gestation and birth. This attitude in itself has a strong nocebo, or noxious, effect.

On top of this is another obstetric layer devoted to correcting the "dysfunctional labour" that such disruption is likely to produce. The resulting distortion of the process of birth – what we might call "disturbed birth" – has come to be what women expect when they have a baby and perhaps, in a strange circularity, it works. Under this model women are almost certain to need the interventions that the medical model employs, and to come away grateful to be saved, no matter how difficult or traumatic their experience.

These disturbances are counterproductive for midwives also. When a midwife's time and focus is taken up with monitoring and recording, she is less able to be "with woman" – the original meaning of the word midwife – as the guardian of normal birth.

When a midwife's intuitive skills and ways of knowing are increasingly sacrificed to technology, more and more invasive procedures will be needed to get information that, in other times, her heart and hands would have illuminated. And when a woman misses out on the ecstasy of birth, so does her midwife, which will influence her job satisfaction as well as her future expectations of birth.

Undisturbed birth

However, our women's bodies have their own wisdom and our innate system of birth, refined over 100,000 generations, is not so easily overpowered. This system, which I am calling undisturbed birth, has the evolutionary stamp of approval not only because it is safe and efficient for the vast majority of mothers and babies, but also because it incorporates our hormonal blueprint for ecstasy in birth.

When birth is undisturbed, our birthing hormones can take us into ecstasy – outside (*ec*) our usual state (*stasis*) – so that we enter motherhood awakened and transformed.

This is not just a good feeling; the post-birth hormones that suffuse the brains of a new mother and her baby also catalyse profound neurological (brain) changes. These changes give the new mother personal empowerment, physical strength, and an intuitive sense of her baby's needs,[3] and prepare both partners for the pleasurable mutual dependency that will ensure a mother's care and protection, and her baby's survival.

Undisturbed birth represents the smoothest hormonal orchestration of the birth process, and therefore the easiest transition possible; physiologically, hormonally, psychologically, and emotionally, from pregnancy and birth to new motherhood and lactation, for each woman. When a mother's hormonal orchestration is undisturbed, her baby's safety is also enhanced, not only during labour and delivery, but also in the critical transition from womb to world. Furthermore, the optimal expression of a woman's motherhood hormones will ensure that her growing child is well nurtured, adding another layer of evolutionary fitness to the process of undisturbed birth.

Undisturbed birth does not mean unsupported birth. Some anthropologists believe that human females have sought assistance in birth since we began to walk on two legs. The change in our pelvic shape that accompanied our upright stance added uniquely complex twists and turns to our babies' journeys during birth, making assistance more necessary than for other mammals.[4] It does mean having supporters whom we have specifically chosen as our familiar and loving companions, who are confident in our abilities, and who will intervene as little and as gently as possible.

Undisturbed birth does not imply that birth will be pain-free. The stress hormones released in birth are equivalent to those of an endurance athlete,[5] a fact which reflects the magnitude of this event, and explains some of the sensations of birth. And like a marathon runner, our task in birth is not so much to avoid the pain – which usually makes it worse – but to realise that birth is a peak bodily performance, for which our bodies are superbly designed. Undisturbed birth gives us the space to follow our instincts and to find our own rhythm in an atmosphere of support and trust, which will also help with the release of our birth hormones, aiding us further in transmuting pain.

Undisturbed birth does not guarantee an easy birth. There are many layers, both individual and cultural, that can impede us at birth, and we must also consider that birth has been significantly disturbed in our culture for many generations. But when we approach birth with the intention of minimum disturbance, we are optimising the functioning of our birth hormones. This, coupled with our unparalleled levels of hygiene and nutrition, gives us a better chance of an easy and safe birth than almost any of our foremothers, from whom we have also inherited, through evolution and natural selection, the female anatomy and physiology that gives birth most easily and efficiently.

The hormones of birth

The hormonal orchestration of birth to which I refer is exceedingly complex. Despite a great amount of research over the last 50 years, involving both humans and other mammals, many fundamental processes are still not understood. For example, we still do not understand what causes the onset of human parturition (childbirth), although recent research implicates a substance secreted into the amniotic fluid by the baby's mature lung.[6]

In this paper, I will be primarily discussing the hormones oxytocin; beta-endorphin; the catecholamines, adrenaline and noradrenaline (epinephrine and norepinephrine); and prolactin. As the hormones of love; transcendence; excitement; and mothering, respectively, these form the major components of an ecstatic cocktail of hormones that nature prescribes to aid birthing mothers of all mammalian species.

Levels of these hormones build during an undisturbed labour, peaking around the time of birth or soon after for both mother and baby, and subsiding or reorganising over the subsequent hours or days. An optimal hormonal orchestration provides safety, ease, and ecstasy during this time for mother and baby. Conversely, interference with this process will also disrupt this delicate hormonal orchestration, making birth more difficult and painful, and potentially less safe.

All of these hormones are produced primarily in the middle or mammalian brain, also called the limbic system. For birth to proceed optimally, this more primitive part of the brain needs to take precedence over our neo-cortex – our new or higher brain – that is the seat of our rational mind. This shift in consciousness, which some call "going to another planet", is aided by (and also aids) the release of birthing hormones such as beta-endorphin, and is inhibited by disturbances such as bright lighting, conversation, and expectations of rationality.

If we were to consider giving birth as the deepest meditation possible, and accord birthing women the appropriate respect, support, and lack of disturbance, we would provide the best physiological conditions for birth. Alternatively, we can consider the parallels between birth and sexual activity, which involves an almost identical pattern of hormone release. In birth, as in lovemaking, we need to feel safe and private so that we can let down our guard, let our hormones flow and reap the rewards of the processes – which include, in both situations, an ultimate dose of hormonal ecstasy.

Mother Nature's pragmatic and efficient principles dictate that these hormones should also help the baby at birth, and this is being increasingly confirmed by scientific research. This hormonal interdependence contradicts the oft-repeated medical response to natural birth as the mother prizing her experience over her baby's safety, and underlines the mutual dependency of mother and baby, even as they begin their physical separation.

Oestrogen and progesterone

In our current understanding, the prime movers – the hormones that are involved in setting the scene, which includes activating, inhibiting, and reorganising other hormone systems – are the sex steroids progesterone and oestrogen, of which there are three distinct types. In pregnancy, progesterone production by the placenta increases 10 to 18 times, while placental production of oestriol, the dominant type of pregnancy oestrogen, rises more than 1,000 times.[7]

These hormones are thought to play a critical but complex role in the initiation of labour, most likely through changes in their levels and/or ratios, or perhaps through their effects at a local (paracrine) level within the expectant mother's uterus.[8]

Oestrogen also increases the number of uterine oxytocin receptors[9] and gap junctions (connections between muscle cells)[10] in late pregnancy, effectively "wiring up" the uterus for co-ordinated contractions in labour. Oestrogen and progesterone together also activate opiate pain-killing pathways in the brain and spinal cord in preparation for labour.[7]

Oxytocin

Oxytocin has been called the hormone of love because of its connection with sexual activity, orgasm, birth, and breastfeeding. In addition, oxytocin is produced in social situations such as sharing a meal[11], making it a hormone of altruism, or, as Michel Odent suggests, of "forgetting oneself".[12]

Oxytocin is made in the hypothalamus, the nervous system's primary communicator with the endocrine (hormone) system. It is then stored, and released in pulses from the posterior pituitary, the master gland of the endocrine system, into the bloodstream. Pulses occur every three to five minutes, becoming stronger later in labour. Levels are difficult to measure in the human because of its pulsatile pattern of release and because, in pregnancy, the placenta makes a specific enzyme to metabolise (break down) oxytocin. Its half-life (the time taken to reduce blood levels by half) has been variously estimated as three and a half minutes,[13] 10 to 12 minutes,[14] and 15 minutes.[15]

The number of oxytocin receptors in a pregnant woman's uterus increases substantially late in pregnancy, increasing her sensitivity to oxytocin. Circulating levels do not actually rise until late in labour, as noted below.[16] Receptors are most dense in the woman's fundus (the top of her uterus),[14] which helps to co-ordinate efficient contractions in labour.

Oxytocin is thought to be the prime initiator of the rhythmic uterine contractions of labour, although it is not the only hormonal system involved – mice who have had their oxytocin gene inactivated are still able to deliver, but not breastfeed, their young.[17] It has been hypothesised that prostaglandins, which are produced locally in the uterus, take over this uterotonic (causing contractions) role later in labour.[13] Oxytocin has also been shown to have a pain-killing effect in rats and mice.[18]

The baby also releases large amounts of oxytocin from the pituitary during labour, and there is some evidence that this oxytocin may be transported back through the placenta into the mother's circulation.[13, 19] Oxytocin is also produced by the placenta and fetal membranes, as well as being present in amniotic fluid.[13] Some researchers have therefore suggested that fetal oxytocin may directly stimulate the mother's uterine muscle, and that this may be important in the process of labour.[20]

Oxytocin catalyses the final powerful uterine contractions that help the mother to birth her baby quickly and easily. At this time, the baby's descending head stimulates stretch receptors in a woman's lower vagina, giving positive feedback to pituitary oxytocin neurons (brain cells) and releasing oxytocin in large quantities.[21] This is also known as the Ferguson reflex. When the labour has been undisturbed, this effect is amplified by adrenaline/noradrenaline, as noted below, producing a more powerful mechanism called the fetal ejection reflex.[22]

After the birth, ongoing high levels of oxytocin, augmented by more pulses released as the baby touches, licks, and nuzzles the mother's breast,[23] help to keep her uterus contracted and so protect her against postpartum haemorrhage. Skin-to-skin and eye-to-eye contact between mother and baby help to optimise oxytocin release.[24] Oxytocin levels peak with the delivery of the placenta and subside over about 60 minutes.[25]

Newborn oxytocin levels peak at around 30 minutes after birth[26] so that during the first hour after birth, both mother and baby are bathed in an ecstatic cocktail of hormones, including oxytocin, the hormone of love. Newborn babies have elevated levels of oxytocin for at least four days after birth,[26] and oxytocin is also present in breastmilk.[27]

Oxytocin is also involved with the olfactory system (smell), which is known to play an important role in mammalian birth. In labour, stimulation of the olfactory sense augments oxytocin release, and after the birth, smell is thought to be important in the establishment of mothering behaviour.[7, 28] For example, one study found that monkeys delivered by caesarean rejected their offspring unless the babies were swabbed with secretions from the mother's vagina.[29] Newborn babies are attracted to the smell of amniotic fluid (which is soothing[30]) and of their mother's nipple,[31] which may help them with breast attachment. The large number of human genes that are involved with smell – one to two percent of the total[32] – suggests that smell is of evolutionary importance in mother–infant bonding in our species.

As well as reaching peak levels after birth, oxytocin is secreted in large amounts in pregnancy, when it acts to enhance nutrient absorption, and conserve energy by making pregnant women more sleepy.[33] The well-documented suppression of the hypotha-lamic-pituitary-adrenal (HPA) stress pathway during pregnancy and lactation, which makes pregnant and breastfeeding mothers more relaxed, more resistant to stress and experience more posi-tive mood states, may be due, at least in part, to oxytocin.[7]

Animal studies have shown that the effects of oxytocin, admin-istered to a caged animal, also extend to its untreated cagemates.[34, 35] It seems likely that there is an olfactory or pheromonal transmission (via hormone-like substances that act outside the body) involving oxytocin. This transmission may also explain the positive emo-tions that birth helpers often feel when attending a woman who is birthing with peak levels of oxytocin.

During breastfeeding (lactation), oxytocin mediates the milk-ejection, or let-down, reflex and is released in pulses as the baby suckles. During the months and years of lactation, oxytocin continues to act to keep the mother relaxed and well nourished. Key oxytocin researcher Kerstin Uvnas Moberg calls it "...a very efficient anti-stress situation, which prevents a lot of disease later on."[33] From her research, mothers who breastfed for more than seven weeks were calmer when their babies were six months old, than mothers who did not breastfeed at all.

The oxytocin system has also been implicated in aggressive-defensive behaviour in lactating females,[36] although opiate mechanisms are also known to be involved.[37]

Other studies indicate that oxytocin is also involved in cognition, tolerance and adaptation, and researchers have recently found that oxytocin also acts as a cardiovascular hormone, with effects such as slowing the heart rate and reducing blood pressure.[38]

Another researcher has ascribed a "relaxation and growth response" to oxytocin release, contrasting this physiologically with the body's fight-or-flight stress response.[39] Other research suggests that the female response to stress is marked by a "tend and befriend" pattern, which may be mediated by oxytocin.[40] Malfunctions of the oxytocin system have been implicated in conditions such as schizophrenia,[41] autism,[42] cardiovascular disease,[43] and drug dependency,[44] and it has been suggested that oxytocin may mediate the antidepressant effect of drugs such as Prozac.[45]

Beta-endorphin

Beta-endorphin is one of a group of naturally occurring opiates (drugs derived from the opium poppy), with properties similar to pethidine (meperidine, Demerol), morphine, and heroin, and has been shown to work on the same receptors of the brain. It is secreted from the pituitary gland under conditions of pain and stress, and high levels are present in pregnancy, birth, and lactation.

Beta-endorphin acts as a natural pain-killer, causing an increasing tolerance to pain in pregnant rats.[46] (It is thought to be the hormone that allows, for example, an injured sportsperson to ignore the pain on the sports field.) Beta-endorphin also suppresses the immune system, which may be important in preventing a pregnant mother's immune system from acting against her baby, whose genetic material is foreign to hers.

Like the addictive opiates, beta-endorphin reduces the effects of stress and induces feelings of pleasure, euphoria, and dependency or, with a partner, mutual dependency. Beta-endorphin levels increase throughout labour,[47] when levels of beta-endorphin and CRH (another stress hormone) reach those found in male endurance athletes during maximal exercise on a treadmill.[5] Maternal levels peak at the time of birth and subside slowly, reaching normal levels one to three days after birth.[48] Such high levels help a labouring woman to transcend pain, as she enters the altered state of consciousness that characterises an undisturbed birth.

The baby also secretes beta-endorphin during labour from the fetal pituitary[49] as well as directly from placental tissue and membranes,[50] and levels in the placenta at birth are even higher than those in maternal blood.[51] Kimball speculates that early cord cutting may "...deprive mothers and infants of placental opioid molecules designed to induce interdependency of mothers and infants."[52]

Beta-endorphin has complex and incompletely understood relationships with other hormonal systems.[46] For example, high levels of beta-endorphin inhibit oxytocin release. It makes sense that, when pain or stress levels are very high, contractions will slow, thus "...rationing labour according to both physiological and psychological stress."[53] Beta-endorphin may also be involved in preventing premature birth by inhibiting the action of oxytocin before labour begins.[54] Beta-endorphin facilitates the release of prolactin during labour,[55] which prepares the mother's breasts for lactation and also aids in lung maturation for the baby.[56]

Beta-endorphin is also important in breastfeeding. Levels peak in the mother at 20 minutes[57] and beta-endorphin is also present in breastmilk,[58] inducing a pleasurable mutual dependency for both mother and baby in their ongoing relationship.

Catecholamines

The fight-or-flight hormones adrenaline and noradrenaline (epinephrine and norepinephrine) are part of the group of hormones known as catecholamines (CAs), and are produced by the body in response to stresses such as hunger, fear and cold. Together they stimulate the sympathetic nervous system for fight or flight.

Catecholamine levels rise during a normal labour;[59] research suggests that adrenaline levels are more responsive to psychological stresses such as pain and anxiety, with noradrenaline increasing in response to the physiological work of labour.[60]

Very high adrenaline levels in the first stage of labour will inhibit oxytocin release, therefore slowing or even stopping labour. Adrenaline also acts to reduce blood flow to the uterus and placenta and therefore to the baby. This makes sense for mammals birthing in the wild, where the presence of danger would activate this fight or flight response, inhibiting labour and diverting blood to the major muscle groups so that the mother can flee to safety. In humans, high levels of adrenaline have been associated with longer labour and adverse fetal heart rate (FHR) patterns, which indicate that the baby is low in oxygen (hypoxic).[60]

After an undisturbed labour, however, when the moment of birth is imminent, these hormones act in a different way. There is a sudden increase in CA levels, especially noradrenaline, which activates the fetal (or fetus) ejection reflex (FER). The mother experiences a sudden rush of energy; she will be upright and alert, with a dry mouth and shallow breathing and perhaps the urge to grasp something. She may express fear, anger, or excitement, and the CA rush will produce, in concert with oxytocin, several very strong contractions, which will birth her baby quickly and easily.[22, 61]

Some birth attendants have made good use of this reflex when a woman is having difficulties in the second (pushing) stage of labour. For example, one anthropologist working with an indigenous Canadian tribe recorded that when a woman was having difficulty in birth, the young people of the village would gather together to help. They would suddenly and unexpectedly shout out close to her, with the shock increasing her catecholamines and triggering her fetal ejection reflex, giving a quick birth.[22]

After the birth, the new mother's CA levels drop steeply. If she is not helped to warm up, the cold stress will keep her CA levels high, which will inhibit her oxytocin production. High CA levels are associated with an increased risk of postpartum haemorrhage.[62]

Noradrenaline, as part of the ecstatic cocktail, is also implicated in instinctive mothering behaviour. Mice bred to be deficient in noradrenaline will not care for their young after birth unless noradrenaline is injected back into their system.[63]

For the baby, too, labour is an exciting and stressful event, reflected in increasing CA levels. In labour these hormones have a very beneficial effect, protecting the baby from the effects of hypoxia (lack of oxygen) and subsequent acidosis by redistributing cardiac output (blood supply)[64] and by increasing the capacity for anaerobic glycolysis (metabolism of glucose at low oxygen levels).[65]

The baby also experiences a marked surge in CA hormones, especially noradrenaline, at the time of birth, probably triggered by pressure on the baby's head.[66] This plays a very important role in the baby's adaptation of extra-uterine life. It aids newborn metabolism by increasing levels of glucose and free fatty acids,[67] which protect the brain from the low blood sugar that can occur (because the baby loses the placental supplies of glucose) in the early newborn period.[68]

In addition, catecholamines enhance respiratory (breathing) adaptation to life outside the womb by increasing the absorption of amniotic fluid from the lungs and stimulating surfactant release.[65] (Surfactant is essential for smooth inflation of the newborn lungs.) CAs also: assist with the necessary newborn shift to non-shivering thermogenesis (heat production); [69] increase cardiac contractility; stimulate breathing; and enhance responsiveness and tone in the newborn.[65]

High CA levels at birth also ensure that the baby is wide-eyed and alert at first contact with the mother. The baby's CA levels also drop steeply after an undisturbed birth, being soothed by contact with the mother, but remain elevated above normal for the first 12 hours.[70]

Prolactin

Prolactin is known as the mothering (or nesting) hormone, and is released from the pituitary gland during pregnancy and lactation. Prolactin is named for its well-known "pro-lactation" effects, preparing a pregnant woman's breasts for lactation and acting postnatally as the major hormone of milk synthesis and breastfeeding.

Prolactin's milk-producing (lactogenic) effect is blocked during pregnancy by high levels of progesterone, produced by the baby's placenta. When progesterone levels drop with delivery of the baby's placenta, prolactin can begin stimulating milk production. All mammalian species also produce a placental hormone with lactogenic effects – in the human this is human placental lactogen (hPL). Human placental lactogen, like prolactin, increases throughout pregnancy and also helps to organise the expectant mother's brain for maternity.[71]

Prolactin is an important hormone in reproduction; mice bred with abnormalities in prolactin release are unsuccessful in reproduction and lacking in maternal behaviour.[72] In all mammalian species, prolactin is thought to play a major role in maternal behaviour through its actions on the nursing mother's brain.[71]

The mother's prolactin levels rise progressively during pregnancy, but decline during labour, reaching the lowest point when her cervix is fully dilated. Prolactin then rises again steeply, peaking in the moments after birth[73] (perhaps due to stimulation of the mother's cervix during delivery[74]) and declining again in the following hours.

During lactation, prolactin levels are directly related to the suckling intensity, duration, and frequency,[71] although prolactin levels actually peak at night.[75] After a nursing episode, breastfeeding mothers are calmer, with an elevation in mood and increased resistance to stress: these effects are likely to be due to the peaks of oxytocin and prolactin, both stress-reducing hormones.[76]

There are more than 300 known bodily effects of prolactin,[72] including: induction of maternal behaviour; increase in appetite and food intake; suppression of fertility; stimulation of motor and grooming activity; reduction of the stress response; stimulation of oxytocin secretion and opioid activity; alteration of the sleep-wake cycle and increase in REM sleep; reduction in body temperature; and stimulation of natural analgesia.[71] Prolactin, along with growth hormone (GH), is one of the hormones of growth and lactation (HGL) and, as such, has a crucial influence in the development and function of the immune system.[77]

This spectrum of prolactin effects has been called the "maternal subroutine" (MS) and is associated psychologically with the perceived need to take care of a child. For example, elevations of prolactin can be triggered by surrogate maternity.[78, 79]

Prolactin is also a hormone of submission or surrender. In some studies of primate troupes, the dominant male has the lowest prolactin level,[80] while other troupe members have higher prolactin levels and are more subordinate and obedient.[12] In the breastfeeding relationship, these prolactin effects may help the mother to put her baby's needs first.

Animal studies show that prolactin release is also increased by carrying infants,[81, 82] and its association with paternal nurturing[83] (including in humans[84]) has earned it the added title "the hormone of paternity".[85] Human studies have shown that, just before the birth, fathers-to-be have elevated prolactin levels, which parallels the rise of prolactin in their partners.[84] Those new fathers with higher prolactin levels are more responsive to newborn cries.[86]

Prolactin levels also peak following male and female orgasm, and levels remain elevated for around an hour afterwards.[87] Prolactin reduces sex drive, which may explain the usual post-coital drop in desire,[87] as well as the lowered libido among people taking antidepressants and antipsychotic drugs,[88] which increase prolactin levels, and among breastfeeding women.

The baby produces prolactin in utero, and prolactin is also present in breast milk, with a significant amount being transferred intact into the newborn circulation, at least in the rat.[89] According to one researcher, "… there is evidence that prolactin plays an important role in the development and maturation of the neonatal [newborn] neuroendocrine [brain-hormone] system."[90] This may partly explain the enhanced IQ and brain development of breastfed babies.[91]

Impact of obstetric procedures

Induction and augmentation with synthetic oxytocin

Induction can be a useful and even life-saving intervention in complicated pregnancies. However, our current rates of induction, and the use of oxytocic ("fast labour") drugs to speed up labour, known as augmentation, stimulation or acceleration, are extreme.

The most commonly used drug for induction and augmentation is synthetic oxytocin, known as Syntocinon or Pitocin (US). In Australia in 2002, more than 25 percent of birthing women had their labour induced, and another 20 percent were augmented during labour, almost all with this drug.[92] In the US in 2002, 44 percent of women reported that their care-givers tried to induce labour; almost one-fifth for solely non-medical reasons. Syntocinon was reportedly used for 85 percent of these inductions, and also administered to the 55 percent of women overall who reported that their labours had been augmented.[93] In the UK[94] and Canada,[95] 20 percent of women in both countries had their labour induced during 2002–3 and 2003–4 respectively.

As with all medical interventions, the balance between benefit and risk becomes weighted towards risk when powerful drugs and procedures are used on essentially healthy individuals. Drugs used for induction and augmentation can cause extra risks for mothers and babies because they produce an abnormal labour. These drugs will also interfere with the orchestration of the mother's ecstatic hormones – and possibly with the brain-hormone system of her baby as well.

Synthetic oxytocin is administered intravenously (IV) in labour, and acts very differently to a labouring woman's intrinsic oxytocin, which is largely released from her middle brain. Firstly, the uterine contractions produced by IV Syntocinon are different to natural contractions – possibly because it is administered continuously rather than in a pulsatile manner[96] – and this can cause detrimental effects to the baby in the womb.

For example, Syntocinon-induced contractions can occur too close together, leaving insufficient time for the baby to recover from the reduced blood flow that occurs when the placenta is compressed with each contraction. Syntocinon also causes the resting tone of the uterus to increase.[97] Such over-stimulation (hyperstimulation) can deprive the baby from the necessary supplies of blood and oxygen, and so produce abnormal FHR patterns, fetal distress (leading to caesarean section), and even uterine rupture.[97]

Birth activist Doris Haire describes the effects of Syntocinon/
Pitocin on the baby:

> The situation is analogous to holding an infant under the sur-
> face of the water, allowing the infant to come to the surface to
> gasp for air, but not to breathe.[98]

With this loss of blood and oxygen, the baby will be at risk, as
the US Pitocin package insert warns, of fetal heart rate abnormalities (bradycardia, premature ventricular contractions and other
arrhythmias – all signs of fetal distress); low five-minute Apgar
scores (signifying poor condition at birth); neonatal jaundice; neonatal retinal hemorrhage; permanent central nervous system or
brain damage and fetal death.[98]

For example, in a US hospital using low or high-dose proto-
cols for induction with Syntocinon (Pitocin), 42 and 55 percent of
induced women respectively experienced hyperstimulation (usually remedied by turning down the infusion rate), and three and six
percent respectively required a caesarean for fetal distress.[99] A Swedish study showed an almost three times higher risk of asphyxia for
babies born after augmentation with Syntocinon,[100] and in a study
in Nepal, where monitoring is not optimal, induced babies were
five times more likely to have signs of brain damage at birth.[101]

Although Syntocinon stimulates uterine contractions, this
has minimal effects on the dilatation of a labouring woman's
cervix, compared to a normal labour.[102] This creates the possibility of a "failed induction" where – despite the presence of regular,
and sometimes very painful, contractions – labour does not progress, the woman's cervix fails to dilate, and a caesarean section
becomes necessary.

Furthermore, oxytocin, whether synthetic or not, cannot cross
from the body back to the brain through the blood–brain barrier.
This means that when it is administered in any way except directly
into the brain, it can cause effects on the body but it cannot act as
the hormone of love. It can, however, interfere with natural oxytocin effects.

For example, there is ample evidence that women who labour
with a Syntocinon infusion are at increased risk of postpartum
haemorrhage.[103–105] Recent research indicates that this is because

prolonged exposure to synthetic oxytocin in labour, for induction or augmentation, leads to a dramatic reduction in the numbers of oxytocin receptors in the labouring woman's uterus.[106] This makes her own postpartum oxytocin release ineffective, and her uterus less likely to contract efficiently in the crucial minutes after birth.

We do not fully understand, however, the psychological, or psychoneuroendocrine (mind-brain-hormone) effects of interference with the oxytocin system at the time of birth.

In one study, women whose labours were augmented with Syntocinon did not experience an increase in beta-endorphin levels in labour,[107] indicating the complexities that may result from interference with any of the hormonal systems of birth. Such hormonal disruption may also explain the findings, in some observational studies, of a reduced rate of breastfeeding following induced labour.[108–110] (This has occurred even among women who intended to breastfeed[110] and when controlling for other variables associated with low breastfeeding rates.[108]) An induced or augmented labour is also more stressful for the mother: stress in labour has been linked with a reduction in breastmilk production.[111]

Other research has suggested that oxytocin may pass through the placenta to the baby unchanged,[19, 112] which implies that the fetal oxytocin system may also be disrupted by administration of synthetic oxytocin in labour. Prairie voles that were exposed to a single dose of synthetic oxytocin a few hours after birth showed abnormalities in sexual and parenting behaviour in adulthood.[113] This raises the possibility of significant long-term effects from perinatal hormone exposure.

There have been few direct studies, animal or human, of the effects of induction and augmentation on the offspring. Observational studies have shown differences in newborn resting brain activity[114] and in neurological development at age two months[115] compared to babies born after spontaneous delivery, but other researchers have found no difference at 30 months (for induction using prostaglandins)[116] and five years of age.[117]

The hypothesis that induction may predispose to neurobehavioral abnormalities such as autism has been proposed,[42, 118, 119] because interference with the oxytocin system has been implicated in autism in animal[120–122] and human studies.[123–125] There is some evidence, from epidemiological (population-based) studies that induction may be a risk factor,[126] but case-control comparisons thus far have not supported this hypothesis.[127–128] It is likely that conditions such as autism have many causative factors,[129] although this may include, especially for vulnerable individuals, exposure to Syntocinon in the perinatal period (around the time of birth).

Note also that, under western obstetric care, synthetic oxytocin is also routinely administered to the mother as her baby is being born, as part of the active management of third stage. If oxytocin can cross the placenta, the majority of newborn babies will be exposed to this substance, with unknown psychoneuroendocrinological effects.[130] (See chapter 15 for more detail about management of the third stage.)

Opiate painkillers

Pethidine (meperidine, Demerol) is the usual opiate administered in Australian and UK labour wards. In Queensland, Australia in 2001, around 40 percent of labouring women used this drug.[131] In the US, other opiates such as nalbuphine (Nubain), butorphanol (Stadol), alphaprodine (Nisentil), hydromorphone (Dilaudid), and fentanyl (Sublimaze) have been traditional mainstays of labour analgesia. Opiate painkillers are reportedly still given to up to 50 percent of women labouring in some US hospitals,[132] despite the increasing popularity of epidural analgesia, which may also contain opiates as discussed below.

Opiates are simple to administer, which partly accounts for their popularity. In many places the midwife or obstetric nurse can prescribe and inject these drugs during labour. However, studies have questioned their efficacy, with some research showing that opiates produce excessive sedation and little pain relief.[133] Studies show an overall reduction in pain of about 20 percent with these drugs.[133–135]

All opiates used in labour can cause side effects, such as maternal nausea, vomiting, sedation, pruritus (itching), hypotension (low blood pressure), and respiratory depression. For the baby, these drugs can cause FHR abnormalities, respiratory depression, impaired early breastfeeding and altered neonatal neurobehaviour (behaviour reflecting brain function),[136] largely due to the sedating effects and their ready passage through the placenta.

Use of these drugs will also reduce a labouring woman's own opioid hormone production,[137] which may be helpful if excessive levels are inhibiting labour. However, the use of pethidine has been shown to slow labour in a dose-response way.[138] In one randomised trial, morphine administered in labour directly reduced oxytocin release,[139] which is consistent with research showing that, within the mammalian brain, opiates reduce the release of oxytocin.[140]

Given that the release of opiates within the brain is connected with maternal behaviour, it is not surprising that animal research has found that these substances (given, in these studies, after the establishment of lactation) can disrupt various aspects of early mothering.[141–144]

Again, we must ask, "What may be the effects for mother and baby of labouring and birthing without peak levels of these hormones of pleasure and transcendence?" Some researchers have nominated our endogenous opiates as the reward system for reproductive acts. That is, the endorphin fix keeps us making babies, having babies, and breastfeeding.[12, 145] Anecdotally I notice that women who have pleasurable experiences of birth and breastfeeding tend to have larger families. On a global scale, countries that have embraced the obstetric model of care, which prizes drugs and interventions above birthing pleasure and empowerment, have experienced steeply declining birth rates in recent years.

More serious are the implications of Swedish research into the use of opiates at birth,[146] recently repeated in a US study.[147] In the first study, researchers looked at the birth records of 200 opiate addicts born between 1945 and 1966, and compared them to their non-addicted siblings. Offspring whose mothers used analgesia in labour (opiates, barbiturates, and nitrous oxide gas) were more likely to become addicted to drugs (opiates, amphetamines) as adults, especially when multiple doses were administered. For example, when a mother had received three doses of any of these drugs in her labour, her child was 4.7 times more likely to become addicted to opiate drugs in adulthood. This figure was replicated almost exactly in the US study.

Animal studies suggest a mechanism for such an effect. It seems that, as with the research on oxytocin and prairie voles quoted above,[113] drugs and hormones administered in the perinatal (late pregnancy and early newborn) period can cause effects in brain structure and function in offspring that may not be obvious until adulthood.[148–152]

For example, Csaba and colleagues have found that, among rats, adult behaviour (and especially reproductive behaviour) becomes abnormal after a single perinatal exposure to substances including beta-endorphin[153] and serotonin[154] (another natural brain chemical).

In one of their studies, changes in brain chemistry after a single dose of beta-endorphin administered in late pregnancy persisted through three generations,[155] and these researchers summarise:

> Perinatally, the first encounter between the maturing receptor and its target hormone results in hormonal imprinting, which adjusts the binding capacity of the receptor for life. In the presence of an excess of the target hormone or foreign molecules than can be bound by the receptor, faulty imprinting carries life-long consequences.[150]

Along with the possibility of hormonal imprinting, there are also potential toxic effects from any drugs that the baby is exposed to during labour and birth. Researchers warn, "During this prenatal period of neuronal [brain cell] multiplication, migration, and interconnection, the brain is most vulnerable to irreversible damage."[156]

Epidural and spinal drugs

Epidural analgesia uses several types of drugs, administered via a catheter (tube) into the epidural space around the coverings of the spinal cord. Traditionally, epidurals have used local anaesthetics, all cocaine derivatives – bupivacaine (Marcaine/Sensoricaine); ropivicaine (Naropin); lidocaine (Xylocaine) – which numb the motor as well as sensory nerves, making lower-limb movement impossible. More recently these have been used in lower doses and/or combined with low-dose opiates, reducing the motor block (paralysing) effect and producing a "walking epidural". Epidural drugs may also include catecholamines, such as adrenaline.

Spinal analgesia involves a single dose of an opiate drug, sometimes with a local anaesthetic, injected through the coverings of the spinal cord. Spinal analgesia is usually short acting, unless given as a combined spinal-epidural (CSE), when an epidural catheter is also put in place.

Epidural pain relief has major effects on all of the above-mentioned hormones of labour. Epidurals inhibit beta-endorphin production[48, 157, 158] (as do spinals[159]) and, therefore, also inhibit the alteration in consciousness that is part of a normal labour. Their popularity may partly reflect our lack of understanding of the physiological process, and of the need for labouring women to shift their state of consciousness. (Most modern birth settings are also lacking the experience, training, and environmental facilities to accommodate this most basic requirement for birth.)

When an epidural is in place, the oxytocin peak that occurs at birth is also inhibited, because the stretch receptors of a birthing woman's lower vagina, which trigger this peak, are numbed. This effect probably persists even when the epidural has worn off and sensation has returned, because the "proprioceptive" nerve fibres involved are smaller than the sensory nerves and therefore more sensitive to drug effects.[160] A woman labouring with an epidural therefore misses out on the final powerful contractions of labour and must use her own effort, often against gravity, to compensate this loss. This explains the increased length of the second stage of labour and the extra need for forceps when an epidural is used.[161]

The use of epidurals also inhibits catecholamine release for mother[162, 163] and, to a lesser extent, for her baby.[164] This may be advantageous for the mother in the first stage of labour; close to the time of birth, however, a reduction in CA levels will likely inhibit the fetal ejection reflex and prolong the second stage. The health of the newborn may also possibly be affected by a reduction in catecholamines under epidural. For example, some studies have shown alterations in lipids and blood glucose levels for epidural babies.[165, 166]

Release of the uterine-stimulating prostaglandin (PG) F2 alpha is also adversely affected by epidurals. Levels of this hormone naturally rise during an unmedicated labour, consistent with its presumed role as the major mediator of uterine contractions later in labour. However, in one study, women with epidurals experienced a decrease in PGF2 alpha, and a prolongation of labour.[167] In this study, average labour times were increased from 4.7 to 7.8 hours.

All of these hormonal disruptions explain some of the most recognised sequelae of epidurals on the processes of labour. According to recent reviews, epidurals lengthen labour (by an average of 26 minutes in first stage and 15 minutes in second stage[168]); double the chance of oxytocin augmentation;[168, 169] double the need for instrumental delivery; [169] double the risk of a severe perineal tear (third or fourth degree); [168] and increase the risk of caesarean by 1.5 times.[161] In six of nine studies reviewed in one paper, less than half of women who received an epidural had a spontaneous vaginal delivery.[161]

Note that most of the comparison groups used in these studies involve women who have used opiate drugs, which also disrupt the hormonal processes of labour, although to a lesser extent. It is likely that a comparison with women using no drugs in labour would have found even more significant effects.

Drugs administered by epidural enter the mother's bloodstream within minutes and go straight to the baby at equal, and sometimes effectively greater, levels than in the mother.[170–171] Almost all will take longer to be eliminated from the baby's immature system after the cord is cut. For example, the half-life (time for blood levels to fall by half) of bupivacaine is 2.7 hours in the adult, but around eight hours in the newborn baby.[172]

Studies using the comprehensive Brazelton Neonatal Assessment Scale (NBAS) have found deficits in newborn abilities consistent with toxicity from these drugs.[161]

Epidural anaesthesia used for caesareans has also been associated with more acidemia (acid blood levels) in healthy newborn babies compared to general anaesthetic, an indication that epidurals can compromise fetal blood and oxygen supply.[173, 174] This effect is probably due to the well-recognised drop in maternal blood pressure that epidurals cause.[161]

Another indication that epidurals may have unintended side effects for mothers and babies comes from French researchers who gave epidurals to labouring sheep.[175] The ewes failed to display their normal mothering behaviour; this effect was especially marked for the ewes in their first lambing that were given epidurals early in labour. Seven out of eight of these mothers showed no interest in their offspring for at least 30 minutes.

Some studies indicate that this disturbance may also apply to humans. Mothers given epidurals in one study spent less time with their babies in hospital, in inverse proportion to the dose of drugs they received and the length of the second stage of labour.[176] In another study, mothers who had epidurals described their babies as more difficult to care for one month later.[177] Such subtle shifts in relationship and reciprocity may reflect hormonal dysfunctions, and/or drug toxicity, and/or the less-than-optimal circumstances that often accompany epidural births: long labours, forceps, and caesareans.

Incredibly, there has been a lack of high-quality research on the long-term effects of epidurals on breastfeeding.[161, 178] There is evidence that babies born after epidural have diminished suckling reflexes and capacity,[179] consistent with drug-related neurobehavioural deficits as noted above. A recent study showed that, for healthy full-term babies born vaginally, being exposed to an epidural reduced their chance of being fully and successfully breastfed before hospital discharge.[180] A large Australian study of first-time mothers found that those who used epidurals breastfed for a shorter duration, compared to women who used nil or another form of analgesia.[181] (For more about epidurals, and the impact on breastfeeding, see chapter 14.)

Caesarean surgery

In the western world we are experiencing an epidemic of caesareans, and we have somehow come to believe that this is a safe – and perhaps even safer – way of delivering our babies. Medical studies do not support this assertion. Caesarean surgery involves major abdominal surgery and increases the risk of maternal death overall by about four times,[182] and, for elective surgery on a healthy mother and baby, by around three times.[183]

Mother's and baby's health may also be compromised, and risk of death increased, in all subsequent pregnancies because of an increased risk of ectopic pregnancy; placental abnormalities such as placenta praevia and placenta accreta;[184] unexplained stillbirth;[185] and rupture of the uterus, even with a repeat elective caesarean.[186] The caesarean rate in Australia in 2002 was 27 percent[92] and in the US in 2003, 27.6 percent[187] – the highest level on record.

With a caesarean, there is an absent or curtailed labour and the maternal hormonal peaks of oxytocin, endorphins, and catecholamines are absent or reduced. The normal multi-phasic pattern of prolactin secretion is abolished in elective caesarean.[188]

Studies of babies delivered by elective caesarean also show significantly lower levels of oxytocin,[189] endorphins,[50] catecholamines,[190] and prolactin.[188, 191] Some of the well-documented risks of caesareans may be due to these hormonal deficits – particularly, for the baby, to absence of the catecholamine surge. This means that babies born after caesareans are at increased risk of respiratory (breathing) compromise[192, 193] for up to a week after birth,[194] as well as low blood sugar[67] and poor temperature regulation.[195]

Brain oxygenation is lower immediately after caesarean versus vaginal birth,[196] possibly because of the lack of blood redistribution from the catecholamine surge and/or the loss of the placental transfusion with caesarean delivery.[130] (See chapter 15, "Leaving Well Alone", for more about the placental transfusion.) These changes may explain the slower neurological (brain and nervous system) adaptation after birth in caesarean babies,[197–199] which may in turn explain the caesarean baby's delay in adapting to a diurnal (day–night) pattern of sleep.[200]

Recent research has found many more differences in the physiology of caesarean newborns. These include differences in levels of the hormones of calcium metabolism,[201] renin-angiotensin (fluid and blood pressure regulating) hormones,[202–204] human atrial natriuretic peptide (a hormone produced by the heart),[205] progesterone,[206] the muscle enzyme creatinine kinase,[207] dopamine (a brain chemical) pathways,[208] nitric oxide synthesis[209] (which helps with lung maturation);[210] the insulin-like hormone IGFBP-1,[211] melatonin,[212] thyroid hormones (which decrease during labour and surge in the hours after birth),[213] and liver enzymes.[214]

In the immune and blood systems, caesarean babies have depressed neutrophil function[215] and survival;[216] fewer neutrophils, lymphocytes and natural killer cells (all white cells that fight infection);[217] less IgG (a type of immunoglobulin or antibody);[218] different phagocyte function (a white cell that ingests bacteria – this difference persists for six months);[219] lower hematocrit (reflecting fewer red cells);[220] less erythropoietin (a substance that signals red cell production);[221] decreased transfer of antibodies against Herpes simplex through the placenta;[222] less activation of monocytes (white cells that make antibodies);[223] decreased ability of monocytes to make cytokines (which kill foreign cells);[224] down-regulated lymohocyte adenoreceptors;[225] changes in coagulation factors[226] and lower levels of leukotrienes (which mediate inflammation and healing).[227]

Gut function also differs for caesarean babies, whose stomachs are less acid after birth;[228] and who secrete less of the gut hormones gastrin;[229] and somatostatin.[189] Caesarean babies have an altered bowel flora (types of "friendly bacteria" present in the intestines) compared to vaginally-born babies, which persists for at least six months, and possibly life-long.[230] This bowel flora abnormality (which occurs because the caesarean baby is not exposed to the mother's bowel flora at birth) may explain the increased susceptibility of premature caesarean babies to newborn gut infections,[231] and possibly the increased risk of asthma[232, 233] and allergies[234] (including food allergies[234]) for caesarean offspring in later life.

The processes of labour and birth are recognised to produce oxidative stress for the baby,[235] which is heightened when the newborn is suddenly exposed to the oxygen-rich environment after birth. Term labor triggers an increase in antioxidants in the baby's blood that may act to protect against this sudden hyperoxia (high levels of oxygen).[236] (Also see chapter 15, "Leaving Well Alone", for information about the antioxidant properties of bilirubin.)

Another protective system is the transfer of tryptophan from mother to baby during labour, which is used by the baby to make kynurenine. This substance protects the newborn's vulnerable brain against, for example, seizures and brain damage due to low oxygen levels. This transfer is reduced for caesarean babies.[237]

Many of these differences may be due to a reduced activation of the baby's stress hormones with caesarean delivery (especially elective caesarean): in a normal labour, the baby's stress hormones are thought to activate many of the hormonal and metabolic systems described above. In more simple terms, we could say that the processes of labour and birth are designed to fully awaken the baby, and prepare for life outside the womb.

These stress hormones – which include cortisol, ACTH (which releases cortisol from the adrenal) and AVP (arginine vasopressin, previously known as antidiuretic hormone, ADH), as well as beta-endorphin and the catecholamines[238] – follow the hormonal pattern described above for vaginally-born babies; they are elevated in labour, peak at birth and slowly decline. Levels in caesarean babies are reduced overall and the pattern may also be different; for example, beta-endorphin levels are elevated at birth but are maintained or continue to rise in the following hours,[239] perhaps reflecting that the caesarean baby lacks the normal preparation for birth, and so is maximally stressed in the hours afterwards.

After a caesarean, mothers and babies are usually separated for some hours (which may be another reason for stress in a caesarean newborn), so the first breastfeed is usually delayed. Both will also be affected to some extent by the drugs used in the procedure (epidural, spinal, or general anaesthetic) and for post-operative pain relief.

The maternal consequences of such radical departures from our maternal blueprint are suggested in the work of Australian researchers who interviewed 242 women in late pregnancy and again after birth. The 50 percent of women who had given spontaneous vaginal birth experienced, in general, a marked improvement in mood and an elevation of self-esteem after delivery. In comparison, the 17 percent who had caesarean surgery were more likely to experience a decline in mood and self-esteem. The remaining women had a forceps or vacuum delivery, and their mood and self-esteem were, on average, unaltered.[240]

Another study looked at the breastfeeding hormones prolactin and oxytocin on day two, comparing women who had given birth vaginally with women who had undergone emergency caesarean surgery. In the caesarean group, prolactin levels did not rise as expected with breastfeeding, and oxytocin pulses were reduced or absent. In this study, first suckling had been at 240 minutes average for caesarean babies, and 75 minutes average for babies vaginally born. The authors of this study believe that these differences may be partly explained by the delay in the first breastfeed, and conclude,

> These data indicate that early breastfeeding and physical close-ness may be associated not only with more interaction between mother and child, but also with endocrine [hormonal] changes in the mother.[241]

The possible effects of these hormonal changes on breastfeeding are explored in a recent study of 185 new mothers and babies. The study found that healthy, breastfeeding, caesarean babies had a significantly lower breastmilk intake for the first six days, compared to babies born after a normal birth, even when controlling for the mothers' previous birth and breastfeeding experience, and for delay in first feeding.

These researchers found that only 20 percent of caesarean babies had regained their birth weight by day six, compared to 40 percent of babies in the normal birth group.[242] The authors conclude that there is a lag in "breastmilk transfer" (BMT) after a caesarean. Other research has shown that early and frequent suckling in the hours after birth positively influences milk production and the duration of breastfeeding.[243, 244]

Many other studies have shown significantly reduced breastfeeding rates after caesarean surgery,[245] which may reflect all of the above effects. These findings also highlight the extra assistance that caesarean mothers and babies may need in establishing breastfeeding.

These caesarean studies not only indicate important links between birth, hormones, and breastfeeding, but also show how an optimal birth experience is designed to enhance the long-term health of mother and baby. For example, successful and long-term breastfeeding confers advantages such as reduced risk of breast cancer and osteoporosis for the mother, and increased intelligence, reduced risk of diabetes, and less obesity long-term for the child.[246]

The connections between events at birth and long-term health certainly deserve more study.[247] But, we cannot afford to wait many years for researchers to prove the benefits of an undisturbed birth. Perhaps the best we can do is to trust our instincts and vote with our birthing bodies, choosing (and supporting) models of care that increase the chances of undisturbed – and therefore safer, easier and more ecstatic – birthing.

Early separation

There are many animal studies that show that removing newborns from their mothers has negative effects on maternal-infant care and on the growing offspring. For some species, there is an inviolable need to lick and smell the offspring; without this, attachment will not occur. There seems also to be a critical period for mammals – the first hour or so after birth – when this process is most easily disrupted.

Human studies also support the importance of not disturbing this early contact. Swedish researchers noted that if an infant's lips touched the mother's nipple in the first hour of life, the mother kept her infant with her for an extra 55 minutes every day compared to mothers who did not experience suckling until later.[248]

Early breastfeeding also confers a lifelong benefit to the baby's gut system. Klaus quotes the research of Uvnas-Moberg,[249] who has found that

> ... when the infant suckles from the breast, there is an outpouring of 19 different gastrointestinal hormones in both the mother and the infant, including insulin, cholesystokinin, and gastrin. Five of these hormones stimulate the growth of intestinal villi in the mother and the infant. As a result, with each feeding, there is an increased intestinal surface area for nutrient absorption. The hormonal release is stimulated by the touch of the mother's nipple by her infant's lips. This increases oxytocin

in both the mother's brain and the infant's brain, which stimulates the vagus nerve, then causes the increase in the output of gastrointestinal hormones. Before the development of modern agriculture and grain storage 10,000 years ago, these responses in the infant and mother were essential for survival when famine was common.[250]

Undisturbed early contact, especially skin-to-skin, fulfils the newborn's physical needs, giving efficient temperature regulation, easy access to the mother's breast, and less crying than babies wrapped and placed in cots.[251] One study showed that newborns who experienced "kangaroo care" – that is, uninterrupted skin-to-skin contact with the mother – in the first hour after birth were less stressed and more organised in their behaviour, cried less, and slept longer, compared to babies who were routinely separated.[252]

Researchers have also identified a separation distress call in the human neonate, equivalent to that in other mammalian species. This cry, which is almost certainly genetically encoded, signals the newborn's need for close body contact with the mother after birth and ceases at reunion. The authors note, "These findings are compatible with the opinion that the most appropriate position of the healthy full-term newborn baby after birth is in close body contact with the mother."[253]

There are also good reasons for continued contact between mother and baby, if the baby is distressed at birth. For example, the baby can be resuscitated with the cord intact, which gives the advantage of an ongoing supply of blood and oxygen to support this transition. (For more about this, see chapter 15, "Leaving Well Alone".)

Beyond the early hours, there is a vulnerable period of several days when attachment is still developing; separation at this time also has negative long-term consequences for mammalian species. For example, researchers found that infant rats removed for five hours a day in the first week of life had increased responsiveness to stress in adulthood, associated with alterations in HPA (stress) hormone regulation.[254]

In humans, extra contact "allowed" in hospital decreases the risks of abandonment, abuse, neglect, and failure to thrive in childhood. These benefits have been noted in many hospitals that have adopted the WHO Baby-Friendly Hospital Initiative, which includes early contact and routine rooming-in for mother and baby (rather than putting the baby in a nursery).[255]

For example, abandonment was reduced in one hospital in Thailand from 36 per 10,000 down to one per 10,000 after becoming "baby-friendly".[256] In an earlier study, a US hospital found substantially less "parental inadequacy", as well as improved child development, for those high-risk mothers randomly allocated to rooming-in with their babies.[257]

In another study, mothers who had experienced extra early contact with their babies spoke differently to their children at two years of age, using more questions, adjectives, and words per proposition, along with fewer commands and content words.[258]

The wisdom of undisturbed mother–baby contact after birth is well described by Joseph Chilton Pearce in his book *Evolution's End: Reclaiming the Potential of Our Intelligence*.[3] According to Pearce, when the newborn baby is in skin-to-skin contact, at the mother's left breast (which is where new mothers in all cultures instinctively cradle their babies) and in contact with her heart rhythm, "...a cascade of supportive, confirmative information activates every sense, instinct, and intelligence needed for the radical change of environment... Thus intelligent learning begins at birth."[259]

For the mother also, "A major block of dormant intelligences is activated... the mother then knows exactly what to do and can communicate with her baby on an intuitive level."[260] Such intuitive capacities are sorely needed in our human culture, where we are heavily reliant on outside advice from books and experts to tell us how to care for our babies.

Researchers are increasingly ratifying Pearce's assertions, although this area is still poorly researched. Lin states, "Parturition [birth] plays a critical role in the full expression of maternal behavior in postpartum females, yet the precise mechanism remains unclear."[261] Animal research is consistent with the hypothesis that the processes of birth activate areas of the brain involved in motherhood via the peaks of hormones such as oxytocin, catecholamines and prolactin.[261–263]

Suggestions for undisturbing birth

For women

- Take responsibility for your health, healing, and wholeness before and during the child-bearing years
- Choose a model of care that enhances the chance of a natural and undisturbed birth; ideally homebirth, birth centre and/or one-on-one midwifery care
- Arrange support according to your individual needs — trust, a loving relationship, and continuity of care with support people are important
- Consider having an advocate at a hospital birth; ideally your own private midwife or doula, who can help to protect your birthing space and also support your partner, if present
- Also note all of the recommendations below

For carers

- Ensure an atmosphere where the labouring woman feels private, safe, and unobserved, and free to follow her own instincts
- Reduce neo-cortical (higher-brain) stimulation by keeping lighting and noises soft, and reducing words to a minimum
- Cover the clock and any other technical equipment
- Avoid procedures (including obvious observations) unless absolutely necessary
- Avoid talking to the labouring woman unless absolutely necessary
- Avoid drugs unless absolutely necessary
- Avoid caesarean surgery unless absolutely necessary
- Keep lighting low during birth, and for the hour following
- Facilitate an undisturbed atmosphere of quiet and calm for mother and baby for at least an hour after birth
- Facilitate skin-to-skin contact between mother and baby for at least the first hour. Bathing and washing are unnecessary at this time
- Facilitate breastfeeding soon after birth, ideally allowing the baby to find the nipple and attach without disturbance
- Don't separate mother and baby for any reason, including resuscitation, which will be more effective with the cord still attached

Pearce believes that the stress caused to the newborn by early separation – which violates an ancient and evolutionary expectation of uninterrupted maternal care – can cause permanent damage, both psychological and neurological, by elevation of the baby's stress hormones. As noted above, the principles of hormonal imprinting would support this assertion. Further, modern concepts of neurological development highlight the plasticity of the developing brain; as Shore states, "Early interactions don't just create a context; they directly affect the way the brain is wired."[264]

Breastfeeding: a second chance

It is noteworthy that breastfeeding involves three of the four ecstatic hormones of labour and birth: oxytocin, beta-endorphin, and prolactin. When birth has been difficult or disturbed; when mother and baby have been separated; or when the mother has missed her ecstatic hormonal cocktail, she can use breastfeeding and skin-to-skin contact with her baby to stimulate these hormones, which will help her to fall in love with her baby, and vice versa.

Constant or near-constant contact between mother and baby (ideally using a sling or baby carrier in the day and co-sleeping at night) will also optimise these pleasurable hormones, which protect both mother and baby from stress, as noted above.

When the baby's breastfeeding behaviour and/or nipple attachment is suboptimal, which may be due to separation in the hours after birth, some midwives have suggested using skin-to-skin contact in a bath to re-enact the time after birth,[265] allowing the baby to use the amazing primitive reflexes (present for the early weeks) to crawl up the mother's body, find the nipple, and self-attach. [266]

Undisturbing birth

How can we avoid disturbing the process of birth, and align our practices with our evolutionary blueprint? This can seem difficult in a culture where birth has been disturbed, one way or another, for many generations. Yet it is really very simple. If we were to provide conditions of privacy, and a sense of safety for birth – which, as Jeannine Parvati Baker reminds us, "… is orgasmic in its essence"[267] – most women would experience a spontaneous, ecstatic, and relatively easy birth.

Dutch professor of obstetrics, G Kloosterman, offers a succinct summary, which would be well placed on the door of every birth room:

> Spontaneous labour in a normal woman is an event marked by a number of processes so complicated and so perfectly attuned to each other that any interference will only detract from the optimal character. The only thing required from the bystanders is that they show respect for this awe-inspiring process by complying with the first rule of medicine – *nil nocere* [Do no harm].[268]

First published in Journal of Prenatal and Perinatal Psychology and Health *17(4), summer 2003, pp 261–288. This version updated March 2005.*

References

1. Buckley SJ. Maia's birth: A family celebration. *The Birthkit* 2001(32):11. See also chapter 8.
2. Buckley SJ. Healing birth, healing the Earth. *The Birthkit* 2002(36):1, 9–10. See also chapter 4.
3. Pearce JC. *Evolution's End: Claiming the Potential of Our Intelligence.* San Francisco: Harper San Francisco, 1992.
4. Rosenberg KR, Trevathan WR. The evolution of human birth. *Sci Am* 2001; 285(5):72–7.
5. Goland RS, et al. Biologically active corticotropin-releasing hormone in maternal and fetal plasma during pregnancy. *Am J Obstet Gynecol* 1988; 159(4):884–90.
6. Mendelson CR, Condon JC. New insights into the molecular endocrinology of parturition. *J Steroid Biochem Mol Biol* 2005; 93(2–5):113–9.
7. Russell JA, et al. Brain preparations for maternity – adaptive changes in behavioral and neuroendocrine systems during pregnancy and lactation. An overview. *Prog Brain Res* 2001; 133:1–38.
8. Weiss G. Endocrinology of parturition. *J Clin Endocrinol Metab* 2000; 85(12):4421–5.
9. Jackson M, Dudley DJ. Endocrine assays to predict preterm delivery. *Clin Perinatol* 1998; 25(4):837–57, vi.
10. Petrocelli T, Lye SJ. Regulation of transcripts encoding the myometrial gap junction protein, connexin-43, by estrogen and progesterone. *Endocrinology* 1993; 133(1):284–90.

11. Verbalis JG, et al. Oxytocin secretion in response to cholecystokinin and food: differentiation of nausea from satiety. *Science* 1986; 232(4756):1417–9.

12. Odent M. *The Scientification of Love.* Revised edn. London: Free Association Books, 2001.

13. Fuchs AR, Fuchs F. Endocrinology of human parturition: a review. *Br J Obstet Gynaecol* 1984; 91(10):948–67.

14. Arias F. Pharmacology of oxytocin and prostaglandins. *Clin Obstet Gynecol* 2000; 43(3):455–68.

15. Gonser M. Labor induction and augmentation with oxytocin: pharmacokinetic considerations. *Arch Gynecol Obstet* 1995; 256(2):63–6.

16. Steer PJ. The endocrinology of parturition in the human. *Baillieres Clin Endocrinol Metab* 1990; 4(2):333–49.

17. Young WS, 3rd, et al. Deficiency in mouse oxytocin prevents milk ejection, but not fertility or parturition. *J Neuroendocrinol* 1996; 8(11):847–53.

18. Lundeberg T, et al. Anti-nociceptive effects of oxytocin in rats and mice. *Neurosci Lett* 1994; 170(1):153–7.

19. Malek A, et al. Human placental transport of oxytocin. *J Matern Fetal Med* 1996; 5(5):245–55.

20. Chard T. Fetal and maternal oxytocin in human parturition. *Am J Perinatol* 1989; 6(2):145–52.

21. Dawood MY, et al. Oxytocin in human pregnancy and parturition. *Obstet Gynecol* 1978; 51(2):138–43.

22. Odent M. The fetus ejection reflex. In: *The Nature of Birth and Breastfeeding.* Sydney: Ace Graphics, 1992:29–43.

23. Matthiesen AS, et al. Postpartum maternal oxytocin release by newborns: effects of infant hand massage and sucking. *Birth* 2001; 28(1):13–9.

24. Uvnas-Moberg K. *The Oxytocin Factor.* Cambridge MA: Da Capo Press, 2003.

25. Nissen E, et al. Elevation of oxytocin levels early post partum in women. *Acta Obstet Gynecol Scand* 1995; 74(7):530–3.

26. Leake RD, et al. Oxytocin concentrations during the neonatal period. *Biol Neonate* 1981; 39(3–4):127–31.

27. Takeda S, et al. Concentrations and origin of oxytocin in breast milk. *Endocrinol Jpn* 1986; 33(6):821–6.

28. Levy F, et al. Olfactory regulation of maternal behavior in mammals. *Horm Behav* 2004; 46(3):284–302.

29. Lundblad EG, Hodgen GD. Induction of maternal–infant bonding in rhesus and cynomolgus monkeys after cesarean delivery. *Lab Anim Sci* 1980; 30(5):913.

30. Varendi H, et al. Soothing effect of amniotic fluid smell in newborn infants. *Early Hum Dev* 1998; 51(1):47–55.

31. Marlier L, et al. Neonatal responsiveness to the odor of amniotic and lacteal fluids: a test of perinatal chemosensory continuity. *Child Dev* 1998; 69(3):611–23.

32. Axel R. The molecular logic of smell. *Sci Am* 1995; 273(4):154–9.

33. Chapman M. Oxytocin has big role in maternal behaviour: interview with Professor K Uvnas-Moberg. *Australian Doctor* 1998, 7 August:38.

34. Agren G, et al. Olfactory cues from an oxytocin-injected male rat can reduce energy loss in its cagemates. *Neuroreport* 1997; 8(11):2551–5.

35. Agren G, et al. Olfactory cues from an oxytocin-injected male rat can induce anti-nociception in its cagemates. *Neuroreport* 1997; 8(14):3073–6.

36. Giovenardi M, et al. Hypothalamic paraventricular nucleus modulates maternal aggression in rats: effects of ibotenic acid lesion and oxytocin antisense. *Physiol Behav* 1998; 63(3):351–9.

37. Kinsley CH, Bridges RS. Opiate involvement in postpartum aggression in rats. *Pharmacol Biochem Behav* 1986; 25(5):1007–11.

38. Gutkowska J, et al. Oxytocin is a cardiovascular hormone. *Braz J Med Biol Res* 2000; 33(6):625–33.

39. Uvnas-Moberg K. Oxytocin linked antistress effects – the relaxation and growth response. *Acta Physiol Scand Suppl* 1997; 640:38–42.

40. Taylor SE, et al. Biobehavioral responses to stress in females: tend-and-befriend, not fight-or-flight. *Psychol Rev* 2000; 107(3):411–29.

41. Feifel D, Reza T. Oxytocin modulates psychotomimetic-induced deficits in sensorimotor gating. *Psychopharmacology (Berl)* 1999; 141(1):93–8.

42. Insel TR, et al. Oxytocin, vasopressin, and autism: is there a connection? *Biol Psychiatry* 1999; 45(2):145–57.

43. Knox SS, Uvnas-Moberg K. Social isolation and cardiovascular disease: an atherosclerotic pathway? *Psychoneuroendocrinology* 1998; 23(8):877–90.

44. Sarnyai Z, Kovacs GL. Role of oxytocin in the neuroadaptation to drugs of abuse. *Psychoneuroendocrinology* 1994; 19(1):85–117.

45. Uvnas-Moberg K, et al. Oxytocin as a possible mediator of SSRI-induced antidepressant effects. *Psychopharmacology (Berl)* 1999; 142(1):95–101.

46. Laatikainen TJ. Corticotropin-releasing hormone and opioid peptides in reproduction and stress. *Ann Med* 1991; 23(5):489–96.

47. Brinsmead M, et al. Peripartum concentrations of beta-endorphin and cortisol and maternal mood states. *Aust N Z J Obstet Gynaecol* 1985; 25(3):194–7.

48. Bacigalupo G, et al. Quantitative relationships between pain intensities during labor and beta-endorphin and cortisol concentrations in plasma. Decline of the hormone concentrations in the early postpartum period. *J Perinat Med* 1990; 18(4):289–96.

49. Facchinetti F, et al. Fetal intermediate lobe is stimulated by parturition. *Am J Obstet Gynecol* 1989; 161(5):1267–70.

50. Facchinetti F, et al. Changes in beta-endorphin in fetal membranes and placenta in normal and pathological pregnancies. *Acta Obstet Gynecol Scand* 1990; 69(7–8):603–7.

51. Jevremovic M, et al. [The opioid peptide, beta-endorphin, in spontaneous vaginal delivery and cesarean section]. *Srp Arh Celok Lek* 1991; 119(9–10):271–4.

52. Kimball CD. Do endorphin residues of beta lipotropin in hormone reinforce reproductive functions? *Am J Obstet Gynecol* 1979; 134(2):127–32, p 128.

53. Jowitt M. Beta-endorphin and stress in pregnancy and labour. *Midwifery Matters* 1993; 56:3–4.

54. Douglas AJ, et al. Pathways to parturition. *Adv Exp Med Biol* 1995; 395:381–94.

55. Rivier C, et al. Stimulation in vivo of the secretion of prolactin and growth hormone by beta-endorphin. *Endocrinology* 1977; 100(1):238–41.

56. Parker CR, Jr., et al. Prolactin levels in umbilical cord blood of human infants: relation to gestational age, maternal complications, and neonatal lung function. *Am J Obstet Gynecol* 1989; 161(3):795–802.

57. Franceschini R, et al. Plasma beta-endorphin concentrations during suckling in lactating women. *Br J Obstet Gynaecol* 1989; 96(6):711–3.

58. Zanardo V, et al. Beta endorphin concentrations in human milk. *J Pediatr Gastroenterol Nutr* 2001; 33(2):160–4.

59. Costa A, et al. Adrenocorticotropic hormone and catecholamines in maternal, umbilical and neonatal plasma in relation to vaginal delivery. *J Endocrinol Invest* 1988; 11(10):703–9.

60. Lederman RP, et al. Anxiety and epinephrine in multiparous women in labor: relationship to duration of labor and fetal heart rate pattern. *Am J Obstet Gynecol* 1985; 153(8):870–7.

61. Odent M. Position in delivery (letter). *Lancet* 1990.

62. Saito M, et al. Plasma catecholamines and microvibration as labour progresses. *Shinshin-Thaku* 1991; 31:381–89.

63. Thomas SA, Palmiter RD. Impaired maternal behavior in mice lacking norepinephrine and epinephrine. *Cell* 1997; 91(5):583–92.

64. Phillippe M. Fetal catecholamines. *Am J Obstet Gynecol* 1983; 146(7):840–55.

65. Irestedt L, et al. Causes and consequences of maternal and fetal sympathoadrenal activation during parturition. *Acta Obstet Gynecol Scand Suppl* 1984; 118:111–5.

66. Lagercrantz H, Slotkin TA. The "stress" of being born. *Sci Am* 1986; 254(4):100–7.

67. Hagnevik K, et al. Catecholamine surge and metabolic adaptation in the newborn after vaginal delivery and caesarean section. *Acta Paediatr Scand* 1984; 73(5):602–9.

68. Colson S. Womb to world: a metabolic perspective. *Midwifery Today Int Midwife* 2002(61):12–7.

69. Lowe NK, Reiss R. Parturition and fetal adaptation. *J Obstet Gynecol Neonatal Nurs* 1996; 25(4):339–49.

70. Eliot RJ, et al. Plasma catecholamine concentrations in infants at birth and during the first 48 hours of life. *J Pediatr* 1980; 96(2):311–5.

71. Grattan DR. The actions of prolactin in the brain during pregnancy and lactation. *Prog Brain Res* 2001; 133:153–71.

72. Harris J, et al. Prolactin and the prolactin receptor: new targets of an old hormone. *Ann Med* 2004; 36(6):414–25.

73. Fernandes PA, et al. Phasic maternal prolactin secretion during spontaneous labor is associated with cervical dilatation and second-stage uterine activity. *J Soc Gynecol Investig* 1995; 2(4):597–601.

74. Fernandes PA, et al. The acute release of maternal prolactin by instrumental cervical dilatation simulates the second stage of labor. *J Soc Gynecol Investig* 1999; 6(1):22–6.

75. Stern JM, Reichlin S. Prolactin circadian rhythm persists throughout lactation in women. *Neuroendocrinology* 1990; 51(1):31–7.

76. Heinrichs M, et al. Effects of suckling on hypothalamic-pituitary-adrenal axis responses to psychosocial stress in postpartum lactating women. *J Clin Endocrinol Metab* 2001; 86(10):4798–804.

77. Berczi I. The role of the growth and lactogenic hormone family in immune function. *Neuroimmunomodulation* 1994; 1(4):201–16.

78. Sobrinho LG, Almeida-Costa JM. Hyperprolactinemia as a result of immaturity or regression: the concept of maternal subroutine. A new model of psychoendocrine interactions. *Psychother Psychosom* 1992; 57(3):128–32.

79. Sobrinho LG. Emotional aspects of hyperprolactinemia. *Psychother Psychosom* 1998; 67(3):133–9.

80. Keverne EB. Sexual and aggressive behaviour in social groups of talapoin monkeys. *Ciba Found Symp* 1978(62):271–97.

81. Roberts RL, et al. Prolactin levels are elevated after infant carrying in parentally inexperienced common marmosets. *Physiol Behav* 2001; 72(5):713–20.

82. Soltis J, et al. Urinary prolactin is correlated with mothering and allomothering in squirrel monkeys. *Physiol Behav* 2005; 84(2):295–301.

83. Ziegler TE. Hormones associated with non-maternal infant care: a review of mammalian and avian studies. *Folia Primatol (Basel)* 2000; 71(1–2):6–21.

84. Storey AE, et al. Hormonal correlates of paternal responsiveness in new and expectant fathers. *Evol Hum Behav* 2000; 21(2):79–95.

85. Schradin C, Anzenberger G. Prolactin, the Hormone of Paternity. *News Physiol Sci* 1999; 14:223–231.

86. Fleming AS, et al. Testosterone and prolactin are associated with emotional responses to infant cries in new fathers. *Horm Behav* 2002; 42(4):399–413.

87. Kruger TH, et al. Orgasm-induced prolactin secretion: feedback control of sexual drive? *Neurosci Biobehav Rev* 2002; 26(1):31–44.

88. Gitlin M. Sexual dysfunction with psychotropic drugs. *Expert Opin Pharmacother* 2003; 4(12):2259–69.

89. Grosvenor CE, Whitworth NS. Accumulation of prolactin by maternal milk and its transfer to circulation of neonatal rat – a review. *Endocrinol Exp* 1983; 17(3–4):271–82.

90. Grattan DR. The actions of prolactin in the brain during pregnancy and lactation. *Prog Brain Res* 2001; 133:153–71, p 165.

91. Horwood LJ, Fergusson DM. Breastfeeding and later cognitive and academic outcomes. *Pediatrics* 1998; 101(1):E9.

92. Laws P, Sullivan E. *Australia's mothers and babies 2002.* Sydney: AIHW National Perinatal Statistics Unit, 2004.

93. Declercq E, et al. *Listening to Mothers: Report of the First U.S. National Survey of Women's Childbearing Experiences.* New York: Maternity Center Association, October 2002.

94. Department of Health. *NHS maternity statistics, England: 2003–4.* London: DoH, 2005.

95. Canadian Institute for Health Information. *Giving Birth in Canada.* Ontario: CIHI 2004.

96. Dawood MY. Novel approach to oxytocin induction-augmentation of labor. Application of oxytocin physiology during pregnancy. *Adv Exp Med Biol* 1995; 395:585–94.

97. Stubbs TM. Oxytocin for labor induction. *Clin Obstet Gynecol* 2000; 43(3):489–94.

98. Haire D. FDA Approved Obstetric Drugs: Their Effects on Mother and Baby. 2001. www.aimsusa.org/obstetricdrugs.htm

99. Satin AJ, et al. High- versus low-dose oxytocin for labor stimulation. *Obstet Gynecol* 1992; 80(1):111–6.

100. Milsom I, et al. Influence of maternal, obstetric and fetal risk factors on the prevalence of birth asphyxia at term in a Swedish urban population. *Acta Obstet Gynecol Scand* 2002; 81(10):909–17.

101. Ellis M, et al. Risk factors for neonatal encephalopathy in Kathmandu, Nepal, a developing country: unmatched case-control study. *Br Med J* 2000; 320(7244):1229–36.

102. Bidgood KA, Steer PJ. A randomized control study of oxytocin augmentation of labour. 2. Uterine activity. *Br J Obstet Gynaecol* 1987; 94(6):518–22.

103. Phillip H, et al. The impact of induced labour on postpartum blood loss. *J Obstet Gynaecol* 2004; 24(1):12–5.

104. Gilbert L, et al. Postpartum haemorrhage – a continuing problem. *Br J Obstet Gynaecol* 1987; 94(1):67–71.

105. Stones RW, et al. Risk factors for major obstetric haemorrhage. *Eur J Obstet Gynecol Reprod Biol* 1993; 48(1):15–8.

106. Phaneuf S, et al. Loss of myometrial oxytocin receptors during oxytocin-induced and oxytocin-augmented labour. *J Reprod Fertil* 2000; 120(1):91–7.

107. Genazzani AR, et al. Lack of beta-endorphin plasma level rise in oxytocin-induced labor. *Gynecol Obstet Invest* 1985; 19(3):130–4.

108. Palmer SR, et al. The influence of obstetric procedures and social and cultural factors on breast-feeding rates at discharge from hospital. *J Epidemiol Community Health* 1979; 33(4):248–52.

109. Zuppa AA, et al. [Assistance procedures in the perinatal period that condition breast feeding at the time of discharge from the hospital]. *Pediatr Med Chir* 1984; 6(3):367–72.

110. Out JJ, et al. Breast-feeding following spontaneous and induced labour. *Eur J Obstet Gynecol Reprod Biol* 1988; 29(4):275–9.

111. Dewey KG. Maternal and fetal stress are associated with impaired lactogenesis in humans. *J Nutr* 2001; 131(11):3012S–5S.

112. Dawood MY, et al. Fetal contribution to oxytocin in human labor. *Obstet Gynecol* 1978; 52(2):205–9.

113. Carter CS. Developmental consequences of oxytocin. *Physiol Behav* 2003; 79(3):383–97.

114. Crowell DH, et al. Effects of induction of labor on the neurophysiologic functioning of newborn infants. *Am J Obstet Gynecol* 1980; 136(1):48–53.

115. Ounsted MK, et al. Induction of labour by different methods in primiparous women. I Some perinatal and postnatal problems. *Early Hum Dev* 1978; 2(3):227–39.

116. De Coster W, et al. Labor induction with prostaglandin F2 alpha. Influence on psychomotor evolution of the child in the first 30 months. *Prostaglandins* 1976; 12(4):559–64.

117. McBride WG, et al. A study of five year old children born after elective induction of labour. *Med J Aust* 1977; 2(14):456–9.

118. Wahl RU. Could oxytocin administration during labor contribute to autism and related behavioral disorders? – A look at the literature. *Med Hypotheses* 2004; 63(3):456–60.

119. Odent M. New reasons and new ways to study birth physiology. *Int J Gynaecol Obstet* 2001; 75 Suppl 1:S39–45.

120. Winslow JT, Insel TR. The social deficits of the oxytocin knockout mouse. *Neuropeptides* 2002; 36(2–3):221–9.

121. Young LJ, et al. Neuropeptides and social behavior: animal models relevant to autism. *Mol Psychiatry* 2002; 7 Suppl 2:S38–9.

122. Lim MM, et al. Neuropeptides and the social brain: potential rodent models of autism. *Int J Dev Neurosci* 2005; 23(2–3):235–43.

123. Hollander E, et al. Oxytocin infusion reduces repetitive behaviors in adults with autistic and Asperger's disorders. *Neuropsychopharmacology* 2003; 28(1):193–8.

124. Green L, et al. Oxytocin and autistic disorder: alterations in peptide forms. *Biol Psychiatry* 2001; 50(8):609–13.

125. Modahl C, et al. Plasma oxytocin levels in autistic children. *Biol Psychiatry* 1998; 43(4):270–7.

126. Glasson EJ, et al. Perinatal factors and the development of autism: a population study. *Arch Gen Psychiatry* 2004; 61(6):618–27.

127. Gale S, et al. Brief report: pitocin induction in autistic and nonautistic individuals. *J Autism Dev Disord* 2003; 33(2):205–8.

128. Fein D, et al. Pitocin induction and autism. *Am J Psychiatry* 1997; 154(3):438–9.

129. Gottesman, II, Hanson DR. Human development: biological and genetic processes. *Annu Rev Psychol* 2005; 56:263–86.

130. Buckley SJ. Leaving well alone – A natural approach to third stage. *Medical Veritas* 2005; 2(2):492–9. See also chapter 15.

131. Queensland Health. Perinatal data collection, Queensland 2002. Brisbane: Queensland Health, 2001.

132. Hawkins J, et al. Update on obstetric anesthesia practices in the US (abstract). *Anesthesiology* 1999; 91:A1060.

133. Olofsson C, et al. Lack of analgesic effect of systemically administered morphine or pethidine on labour pain. *Br J Obstet Gynaecol* 1996; 103(10):968–72.

134. Tsui MH, et al. A double blinded randomised placebo-controlled study of intramuscular pethidine for pain relief in the first stage of labour. *Bjog* 2004; 111(7):648–55.

135. Soontrapa S, et al. Effectiveness of intravenous meperidine for pain relief in the first stage of labour. *J Med Assoc Thai* 2002; 85(11):1169–75.

136. American College of Obstetricians and Gynecologists. Obstetric Analgesia and Anesthesia. *ACOG Technical Bulletin* 1996; 225(July).

137. Thomas TA, et al. Influence of medication, pain and progress in labour on plasma beta-endorphin-like immunoreactivity. *Br J Anaesth* 1982; 54(4):401–8.

138. Thomson AM, Hillier VF. A re-evaluation of the effect of pethidine on the length of labour. *J Adv Nurs* 1994; 19(3):448–56.

139. Lindow SW, et al. The effect of morphine and naloxone administration on plasma oxytocin concentrations in the first stage of labour. *Clin Endocrinol (Oxf)* 1992; 37(4):349–53.

140. Russell JA, et al. Interruption of parturition in rats by morphine: a result of inhibition of oxytocin secretion. *J Endocrinol* 1989; 121(3):521–36.

141. Kinsley CH, et al. Intracerebroventricular infusions of morphine, and blockade with naloxone, modify the olfactory preferences for pup odors in lactating rats. *Brain Res Bull* 1995; 37(1):103–7.

142. Misiti A, et al. Heroin induces changes in mother–infant monkey communication and subsequent disruption of their dyadic interaction. *Pharmacol Res* 1991; 24(1):93–104.

143. Bridges RS, Grimm CT. Reversal of morphine disruption of maternal behavior by concurrent treatment with the opiate antagonist naloxone. *Science* 1982; 218(4568):166–8.

144. Stafisso-Sandoz G, et al. Opiate disruption of maternal behavior: morphine reduces, and naloxone restores, c-fos activity in the medial preoptic area of lactating rats. *Brain Res Bull* 1998; 45(3):307–13.

145. Kimball CD. Do endorphin residues of beta lipotropin in hormone reinforce reproductive functions? *Am J Obstet Gynecol* 1979; 134(2):127–32.

146. Jacobson B, et al. Opiate addiction in adult offspring through possible imprinting after obstetric treatment. *Br Med J* 1990; 301(6760):1067–70.

147. Nyberg K. Long-term effects of labor analgesia. *J Obstet Gynecol Neonatal Nurs* 2000; 29(3):226.

148. Kellogg CK. Sex differences in long-term consequences of prenatal diazepam exposure: possible underlying mechanisms. *Pharmacol Biochem Behav* 1999; 64(4):673–80.

149. Livezey GT, et al. Prenatal exposure to phenobarbital and quantifiable alterations in the electroencephalogram of adult rat offspring. *Am J Obstet Gynecol* 1992; 167(6):1611–5.

150. Csaba G, et al. Endorphin excess at weaning durably influences sexual activity, uterine estrogen receptor's binding capacity and brain serotonin level of female rats. *Horm Metab Res* 2004; 36(1):39–43.

151. Meyerson BJ. Socio-sexual behaviours in rats after neonatal and adult beta-endorphin treatment. *Scand J Psychol* 1982; Suppl 1:85–9.

152. Mirmiran M, Swaab D. Effects of perinatal medication on the developing brain. In: Nijhuis J, editor. *Fetal behaviour*. Oxford: Oxford University Press, 1992.

153. Csaba G, et al. Effect of neonatal beta-endorphin imprinting on sexual behavior and brain serotonin level in adult rats. *Life Sci* 2003; 73(1):103–14.

154. Csaba G, et al. Single treatment (hormonal imprinting) of newborn rats with serotonin increases the serotonin content of cells in adults. *Cell Biol Int* 2002; 26(8):663–8.

155. Csaba G, et al. Three-generation investigation on serotonin content in rat immune cells long after beta-endorphin exposure in late pregnancy. *Horm Metab Res* 2005; 37(3):172–7.

156. Livezey GT, et al. Prenatal exposure to phenobarbital and quantifiable alterations in the electroencephalogram of adult rat offspring. *Am J Obstet Gynecol* 1992; 167(6):1611–5, p 1614.

157. Browning AJ, et al. Maternal and cord plasma concentrations of beta-lipotrophin, beta-endorphin and gamma-lipotrophin at delivery; effect of analgesia. *Br J Obstet Gynaecol* 1983; 90(12):1152–6.

158. Raisanen I, et al. Pain and plasma beta-endorphin level during labor. *Obstet Gynecol* 1984; 64(6):783–6.

159. Abboud TK, et al. Effect of intrathecal morphine during labor on maternal plasma beta-endorphin levels. *Am J Obstet Gynecol* 1984; 149(7):709–10.

160. Goodfellow CF, et al. Oxytocin deficiency at delivery with epidural analgesia. *Br J Obstet Gynaecol* 1983; 90(3):214–9.

161. Lieberman E, O'Donoghue C. Unintended effects of epidural analgesia during labor: a systematic review. *Am J Obstet Gynecol* 2002; 186(5 Suppl Nature):S31–68.

162. Jones CR, et al. Plasma catecholamines and modes of delivery: the relation between catecholamine levels and in-vitro platelet aggregation and adrenoreceptor radioligand binding characteristics. *Br J Obstet Gynaecol* 1985; 92(6):593–9.

163. Jouppila R, et al. Maternal and umbilical cord plasma noradrenaline concentrations during labour with and without segmental extradural analgesia, and during caesarean section. *Br J Anaesth* 1984; 56(3):251–5.

164. Hirsimaki H, et al. Mode of delivery, plasma catecholamines and Doppler-derived cardiac output in healthy term newborn infants. *Biol Neonate* 1992; 61(5):285–93.

165. Swanstrom S, Bratteby LE. Metabolic effects of obstetric regional analgesia and of asphyxia in the newborn infant during the first two hours after birth. I. Arterial blood glucose concentrations. *Acta Paediatr Scand* 1981; 70(6):791–800.

166. Swanstrom S, Bratteby LE. Metabolic effects of obstetric regional analgesia and of asphyxia in the newborn infant during the first two hours after birth. II. Arterial plasma concentrations of glycerol, free fatty acids and beta-hydroxybutyrate. *Acta Paediatr Scand* 1981; 70(6):801–9.

167. Behrens O, et al. Effects of lumbar epidural analgesia on prostaglandin F2 alpha release and oxytocin secretion during labor. *Prostaglandins* 1993; 45(3):285–96.

168. Leighton BL, Halpern SH. The effects of epidural analgesia on labor, maternal, and neonatal outcomes: a systematic review. *Am J Obstet Gynecol* 2002; 186(5 Suppl Nature):S69–77.

169. Howell CJ. Epidural versus non-epidural analgesia for pain relief in labour. *Cochrane Database Syst Rev* 2000(2):CD000331.

170. Brinsmead M. Fetal and neonatal effects of drugs administered in labour. *Med J Aust* 1987; 146(9):481–6.

171. Fernando R, et al. Neonatal welfare and placental transfer of fentanyl and bupivacaine during ambulatory combined spinal epidural analgesia for labour. *Anaesthesia* 1997; 52(6):517–24.

172. Hale T. *Medications and Mother's Milk*. Amarillo TX: Pharmasoft, 1997.

173. Mueller MD, et al. Higher rate of fetal acidemia after regional anesthesia for elective cesarean delivery. *Obstet Gynecol* 1997; 90(1):131–4.

174. Roberts SW, et al. Fetal acidemia associated with regional anesthesia for elective cesarean delivery. *Obstet Gynecol* 1995; 85(1):79–83.

175. Krehbiel D, et al. Peridural anesthesia disturbs maternal behavior in primiparous and multiparous parturient ewes. *Physiol Behav* 1987; 40(4):463–72.

176. Sepkoski CM, et al. The effects of maternal epidural anesthesia on neonatal behavior during the first month. *Dev Med Child Neurol* 1992; 34(12):1072–80.

177. Murray AD, et al. Effects of epidural anesthesia on newborns and their mothers. *Child Dev* 1981; 52(1):71–82.

178. Walker M. Do labor medications affect breastfeeding? *J Hum Lact* 1997; 13(2):131–7.

179. Riordan J, et al. The effect of labor pain relief medication on neonatal suckling and breastfeeding duration. *J Hum Lact* 2000; 16(1):7–12.

180. Baumgarder DJ, et al. Effect of labor epidural anesthesia on breastfeeding of healthy full-term newborns delivered vaginally. *J Am Board Fam Pract* 2003; 16(1):7–13.

181. Henderson JJ, et al. Impact of intrapartum epidural analgesia on breastfeeding duration. *Aust N Z J Obstet Gynaecol* 2003; 43(5):372–7.

182. Enkin M, et al. *Effective Care in Pregnancy and Childbirth*. 3rd edn. Oxford: Oxford University Press, 2000.

183. Bewley S, Cockburn J. II. The unfacts of 'request' caesarean section. *Br J Obstet Gynaecol* 2002; 109(6):597–605.

184. Hemminki E. Impact of caesarean section on future pregnancy – a review of cohort studies. *Paediatr Perinat Epidemiol* 1996; 10(4):366–79.

185. Smith GC, et al. Caesarean section and risk of unexplained stillbirth in subsequent pregnancy. *Lancet* 2003; 362(9398):1779–84.

186. Lydon-Rochelle M, et al. Risk of uterine rupture during labor among women with a prior cesarean delivery. *N Engl J Med* 2001; 345(1): 3–8.

187. Hamilton B, et al. Births: Preliminary data for 2003. *National vital statistics reports* 2004; 53(9).

188. Rigg LA, Yen SS. Multiphasic prolactin secretion during parturition in human subjects. *Am J Obstet Gynecol* 1977; 128(2):215–8.

189. Marchini G, et al. Fetal and maternal plasma levels of gastrin, somatostatin and oxytocin after vaginal delivery and elective cesarean section. *Early Hum Dev* 1988; 18(1):73–9.

190. Jones CR, et al. Plasma catecholamines and modes of delivery: the relation between catecholamine levels and in-vitro platelet aggregation and adrenoreceptor radioligand binding characteristics. *Br J Obstet Gynaecol* 1985; 92(6):593–9.

191. Heasman L, et al. Plasma prolactin concentrations after caesarean section or vaginal delivery. *Arch Dis Child Fetal Neonatal Ed* 1997; 77(3): F237–8.

192. Faxelius G, et al. Catecholamine surge and lung function after delivery. *Arch Dis Child* 1983; 58(4):262–6.

193. Zanardo V, et al. Neonatal respiratory morbidity risk and mode of delivery at term: influence of timing of elective caesarean delivery. *Acta Paediatr* 2004; 93(5):643–7.

194. Richardson BS, et al. The impact of labor at term on measures of neonatal outcome. *Am J Obstet Gynecol* 2005; 192(1):219–26.

195. Christensson K, et al. Lower body temperatures in infants delivered by caesarean section than in vaginally delivered infants. *Acta Paediatr* 1993; 82(2):128–31.

196. Isobe K, et al. Measurement of cerebral oxygenation in neonates after vaginal delivery and cesarean section using full-spectrum near infrared spectroscopy. *Comp Biochem Physiol A Mol Integr Physiol* 2002; 132(1):133–8.

197. Otamiri G, et al. Delayed neurological adaptation in infants delivered by elective cesarean section and the relation to catecholamine levels. *Early Hum Dev* 1991; 26(1):51–60.

198. Kim HR, et al. Delivery modes and neonatal EEG: spatial pattern analysis. *Early Hum Dev* 2003; 75(1–2):35–53.

199. Vladimirova E, Smirnova EE. [The CNS status of newborn infants delivered by cesarean section (based on EEG data)]. *Zh Nevropatol Psikhiatr Im S S Korsakova* 1994; 94(3):16–8.

200. Freudigman KA, Thoman EB. Infants' earliest sleep/wake organization differs as a function of delivery mode. *Dev Psychobiol* 1998; 32(4):293–303.

201. Bagnoli F, et al. Relationship between mode of delivery and neonatal calcium homeostasis. *Eur J Pediatr* 1990; 149(11):800–3.

202. Broughton Pipkin F, Symonds EM. Factors affecting angiotensin II concentrations in the human infant at birth. *Clin Sci Mol Med* 1977; 52(5):449–56.

203. Fujimura A, et al. The influence of delivery mode on biological inactive renin level in umbilical cord blood. *Am J Hypertens* 1990; 3(1):23–6.

204. Tetlow HJ, Broughton Pipkin F. Studies on the effect of mode of delivery on the renin-angiotensin system in mother and fetus at term. *Br J Obstet Gynaecol* 1983; 90(3):220–6.

205. Okamoto E, et al. Plasma concentrations of human atrial natriuretic peptide at vaginal delivery and elective cesarean section. *Asia Oceania J Obstet Gynaecol* 1989; 15(2):199–202.

206. Aisien AO, et al. Umbilical cord venous progesterone at term delivery in relation to mode of delivery. *Int J Gynaecol Obstet* 1994; 47(1):27–31.

207. Malamitsi-Puchner A, et al. Serum levels of creatine kinase and its isoenzymes during the 1st postpartum day in healthy newborns delivered vaginally or by cesarean section. *Gynecol Obstet Invest* 1993; 36(1):25–8.

208. Boksa P, El-Khodor BF. Birth insult interacts with stress at adulthood to alter dopaminergic function in animal models: possible implications for schizophrenia and other disorders. *Neurosci Biobehav Rev* 2003; 27(1–2):91–101.

209. Endo A, et al. Spontaneous labor increases nitric oxide synthesis during the early neonatal period. *Pediatr Int* 2001; 43(4):340–2.

210. Endo A, et al. Physiologic significance of nitric oxide and endothelin-1 in circulatory adaptation. *Pediatr Int* 2000; 42(1):26–30.

211. Hills FA, et al. IGFBP-1 in the placenta, membranes and fetal circulation: levels at term and preterm delivery. *Early Hum Dev* 1996; 44(1):71–6.

212. Mitchell MD, et al. Melatonin in the maternal and umbilical circulations during human parturition. *Br J Obstet Gynaecol* 1979; 86(1):29–31.

213. Bird JA, et al. Endocrine and metabolic adaptation following caesarean section or vaginal delivery. *Arch Dis Child Fetal Neonatal Ed* 1996; 74(2):F132–4.

214. Mongelli M, et al. Effect of labour and delivery on plasma hepatic enzymes in the newborn. *J Obstet Gynaecol Res* 2000; 26(1):61–3.

215. Banasik M, et al. [Effect of maternal labor and mode of delivery on function of neonatal cord blood neutrophils]. *Ginekol Pol* 2000; 71(6):559–65.

216. Molloy EJ, et al. Labor promotes neonatal neutrophil survival and lipopolysaccharide responsiveness. *Pediatr Res* 2004; 56(1):99–103.

217. Thilaganathan B, et al. Labor: an immunologically beneficial process for the neonate. *Am J Obstet Gynecol* 1994; 171(5):1271–2.

218. Agrawal S, et al. Comparative study of immunoglobulin G and immunoglobulin M among neonates in caesarean section and vaginal delivery. *J Indian Med Assoc* 1996; 94(2):43–4.

219. Gronlund MM, et al. Mode of delivery directs the phagocyte functions of infants for the first 6 months of life. *Clin Exp Immunol* 1999; 116(3):521–6.

220. Lubetzky R, et al. Mode of delivery and neonatal hematocrit. *Am J Perinatol* 2000; 17(3):163–5.

221. Stevenson DK, et al. Increased immunoreactive erythropoietin in cord plasma and neonatal bilirubin production in normal term infants after labor. *Obstet Gynecol* 1986; 67(1):69–73.

222. Bujko M, et al. Mode of delivery and level of passive immunity against herpes simplex virus. *Clin Exp Obstet Gynecol* 1989; 16(1):6–8.

223. Steinborn A, et al. Spontaneous labour at term is associated with fetal monocyte activation. *Clin Exp Immunol* 1999; 117(1):147–52.

224. Brown MA, et al. Method of birth alters interferon-gamma and interleukin-12 production by cord blood mononuclear cells. *Pediatr Allergy Immunol* 2003; 14(2):106–11.

225. Santala M. Mode of delivery and lymphocyte beta 2-adrenoceptor density in parturients and newborns. *Gynecol Obstet Invest* 1989; 28(4):174–7.

226. Franzoi M, et al. Effect of delivery modalities on the physiologic inhibition system of coagulation of the neonate. *Thromb Res* 2002; 105(1):15–8.

227. Pasetto N, et al. Leukotrienes in human umbilical plasma at birth. *Br J Obstet Gynaecol* 1989; 96(1):88–91.

228. Miclat NN, et al. Neonatal gastric pH. *Anesth Analg* 1978; 57(1):98–101.

229. Sangild PT, et al. Vaginal birth versus elective caesarean section: effects on gastric function in the neonate. *Exp Physiol* 1995; 80(1):147–57.

230. Gronlund MM, et al. Fecal microflora in healthy infants born by different methods of delivery: permanent changes in intestinal flora after cesarean delivery. *J Pediatr Gastroenterol Nutr* 1999; 28(1):19–25.

231. Hallstrom M, et al. Effects of mode of delivery and necrotising enterocolitis on the intestinal microflora in preterm infants. *Eur J Clin Microbiol Infect Dis* 2004; 23(6):463–70.

232. Kero J, et al. Mode of delivery and asthma – is there a connection? *Pediatr Res* 2002; 52(1):6–11.

233. Hakansson S, Kallen K. Caesarean section increases the risk of hospital care in childhood for asthma and gastroenteritis. *Clin Exp Allergy* 2003; 33(6):757–64.

234. Laubereau B, et al. Caesarean section and gastrointestinal symptoms, atopic dermatitis, and sensitisation during the first year of life. *Arch Dis Child* 2004; 89(11):993–7.

235. Rogers MS, et al. Lipid peroxidation in cord blood at birth: the effect of labour. *Br J Obstet Gynaecol* 1998; 105(7):739–44.

236. Buhimschi IA, et al. Beneficial impact of term labor: nonenzymatic antioxidant reserve in the human fetus. *Am J Obstet Gynecol* 2003; 189(1):181–8.

237. Kazda H, et al. Maternal, umbilical, and amniotic fluid concentrations of tryptophan and kynurenine after labor or cesarean section. *Pediatr Res* 1998; 44(3):368–73.

238. Pohjavuori M, Fyhrquist F. Vasopressin, ACTH and neonatal haemodynamics. *Acta Paediatr Scand Suppl* 1983; 305:79–83.

239. Pohjavuori M, et al. Plasma immunoreactive beta-endorphin and cortisol in the newborn infant after elective caesarean section and after spontaneous labour. *Eur J Obstet Gynecol Reprod Biol* 1985; 19(2):67–74.

240. Fisher J, et al. Adverse psychological impact of operative obstetric interventions: a prospective longitudinal study. *Aust N Z J Psychiatry* 1997; 31(5):728–38.

241. Nissen E, et al. Different patterns of oxytocin, prolactin but not cortisol release during breastfeeding in women delivered by caesarean section or by the vaginal route. *Early Hum Dev* 1996; 45(1–2):103–18, p 116.

242. Evans KC, et al. Effect of caesarean section on breast milk transfer to the normal term newborn over the first week of life. *Arch Dis Child Fetal Neonatal Ed* 2003; 88(5):F380–2.

243. Salariya EM, et al. Duration of breast-feeding after early initiation and frequent feeding. *Lancet* 1978; 2(8100):1141–3.

244. de Chateau P, Wiberg B. Long-term effect on mother–infant behaviour of extra contact during the first hour post partum. II. A follow-up at three months. *Acta Paediatr Scand* 1977; 66(2):145–51.

245. DiMatteo MR, et al. Cesarean childbirth and psychosocial outcomes: a meta-analysis. *Health Psychol* 1996; 15(4):303–14.

246. Burby L. *101 Reasons to Breastfeed Your Child*: Promotion of Mothers' Milk Inc, 2001. www.promom.org/101/

247. Odent M. Primal Health Database: Birthworks, 2003. www.birthworks.org/primalhealth/

248. Widstrom AM, et al. Short-term effects of early suckling and touch of the nipple on maternal behaviour. *Early Hum Dev* 1990; 21(3): 153–63.

249. Uvnas-Moberg K. The gastrointestinal tract in growth and reproduction. *Sci Am* 1989; 261(1):78–83.

250. Klaus M. Mother and infant: early emotional ties. *Pediatrics* 1998; 102(5 Suppl E):1244–6, p 1246.

251. Christensson K, et al. Temperature, metabolic adaptation and crying in healthy full-term newborns cared for skin-to-skin or in a cot. *Acta Paediatr* 1992; 81(6–7):488–93.

252. Ferber SG, Makhoul IR. The effect of skin-to-skin contact (kangaroo care) shortly after birth on the neurobehavioral responses of the term newborn: a randomized, controlled trial. *Pediatrics* 2004; 113(4):858–65.

253. Christensson K, et al. Separation distress call in the human neonate in the absence of maternal body contact. *Acta Paediatr* 1995; 84(5):468–73, p 468.

254. Biagini G, et al. Postnatal maternal separation during the stress hyporesponsive period enhances the adrenocortical response to novelty in adult rats by affecting feedback regulation in the CA1 hippocampal field. *Int J Dev Neurosci* 1998; 16(3–4):187–97.

255. Klaus M. Mother and infant: early emotional ties. *Pediatrics* 1998; 102(5 Suppl E):1244–6.

256. Buranasin B. The effects of rooming-in on the success of breastfeeding and the decline in abandonment of children. *Asia Pac J Public Health* 1991; 5(3):217–20.

257. O'Connor S, et al. Reduced incidence of parenting inadequacy following rooming-in. *Pediatrics* 1980; 66(2):176–82.

258. Ringler NM, et al. Mother-to-child speech at 2 years – effects of early postnatal contact. *J Pediatr* 1975; 86(1):141–4.

259. Pearce JC. *Evolution's End: Claiming the Potential of Our Intelligence*. San Francisco: Harper San Francisco, 1992 pp 114–5.

260. Pearce JC. *Evolution's End: Claiming the Potential of Our Intelligence*. San Francisco: Harper San Francisco, 1992 p 115.

261. Lin SH, et al. Maternal behavior: activation of the central oxytocin receptor system in parturient rats? *Neuroreport* 2003; 14(11):1439–44, p 1444.

262. Luckman SM. Fos expression within regions of the preoptic area, hypothalamus and brainstem during pregnancy and parturition. *Brain Res* 1995; 669(1):115–24.

263. Bridges RS. Long-term effects of pregnancy and parturition upon maternal responsiveness in the rat. *Physiol Behav* 1975; 14(3):245–9.

264. Shore R. *Rethinking the Brain: New Insights into Early Development*. New York: Families and Work Institute, 1997, p 15.

265. Brown T. Back to Basics: Regressive Therapy Could Give You and Baby a Fresh Start. breastfeed.com/resources/articles/btob.htm, n.d.

266. Righard L, Alade MO. Effect of delivery room routines on success of first breast-feed. *Lancet* 1990; 336(8723):1105–7.

267. Baker JP. *Prenatal Yoga and Natural Childbirth*. 3rd edn. Berkley: North Atlantic Books, 2001 p 90.

268. Kloosterman G. The universal aspects of childbirth: Human birth as a socio-psychosomatic paradigm. *J Psychosom Obstet Gynaecol* 1982; 1(1):35–41, p 40.

14

Epidurals ~
risks and concerns
for mother and baby

T HE first recorded use of an epidural was in 1885, when New York neurologist J Leonard Corning injected cocaine into the back of a patient suffering from "spinal weakness and seminal incontinence".[1] More than a century later, epidurals have become the most popular method of pain relief (analgesia) in US birth rooms. In 2002, almost two-thirds of labouring women reported that they were administered an epidural, including 59 percent of women who had a vaginal birth.[2] In Canada, around half of women who birthed vaginally in 2001–2 used an epidural,[3] and in the UK, 21 percent of women had an epidural before or during delivery in 2003–04.[4]

Epidurals involve the injection of one or more drugs into the epidural space – the space around (*epi*) the tough coverings (*dura*) that protect the spinal cord and cerebrospinal fluid. Epidurals are also sometimes called peridurals or extradurals.

The drugs conventionally injected into the epidural space – including bupivacaine (Marcaine), ropivacaine (Naropin), and lidocaine (Xylocaine) – are all derivatives of the cocaine that Corning originally used. These drugs work through their local anaesthetic effect, numbing the nerves that are exiting the spinal cord through the epidural space. In the case of a labour epidural, the nerves that are numbed are those that provide sensation and motor function to the lower part of the body. A conventional epidural can stop the pain of contractions in labour by numbing the sensory nerves, but will also, to some extent, numb (block) the motor nerves, making the recipient unable to move the lower part of their body. Women given conventional epidurals will therefore usually be unable to walk during labour, or to push their baby out at birth.

More recently, obstetric anaesthetists (anesthesiologists) – the specialists who administer epidurals – have been experimenting with lower strengths of local anaesthetic drugs, and with combinations of local anesthetics and opiate pain killers (drugs similar to morphine and pethidine) to reduce the motor block, and to produce a so-called walking epidural. For the same reasons, anaesthetists have begun to use spinal analgesia for labouring women, where drugs are injected right through the dura and into the spinal (intrathecal) space, which contains the spinal cord and cerebrospinal fluid.

Spinals have been used successfully for many years in the operating theatre; however, they provide only short-term pain relief (an hour or two at most), which is usually insufficient in labour. (It is not considered safe to re-inject into this delicate space, nor to place an indwelling catheter (tube) for further administration of drugs, as occurs with an epidural.) To prolong the pain-relieving effect for labour, spinals are now being combined with epidurals as a combined spinal epidural (CSE), where ongoing pain relief can be administered via the epidural catheter, which is put in place with the same injection that administers the spinal.

Epidurals and spinals – sometimes collectively called regional or neuraxial analgesia – offer labouring women the most effective form of pain relief that is available, and women who have used these analgesics rate their satisfaction with pain relief as very high. However, satisfaction with pain relief does not equate with overall satisfaction with birth,[5] and epidurals are also associated with major disruptions to the processes of birth. These disruptions can interfere with a woman's ultimate enjoyment of, and satisfaction with, her labour experience, and may also compromise the safety of birth for mother and baby.

For example, when an epidural is in place, continuous monitoring of the baby's heart rate (electronic fetal monitoring, EFM) is necessary, because epidurals can cause abnormalities in the baby's heart rate (fetal heart rate, FHR) that signal that the baby has insufficient supplies of oxygen (fetal distress). Women using an epidural also require intravenous (IV) fluids to counteract the drop in blood pressure that epidurals cause in all women, and also in case drugs are needed to treat fetal distress. The need for EFM monitoring (usually with a monitor strapped to the labouring woman's belly) and IV fluids will usually confine a woman with an epidural to bed. When an epidural is in place, a catheter is often needed to pass urine, because the nerves to the bladder are also numbed.

A woman labouring with an epidural is very likely to require synthetic oxytocin (Syntocinon, Pitocin) to speed up (augment, stimulate) her labour, which will be slowed by using an epidural. She is also more likely to need instrumental assistance (forceps, vacuum) to give birth, which increases her chance of a major tear, and of resulting damage to her pelvic floor. She also may have a higher chance of having a caesarean, especially with her first baby.

The baby may also be affected by these procedures; by the drugs administered via epidural; and by the disruption to the processes of birth. Incredibly, there has been a lack of high-quality research on the impact of epidurals for the baby, both in the womb and postnatally, and on the effect of epidurals on breastfeeding success.

Epidurals and the processes of labour

Labour hormones

The processes of labour and birth are complex and exquisitely orchestrated. This orchestration is thought to originate in the labouring mother's middle brain, through her production of birthing hormones such as oxytocin, beta-endorphin, adrenaline and noradrenaline (epinephrine and norepinephrine) and prolactin. As the hormones of love, pleasure and transcendence, excitement, and tender mothering respectively, these hormones form an ecstatic hormonal cocktail that catalyses the processes of labour and produces, in the minutes after birth, feelings of love, pleasure, excitement and tenderness as mother and baby meet for the first time.[6–8] (For more about the hormonal orchestration of labour, see chapter 13, "Undisturbed Birth".) Epidurals interfere with all of these hormones, which may explain their negative effect on the processes of labour.

For example, oxytocin is the hormone that naturally causes a woman's uterus to contract (uterotonic) in labour. Epidurals lower the mother's release of oxytocin,[9] or stop its normal rise during labour.[10] The effect of spinals on oxytocin release is even more marked.[10] Epidurals also obliterate the maternal oxytocin peak that occurs at birth[11] – the highest of a mother's lifetime – that catalyses the final powerful contractions of labour, and helps mother and baby to fall in love at first meeting. Another important uterotonic hormone, prostaglandin F2 alpha, is also reduced in women using an epidural.[12]

Beta-endorphin is the stress hormone that builds up in a natural labour to help the labouring woman to transcend pain. Beta-endorphin is also associated with the altered state of consciousness that is normal in labour, and helps the mother-to-be to follow her own instincts and intuition in birth. Epidurals reduce the labouring woman's release of beta-endorphin.[13, 14] Perhaps the widespread use of epidurals reflects our difficulty with supporting women in this altered state, and our cultural preference for labouring women to be quiet and acquiescent.

Adrenaline and noradrenaline (epinephrine and norepinephrine, collectively known as catecholamines, or CAs) are also released under stressful conditions, and levels naturally increase during labour.[15] At the end of an undisturbed labour, a natural surge in these hormones gives the mother the energy to push her baby out, and makes her excited and fully alert at first meeting with her baby. This is known as the fetal ejection reflex.[16]

However, labour is inhibited in the earlier stages by very high CA levels, which may be released when the labouring woman feels hungry, cold, fearful, or unsafe.[17] This makes evolutionary sense: if the mother senses danger, her hormones will slow or stop labour and give her time to flee to find a safer place to birth.

Epidurals reduce the labouring woman's release of CAs,[18, 19] which may be helpful if high levels are inhibiting her labour. However, a reduction in the final CA surge (fetal ejection reflex) may contribute to the difficulty that women labouring with an epidural can experience in pushing out their babies, and the increased risk of instrumental delivery (forceps and vacuum) that accompanies the use of an epidural, as noted below.

Prolactin, the mothering hormone, is also involved in the ecstatic hormonal cocktail, reaching peak levels in the minutes after birth. Prolactin is the major hormone of breastmilk synthesis, and its secretion is stimulated by beta-endorphin.[20] This implies that decreases in beta-endorphin, as caused by epidurals, may also interfere with prolactin. As noted below, there is evidence that epidurals have a negative impact on breastfeeding and breast-milk production.

Birth interventions

These hormonal deviations translate into major disruptions for the labouring woman. As the World Health Organization comments, "… epidural analgesia is one of the most striking examples of the medicalisation of normal birth, transforming a physiological event into a medical procedure."[21]

Epidurals slow labour, possibly through the above effects on the labouring woman's oxytocin release, although there is also evidence from animal research that the local anaesthetic drugs used in epidurals may inhibit contractions by a direct effect on the muscle of the uterus.[22]

Such tocolytic (labour-slowing) effects translate into a first stage of labour that is, on average, 26 minutes longer in women who use an epidural, and a second (pushing) stage that is 15 minutes longer.[23] Loss of the final oxytocin peak probably also contributes to the doubled risk of an instrumental delivery – vacuum or forceps – for women who use an epidural,[23] although other mechanisms may be involved.

For example, the motor block caused by a conventional epidural paralyses the labouring woman's pelvic floor muscles, which are important in guiding her baby's head into a good position for birth. When an epidural is in place, the baby is four times more likely to be persistently posterior (POP, face up) in the final stages of labour – 13 percent compared to three percent for women without an epidural in one study.[24] A POP position decreases the chance of a spontaneous vaginal birth (SVD); in one study, only 26 percent of first-time mothers (and 57 percent of experienced mothers) with POP babies experienced a SVD; the remaining mothers had an instrumental birth (forceps or vacuum) or a caesarean.[25]

Anaesthetists have hoped that low-dose or CSE will increase the chances of a spontaneous vaginal birth, but the improvement seems to be modest. In one study, (known as COMET – Conventional Obstetric Mobile Epidural Trial), 37 percent of women with a conventional epidural experienced instrumental births, compared with 29 percent of women using low-dose and 28 percent of women using CSE.[26]

Other centres have attempted to increase the rate of spontaneous vaginal birth by allowing the epidural to wear off late in labour. A recent review concluded that this policy is associated with more pain (possibly worsened because the labouring mother's beta-endorphin levels have not built up), but there is not enough evidence to suggest that it is useful in avoiding instrumental delivery.[27]

The impact of an instrumental delivery is substantial for both mother and baby. For the mother, instrumental delivery increases her risks of episiotomy and tears to her vagina and perineum, and of major tears that can damage her anal sphincter. Two studies have shown that severe perineal lacerations are around twice as common after epidurals.[28, 29]

After an instrumental delivery, women report more sexual problems, perineal pain and urinary incontinence, compared to women who have had a spontaneous birth.[30–32] For example, an Australian population survey of women six to seven months after birth found that, compared to women who had spontaneous vaginal births, women who had instrumental deliveries were four times more likely to have perineal pain; twice as likely to have sexual problems; and almost twice as likely to experience urinary incontinence.[31]

For the baby, instrumental delivery can increase the short-term risks of bruising, facial injuries, displacement of the skull bones and cephalohematoma (blood clot in the scalp).[33] The risk of intracranial haemorrhage (bleeding inside the brain) was increased in one study by more than four times for babies born by forceps compared to spontaneous birth,[34] although two studies showed no detectable developmental differences for forceps-born children at five years old.[35, 36] Another study showed that, when women with an epidural had a forceps delivery, the force used by the clinician to deliver the baby was almost doubled, compared to the force used when an epidural was not in place.[37]

Epidurals also increase the need for Syntocinon (Pitocin) to augment labour, probably due to the negative effect on the labouring woman's own oxytocin release, and subsequent slowing of labour. Women labouring with an epidural in place are almost three times more likely to be administered Syntocinon.[23] The combination of epidurals and Syntocinon, both of which can cause FHR abnormalities and fetal distress, markedly increases the risks of operative delivery (forceps, vacuum or cesarean delivery). In an Australian survey, up to two-thirds of first-time mothers who were administered both an epidural and Syntocinon had an operative delivery.[38]

The impact of epidurals on the risk of cesarean is contentious, with studies suggesting no increased risk[23] and a 50 percent increased risk.[39] The risk is probably most significant for women having their first baby, who, according to one study, may be three times more likely to have a caesarean.[40]

Note that the studies used to arrive at these conclusions are mostly randomised controlled trials (RCTs), where the women who agree to participate are randomly assigned to epidural or non-epidural pain relief. Non-epidural pain relief usually involves opiates such as pethidine (meperidine), which can itself significantly impact labour and birth for mother and baby. Many of these studies are also flawed from high rates of crossover – women who were assigned to non-epidurals but who ultimately had an epidural, and vice versa. Also, note that there are no true controls – that is, women who are not using any form of pain relief – so we cannot know the impact of epidurals on mothers and babies compared to birth without analgesic drugs from these studies.

Epidural techniques and side effects

The drugs used in labour epidurals are powerful enough to numb and usually paralyse the mother's lower body, so it is not surprising that there can be significant side effects for mother and baby. Side effects range from minor to life threatening and depend, to some extent, on the specific drugs used.

Local anaesthetic drugs depress the electrical conduction of nerve impulses, leading to numbing at the site of injection, making them useful for dental procedures and minor skin surgery. When injected via epidural, these drugs numb the nerves as they exit the spinal cord. Opiate drugs injected into the epidural space act on opiate receptors in the spinal cord (as does a labouring woman's own beta-endorphin release).

However, any epidural drug will also enter the mother's blood stream within minutes, generating possible whole body (systemic) effects for the mother. Epidural drugs also cross the placenta, creating potential side effects for the baby. As Golub notes, "Probably the most widespread exposure of the developing brain to central nervous system active agents occurs at birth."[41]

Opiate drugs administered via spinal also act on spinal receptors, and have been shown to move rapidly upwards in the cerebrospinal fluid to the brainstem (lower brain),[42] where they can cause breathing (respiratory) problems, as noted below, by depressing the brainstem respiratory centre.

Many of the epidural side effects mentioned below are not improved with low-dose or walking epidurals, because women using these techniques may receive the same total dose of local anaesthetic, especially when continuous infusions and/or patient-controlled boluses (single large doses) are used.[26] The addition of opiate drugs in epidurals or CSE can introduce further risks, such as pruritis (itching) and respiratory depression, mentioned above.

Further, the ability of women with a "walking epidural" to actually walk will be compromised by the presence of an IV and monitor, and the need for constant one-to-one caregiver support

while walking. Some studies show that women using a walking epidural may have impaired balance[43] and circulatory adjustments.[44]

Maternal side effects

The most common side effect of epidurals is a drop in maternal
blood pressure. This effect is almost universal, and usually pre-
empted by administering IV fluids before placing an epidural. Even
with this "preloading", episodes of significant low blood pressure
(hypotension) occur for up to half of all women labouring with an
epidural,[45, 46] especially in the minutes following the administration
of a drug bolus. Hypotension can cause complications ranging from
feeling faint to cardiac arrest,[47] and can also affect the baby's blood
supply, as noted below. Hypotension can be treated with more IV
fluids and, if severe, with injections of adrenaline (epinephrine).

Some researchers believe that the hypotensive effect of epidurals and spinals may be caused by the sudden relief of pain,
which disrupts the labouring mother's balance of CA hormones.
These hormones help to maintain and equalise the mother's blood
pressure and heart rate, as well as influencing the strength of her
contractions. A shift in CA hormones can also cause her uterus
to contract too strongly (hyperstimulation). Hyperstimulation reduces the baby's supplies of blood and oxygen, and can lead to
fetal distress.

Other common side effects of epidurals include: inability to
pass urine (and requirement for a urinary catheter) for up to two-
thirds of women;[46] itching of the skin (pruritis) for up to two-thirds
of women administered an opiate drug via epidural;[45, 46] shivering
for up to one in three women;[48] sedation for around one in five
women;[46] and nausea and vomiting for one in 20 women.[46]

Epidurals can also cause a rise in temperature in labouring
women. Fever over 38 °C (100.4 °F) during labour is five times
more likely overall for women using an epidural;[23] this rise in
temperature is more common in women having their first baby
and more marked with prolonged exposure to epidurals.[39] For example, in one study, seven percent of first-time mothers labouring
with an epidural were feverish (febrile) after six hours, increasing
to 36 percent after 18 hours.[49]

The cause of this fever is not known although various explanations have been proposed. These include: a direct effect on the woman's heat-regulating system; infection of the uterus and membranes (chorioamnionitis) and a false effect, because most trials compare women having epidurals with women administered opiate drugs, which reduce temperature.[50] Maternal fever can have a significant effect on the baby, as noted below.

Opiate drugs, especially administered as spinals, can cause unexpected breathing difficulties for the mother, which may come on hours after birth and may progress to respiratory arrest. DeBalli comments: "Respiratory depression remains one of the most feared and least predictable complications of … intrathecal [spinal] opioids."[51]

Many observational studies have found an association between epidural use and bleeding after birth (postpartum haemorrhage, PPH).[52–57] For example, a large UK study found that women were twice as likely to experience a PPH if they had used an epidural in labour.[52] This may be related to the increase in instrumental births and perineal trauma (causing bleeding) or may reflect some of the hormonal disruptions, as noted above.

An epidural gives inadequate pain relief for around 10 percent of women;[45] and the epidural catheter needs to be reinserted in about five percent.[58] For around one percent of women, the epidural needle punctures the dura (dural tap); this usually causes a severe headache, which can last up to six weeks, but can usually be treated by an injection into the epidural space.[59, 60]

More serious side effects are rare. If the epidural drugs are inadvertently injected into the blood stream, local anaesthetics can cause toxic effects such as slurred speech, drowsiness and at high doses, convulsions. This occurs in around one in 2,800 epidural insertions.[58] Overall, life-threatening reactions occur for around one in 4,000 women.[47, 58, 61, 62] Death associated with an obstetric epidural is very rare,[63] but may be caused by cardiac or respiratory arrest, or by an epidural abscess that can develop days or weeks afterwards.

Later complications include weakness and numbness in four to 18 per 10,000 women, most of which resolve within three months.[47, 61–64] Longer term or permanent problems can arise from: damage to a nerve during epidural placement; from abscess or haematoma (blood clot) which can compress the spinal cord; and from loss of blood supply to the spinal cord, which can lead to paraplegia.[47]

A recent review found some evidence that women who had used an epidural were more likely to experience urinary retention in hospital, and stress urinary incontinence in the first year after birth. This may be related to the longer labours and higher rates of instrumental delivery associated with epidurals.[39]

Side effects for the baby

Some of the most significant and well-documented side effects for the unborn baby (fetus) and newborn derive from effects on the mother. These include, as noted above, effects on her hormonal orchestration, her blood pressure and her temperature regulation. Drug levels in the fetus and newborn may be even higher than the mother's drug levels,[65] which may cause directly toxic effects.

FHR changes

For example, epidurals can cause changes in the fetal heart rate (FHR) that indicate that the unborn baby is lacking blood and oxygen. This effect is well recognised soon after the administration of an epidural (usually within the first 30 minutes), can last for 20 minutes, and is particularly likely following the use of opiate drugs administered via epidural and spinal. In these situations, the fetal heart rate can drop to very low levels (fetal bradycardia).

This fetal bradycardia (and other FHR abnormalities) may relate to the sudden drop in maternal CA hormones, which can cause hypotension and uterine hyperstimulation, as noted above.[66] Drug toxicity may also contribute to the FHR effects: Capogna notes that FHR abnormalities peak at the same time as maternal drug levels,[66] and Hill proposes that high doses of local anaesthetics may cause spasm in the uterine arteries, impairing the blood supply to the uterus and baby.[67]

Note that the use of pethidine (meperidine) for labour analgesia can also cause FHR abnormalities. This makes the real effects of epidurals on FHR hard to assess because, in almost all randomised trials, epidurals are compared with meperidine and other opiate drugs.

Studies looking at FHR abnormalities after the administration of spinal opiates have found that 10 to 15 percent of babies develop FHR changes,[66] and one in 28 develop a significant bradycardia.[68] Most of these changes in FHR will resolve spontaneously, with a change in position or, more rarely, may require drug treatment.[69] More severe changes, and the fetal distress that they reflect, may require an urgent cesarean.

Capogna notes that the supine position (lying on the back) may contribute significantly to hypotension and FHR abnormalities when an epidural is in place:[66] one researcher found that the supine position (plus epidural) was associated with a significant decrease in fetal cerebral oxygenation (oxygen supply to the baby's brain).[70]

Effects from maternal fever

The baby can also be affected by an epidural-induced rise in the labouring mother's temperature. In one large study of first-time mothers, babies born to febrile mothers, 97 percent of whom had received epidurals, were more likely to be in poor condition (low APGAR) at birth; to have poor tone; to require resuscitation (11.5 percent versus three percent); and to have seizures in the newborn period, compared to babies born to afebrile (not feverish) mothers.[71]

The authors of this study express concerns about these effects and note that, in primate studies, maternal hyperthermia (high temperature), even without infection, can cause low oxygen and low blood pressure in the unborn baby as well as signs of poor condition (acidosis) at birth. They note further, "Other animal studies have demonstrated that an increase in brain temperature of even 1°C or 2°C increases the degree of brain damage resulting from an ischemic insult" (acute lack of blood). One researcher has noted a ten-times increased risk of newborn encephalopathy (brain damage) in babies born to febrile mothers.[72]

Maternal fever in labour can also directly cause problems for the newborn. Because fever can be a sign of infection involving the uterus, babies born to febrile mothers are almost always evaluated for sepsis (infection). Sepsis evaluation involves prolonged separation from the mother, admission to special care, invasive tests and most likely administration of antibiotics until tests results are available. In one study of first-time mothers, 34 percent of epidural babies were given a sepsis evaluation compared to 9.8 percent of non-epidural babies.[71]

Drugs and toxicity

These effects on the baby are likely to be increased where other drugs and interventions are used although, incredibly, this has not been well studied.

In older studies, babies born to women who were induced with Syntocinon and also received an epidural were mildly hypoxic (lacking in oxygen) at birth,[73] and mothers who received (intravenous) prostaglandin induction along with an epidural had an extremely high incidence of hyperstimulation, and their babies had some severe, although temporary, FHR abnormalities. The authors comment, "… the combined application of an intravenous prostaglandin and continuous epidural analgesia should not be introduced into obstetrical practice."[74] There are no similar studies, to my knowledge, using modern vaginally administered prostaglandins, which are commonly used with epidurals.

There are also few studies of the condition of epidural babies at birth, and almost all of these compare babies born after epidurals with babies born after exposure to opiate drugs, which are known to cause drowsiness and difficulty with breathing. These studies show little difference between epidural and non-epidural (usually opiate-exposed) babies in terms of APGAR score and umbilical cord pH (both of which reflect the baby's condition at birth).[39] However, a large population survey from Sweden found that use of an epidural was significantly associated with a low APGAR score at birth.[75]

There are also reports of drug toxicity from epidural drugs, especially opiates,[76] which are administered via epidural at similar doses to those given parenterally (by injection into muscle or vein). These drugs will enter the mother's and then the baby's circulation within minutes. Opiate overdose can make the baby unresponsive and not breathing at birth. Newborn opiate toxicity seems more likely when higher dose regimes are used, including those where the mother is able to self-administer extra doses, although it also seems that there are wide differences in individual sensitivity.[76]

It is also important to note that a newborn baby's ability to process and excrete drugs is much less than an adult. For example, the half-life (time to reduce drug blood levels by one-half) for the local anaesthetic bupivacaine (Marcaine) is 8.1 hours in the newborn, compared to 2.7 hours in the mother.[77] As well, drug levels may not accurately reflect the baby's toxic load because drugs may be taken up from the blood and stored in newborn tissues such as brain and liver (or bound to blood proteins)[65] from where they are more slowly released. This is especially likely for drugs such as the opiate fentanyl, which are very fat-soluble (lipophilic).[78]

A recent review also found higher rates of jaundice for epidural-exposed babies, which may be related to the increase in instrumental deliveries or to the increased use of Syntocinon.[39]

Neurobehavioural effects

The effects of epidural drugs on newborn neurobehaviour (behaviour that reflects brain state) are controversial.

Older studies comparing babies exposed to epidurals with un-drugged babies have found significant neurobehavioural effects, whereas more recent findings from randomised controlled trials (which compare epidural- and opiate-exposed newborns) have found no differences. However, these older studies used the more comprehensive (and difficult to administer) Brazelton Neonatal Behavioural Assessment Scale (NBAS, devised by paediatricians) whereas more recent tests have used less complex tests, especially the Neurologic and Adaptive Capacity Score (NACS, devised by anaesthetists) which aggregates all data into a single figure and which has been criticised as insensitive and unreliable.[50, 79, 80]

For example, all three studies comparing epidural-exposed with unmedicated babies, and using the NBAS, found significant differences between groups.[39]

Murray compared 15 unmedicated with 40 epidural-exposed babies, and found that the epidural babies still had a depressed NBAS score at five days, with particular difficulty controlling their state. The 20 babies whose mothers had received oxytocin as well as an epidural had even more depression of NBAS scores, which may be explained by these babies' higher rates of jaundice. At one month, epidural mothers found their babies "… less adaptable, more intense and more bothersome in their behaviour." These differences could not be explained by the more difficult deliveries and subsequent maternal–infant separations associated with epidurals.[81]

Sepkoski compared 20 epidural babies with 20 undrugged babies, and found less alertness and ability to orient for the first month of life. The epidural mothers spent less time with their babies in hospital, which was in proportion to the dose of bupivacaine administered.[82] Rosenblatt tested epidural babies with NBAS over six weeks and found maximal depression on the first day. Although there was some recovery, at three days epidural babies still cried more easily and more often, and aspects of this problem ("control of state") persisted for the full six weeks.[83]

Although these older studies used conventional epidurals, the total dose of bupivacaine administered to the mothers (mean doses 61.6 mg;[81] 112.7mg;[82] and 119.8mg[83] respectively in these studies) was largely comparable to more recent low-dose studies (for example, 67.5mg;[65] 91.1mg;[84] 101.1mg[26]).

These neurobehavioural studies highlight the possible impact of epidurals on newborns and on the evolving mother–infant relationships. The researchers have emphasised, in their conclusions, "The importance of first contact with a disorganized baby in shaping maternal expectations and interactive styles…"[85]

Animal studies

Animal studies suggest that the disruption of maternal hormones caused by epidurals may also contribute to maternal–infant difficulties. Researchers who administered epidurals to labouring sheep found that the epidural ewes had difficulty bonding with their newborn lambs, especially those in first lambing with an epidural administered early in labour.[86] This effect was substantially reversed when these ewes had oxytocin administered directly into the brain,[87] implying that disruption of the oxytocin system may account for these epidural maternal–infant effects.

There are no long-term studies of the possible effects of epidural analgesia on exposed human offspring. However, studies on some of our closest animal relatives give cause for concern. Golub administered epidural bupivacaine to pregnant rhesus monkeys at term, and followed the development of the exposed offspring to age 12 months (equivalent to four years in children). She found that milestone achievement was abnormal in these monkeys; at six to eight weeks they were slow in starting to manipulate, and at 10 months the increase in "motor disturbance behaviours" that normally occurs was prolonged.[88]

The author concludes, "These effects could occur as a result of effects on vulnerable brain processes during a sensitive period, interference with programming of brain development by endogenous [external] agents or alteration in early experiences."[41]

Breastfeeding

As with neurobehaviour, effects on breastfeeding are poorly studied, and more recent RCTs comparing exposure to epidural and opiates are especially misleading, because opiates have a well-recognised negative effect on early breastfeeding behaviour and success.[89–93]

Epidurals may affect the experience and success of breastfeeding through several mechanisms. First, the epidural-exposed baby may have neurobehavioural abnormalities caused by drug exposure, which are likely to be maximal in the hours following birth. This is a critical time for the initiation of breastfeeding. Recent epidural research has found (rather obviously) that the higher the baby's neurobehaviour (NACS) score one hour after birth, the higher their score for early breastfeeding behaviour.[94]

In another study, the baby's breastfeeding abilities – as measured by the Infant Breastfeeding Assessment Tool (IBFAT) – were highest amongst unmedicated babies, lower for babies exposed to epidurals or IV opiates and lowest for babies exposed to both. Infants with lower scores were weaned earlier although overall, similar numbers in all groups were breastfeeding at six weeks.[95]

In other research, babies exposed to epidurals and spinals were more likely to lose weight in hospital, which may reflect poor feeding efficiency.[96] Other research has suggested that newborn breastfeeding behaviour and NACS score may be normal when ultra-low dose epidural is used, although even in this study, babies with higher drug levels had lower neurobehaviour (NACS) scores at two hours.[97]

Second, epidurals may affect the new mother, so that breastfeeding is more difficult. This is likely if she has experienced a long labour, an instrumental delivery, or separation from her baby, all of which are more likely following an epidural. Hormonal disruptions may also contribute, as oxytocin is a major hormone of breastfeeding.

Baumgarder found that babies born after epidurals were less likely to be fully breastfed on hospital discharge; this was a special risk for epidural babies who did not feed in the first hour after birth.[98] A Finnish survey records that 67 percent of women who had laboured with an epidural reported partial or full formula-feeding in the first 12 weeks compared to 29 percent of non-epidural mothers; epidural mothers were also more likely to report having "not enough milk".[99] Australian researchers found that epidural first-time mothers weaned their babies earlier than mothers who had used alternative labour analgesia.[100] An observational US study also found earlier weaning by epidural mothers,[101] although other US research did not concur.[102] (The latter hospital had policies that were strongly supportive of breastfeeding – including not separating mothers and babies after birth – and an exceptional rate of breastfeeding in all groups: over 70 percent at six weeks. This study highlights the positive effects of breastfeeding support for epidural mothers).

Two groups of Swedish researchers have looked at the subtle but complex breastfeeding and pre-breastfeeding behaviour of un-medicated newborns. Righard has documented that, when placed skin-to-skin on the mother's chest, a newborn can crawl up, find the nipple and self-attach. Newborns affected by opiate drugs in labour or separated from their mothers briefly after birth lose much of this ability.[89] Ransjo-Arvidson found that newborns exposed to labour analgesia (mostly opiates, but including some epidural-affected newborns) were also disorganised in their pre-feeding behaviour – nipple massage and licking and hand sucking – compared to unmedicated newborns.[91]

Satisfaction with birth

Obstetric care providers have assumed that control of pain is the foremost concern of labouring women, and that effective pain relief will ensure a positive birth experience. This belief has resulted in the development and promotion of obstetric techniques that very effectively relieve pain, but these developments have not necessarily lead to improvements in overall satisfaction with the experience of birth.

In fact, there is evidence that the opposite may be true. Several studies have shown that women who use no labour medication are the most satisfied with their birth experience at the time,[103] at six weeks,[104] and one year after the birth.[105] In a UK survey of 1,000 women, those who had used epidurals reported the highest levels of pain relief but the lowest levels of satisfaction with the birth, possibly because of the higher rates of intervention. The authors conclude, "This survey shows that epidural analgesia does not confer an improved maternal experience even when technically satisfactory and giving good analgesia."[106]

A recent review of satisfaction after childbirth found that personal expectations; support from caregivers; the caregiver–patient relationship; and involvement in decision-making are the most important factors in determining satisfaction with the experience of childbirth.[5] Note that, contrary to medical belief, women with high expectations are more likely to be satisfied. The reviewer also notes that the highest rates of dissatisfaction are among women who had an emergency caesarean or an instrumental birth.

Finally, it is noteworthy that caregiver preferences may dictate, to a large extent, the use of epidurals and other medical procedures for labouring women. Klein found that women under the care of family physicians with a low mean use of epidurals were less likely to receive monitoring and Pitocin (Syntocinon), to deliver by caesarean, and to have their baby admitted to newborn special care.[107]

Summary and conclusions

Epidural analgesia offers the most effective form of pain relief, and its use is widespread. However, epidurals, spinals, and combined spinal-epidurals also cause major disruptions to the processes of birth, increasing the chances of slower labour, augmentation, instrumental birth, and possibly caesarean, and causing significant unwanted effects, which include dissatisfaction with the birth experience.

Other possible side effects for the mother include low blood pressure, itching, shivering, fever, sedation, need for urinary catheter, postpartum haemorrhage, and breathing difficulties. For the baby, risks include abnormal FHR (suggesting lack of blood or oxygen), toxic effects from drugs, sepsis evaluation, and jaundice.

There is also evidence that epidurals cause subtle neurobehavioural effects, which may have ongoing negative effects for the newborn, the infant–mother relationship, and for breastfeeding. These important areas urgently need more high-quality research.

In conclusion, epidurals have possible benefits, but also significant risks, for the labouring mother and her baby. Women who wish to avoid the use of epidurals are advised to choose carers, and models of care, that promote, support, and understand the principles and practice of natural and undisturbed birth.

An edited version of this article was published in Mothering, *November–December 2005, issue 133.*

References

1. Hamilton GR, Baskett TF. In the arms of Morpheus: the development of morphine for postoperative pain relief. *Can J Anaesth* 2000; 47(4): 367–74.

2. Declercq E, et al. *Listening to Mothers: Report of the First U.S. National Survey of Women's Childbearing Experiences.* New York: Maternity Center Association, October 2002.

3. Canadian Institute for Health Information. *Giving Birth in Canada.* Ontario: CIHI, 2004.

4. Department of Health. NHS Maternity Statistics, England: 2003–4: London: DOH, 2005.

5. Hodnett ED. Pain and women's satisfaction with the experience of childbirth: a systematic review. *Am J Obstet Gynecol* 2002; 186(5 Suppl Nature):S160–72.

6. Buckley SJ. Ecstatic Birth – Nature's hormonal blueprint for labor. *Mothering* March–April 2002. www.sarahjbuckley.com/articles/ecstatic-birth.htm

7. Buckley SJ. Undisturbed birth: Nature's hormonal blueprint for safety, ease and ecstasy. *MIDIRS Midwifery Digest* 2004; 14(2):203–9. See also chapter 13, Undisturbed Birth.

8. Buckley SJ. What disturbs birth? *MIDIRS Midwifery Digest* 2004; 14(3):353–9. See also chapter 13, Undisturbed Birth.

9. Rahm VA, et al. Plasma oxytocin levels in women during labor with or without epidural analgesia: a prospective study. *Acta Obstet Gynecol Scand* 2002; 81(11):1033–9.

10. Stocche RM, et al. Effects of intrathecal sufentanil on plasma oxytocin and cortisol concentrations in women during the first stage of labor. *Reg Anesth Pain Med* 2001; 26(6):545–50.

11. Goodfellow CF, et al. Oxytocin deficiency at delivery with epidural analgesia. *Br J Obstet Gynaecol* 1983; 90(3):214–9.

12. Behrens O, et al. Effects of lumbar epidural analgesia on prostaglandin F2 alpha release and oxytocin secretion during labor. *Prostaglandins* 1993; 45(3):285–96.

13. Brinsmead M, et al. Peripartum concentrations of beta endorphin and cortisol and maternal mood states. *Aust N Z J Obstet Gynaecol* 1985; 25(3):194–7.

14. Bacigalupo G, et al. Quantitative relationships between pain intensities during labor and beta-endorphin and cortisol concentrations in plasma. Decline of the hormone concentrations in the early postpartum period. *J Perinat Med* 1990; 18(4):289–6.

15. Costa A, et al. Adrenocorticotropic hormone and catecholamines in maternal, umbilical and neonatal plasma in relation to vaginal delivery. *J Endocrinol Invest* 1988; 11(10):703–9.

16. Odent M. The fetus ejection reflex. *The Nature of Birth and Breastfeeding*. Sydney: Ace Graphics, 1992:29–43.

17. Lederman RP, et al. Anxiety and epinephrine in multiparous women in labor: relationship to duration of labor and fetal heart rate pattern. *Am J Obstet Gynecol* 1985; 153(8):870–7.

18. Jouppila R, et al. Maternal and umbilical cord plasma noradrenaline concentrations during labour with and without segmental extradural analgesia, and during caesarean section. *Br J Anaesth* 1984; 56(3):251–5.

19. Jones CR, et al. Plasma catecholamines and modes of delivery: the relation between catecholamine levels and in-vitro platelet aggregation and adrenoreceptor radioligand binding characteristics. *Br J Obstet Gynaecol* 1985; 92(6):593–9.

20. Rivier C, et al. Stimulation in vivo of the secretion of prolactin and growth hormone by beta-endorphin. *Endocrinology* 1977; 100(1):238–41.

21. World Health Organization. *Care in Normal Birth: a Practical Guide. Report of a Technical Working Group*. Geneva: World Health Organization, 1996, p 16.

22. Arici G, et al. The effects of bupivacaine, ropivacaine and mepivacaine on the contractility of rat myometrium. *Int J Obstet Anesth* 2004; 13(2):95–8.

23. Leighton BL, Halpern SH. The effects of epidural analgesia on labor, maternal, and neonatal outcomes: a systematic review. *Am J Obstet Gynecol* 2002; 186(5 Suppl Nature):S69–77.

24. Lieberman E, et al. Changes in fetal position during labor and their association with epidural analgesia. *Obstet Gynecol* 2005; 105(5):974–82.

25. Ponkey SE, et al. Persistent fetal occiput posterior position: obstetric outcomes. *Obstet Gynecol* 2003; 101(5 Pt 1):915–20.

26. COMET Study Group UK. Effect of low-dose mobile versus traditional epidural techniques on mode of delivery: a randomised controlled trial. *Lancet* 2001; 358(9275):19–23.

27. Torvaldsen S, et al. Discontinuation of epidural analgesia late in labour for reducing the adverse delivery outcomes associated with epidural analgesia. *Cochrane Database Syst Rev* 2004(4):CD004457.

28. Carroll TG, et al. Epidural analgesia and severe perineal laceration in a community-based obstetric practice. *J Am Board Fam Pract* 2003; 16(1):1–6.

29. Robinson JN, et al. Epidural analgesia and third- or fourth-degree lacerations in nulliparas. *Obstet Gynecol* 1999; 94(2):259–62.

30. Thompson JF, et al. Prevalence and persistence of health problems after childbirth: associations with parity and method of birth. *Birth* 2002; 29(2):83–94.

31. Brown S, Lumley J. Maternal health after childbirth: results of an Australian population based survey. *Br J Obstet Gynaecol* 1998; 105(2):156–61.

32. Johanson RB, et al. Maternal and child health after assisted vaginal delivery: five-year follow up of a randomised controlled study comparing forceps and ventouse. *Br J Obstet Gynaecol* 1999; 106(6):544–9.

33. Johnson JH, et al. Immediate maternal and neonatal effects of forceps and vacuum-assisted deliveries. *Obstet Gynecol* 2004; 103(3):513–8.

34. Jhawar BS, et al. Risk factors for intracranial hemorrhage among full-term infants: a case-control study. *Neurosurgery* 2003; 52(3):581–90; discussion 588–90.

35. McBride WG, et al. Method of delivery and developmental outcome at five years of age. *Med J Aust* 1979; 1(8):301–4.

36. Wesley BD, et al. The effect of forceps delivery on cognitive development. *Am J Obstet Gynecol* 1993; 169(5):1091–5.

37. Poggi SH, et al. Effect of epidural anaesthesia on clinician-applied force during vaginal delivery. *Am J Obstet Gynecol* 2004; 191(3):903–6.

38. Roberts CL, et al. Rates for obstetric intervention among private and public patients in Australia: population based descriptive study. *Br Med J* 2000; 321(7254):137–41.

39. Lieberman E, O'Donoghue C. Unintended effects of epidural analgesia during labor: a systematic review. *Am J Obstet Gynecol* 2002; 186(5 Suppl Nature):S31–68.

40. Thorp JA, et al. The effect of continuous epidural analgesia on cesarean section for dystocia in nulliparous women. *Am J Obstet Gynecol* 1989; 161(3):670–5.

41. Golub MS. Labor analgesia and infant brain development. *Pharmacol Biochem Behav* 1996; 55(4):619–28, p 619.

42. DeBalli P, Breen TW. Intrathecal opioids for combined spinal-epidural analgesia during labour. *CNS Drugs* 2003; 17(12):889–904.

43. Buggy D, et al. Posterior column sensory impairment during ambulatory extradural analgesia in labour. *Br J Anaesth* 1994; 73(4):540–2.

44. Shennan A, et al. Blood pressure changes during labour and whilst ambulating with combined spinal epidural analgesia. *Br J Obstet Gynaecol* 1995; 102(3):192–7.

45. Goetzl LM. ACOG Practice Bulletin. Clinical Management Guidelines for Obstetrician-Gynecologists Number 36, July 2002. Obstetric analgesial and anesthesia. *Obstet Gynecol* 2002; 100(1):177–91.

46. Mayberry LJ, et al. Epidural analgesia side effects, co-interventions, and care of women during childbirth: a systematic review. *Am J Obstet Gynecol* 2002; 186(5 Suppl Nature):S81–93.

47. Scott DB, Hibbard BM. Serious non-fatal complications associated with extradural block in obstetric practice. *Br J Anaesth* 1990; 64(5):537–41.

48. Buggy D, Gardiner J. The space blanket and shivering during extradural analgesia in labour. *Acta Anaesthesiol Scand* 1995; 39(4):551–3.

49. Lieberman E, et al. Epidural analgesia, intrapartum fever, and neonatal sepsis evaluation. *Pediatrics* 1997; 99(3):415–9.

50. Gaiser R. Neonatal effects of labor analgesia. *Int Anesthesiol Clin* 2002; 40(4):49–65.

51. DeBalli P, Breen TW. Intrathecal opioids for combined spinal-epidural analgesia during labour. *CNS Drugs* 2003; 17(12):889–904, pp 892–3.

52. Saunders NS, et al. Neonatal and maternal morbidity in relation to the length of the second stage of labour. *Br J Obstet Gynaecol* 1992; 99(5):381–5.

53. St George L, Crandon AJ. Immediate postpartum complications. *Aust N Z J Obstet Gynaecol* 1990; 30(1):52–6.

54. Magann EF, et al. Postpartum hemorrhage after vaginal birth: an analysis of risk factors. *South Med J* 2005; 98(4):419–22.

55. Eggebo TM, Gjessing LK. [Hemorrhage after vaginal delivery]. *Tidsskr Nor Laegeforen* 2000; 120(24):2860–3.

56. Ploeckinger B, et al. Epidural anaesthesia in labour: influence on surgical delivery rates, intrapartum fever and blood loss. *Gynecol Obstet Invest* 1995; 39(1):24–7.

57. Gilbert L, et al. Postpartum haemorrhage—a continuing problem. *Br J Obstet Gynaecol* 1987; 94(1):67–71.

58. Paech MJ, et al. Complications of obstetric epidural analgesia and anaesthesia: a prospective analysis of 10,995 cases. *Int J Obstet Anesth* 1998; 7(1):5–11.

59. Stride PC, Cooper GM. Dural taps revisited. A 20-year survey from Birmingham Maternity Hospital. *Anaesthesia* 1993; 48(3):247–55.

60. Costigan SN, Sprigge JS. Dural puncture: the patients' perspective. A patient survey of cases at a DGH maternity unit 1983–1993. *Acta Anaesthesiol Scand* 1996; 40(6):710–4.

61. Scott DB, Tunstall ME. Serious complications associated with epidural/spinal blockade in obstetrics: a two-year prospective study. *Int J Obstet Anesth* 1995; 4(3):133–9.

62. Crawford JS. Some maternal complications of epidural analgesia for labour. *Anaesthesia* 1985; 40(12):1219–25.

63. Reynolds F. Epidural analgesia in obstetrics. *Br Med J* 1989; 299(6702):751–2.

64. MIDIRS and The NHS Centre for Reviews and Dissemination. Epidural pain relief during labour. *Informed choice for professionals.* Bristol: MIDIRS, 1999.

65. Fernando R, et al. Neonatal welfare and placental transfer of fentanyl and bupivacaine during ambulatory combined spinal epidural analgesia for labour. *Anaesthesia* 1997; 52(6):517–24.

66. Capogna G. Effect of epidural analgesia on the fetal heart rate. *Eur J Obstet Gynecol Reprod Biol* 2001; 98(2):160–4.

67. Hill JB, et al. A comparison of the effects of epidural and meperidine analgesia during labor on fetal heart rate. *Obstet Gynecol* 2003; 102(2):333–7.

68. Mardirosoff C, et al. Fetal bradycardia due to intrathecal opioids for labour analgesia: a systematic review. *Br J Obstet Gynaecol* 2002; 109(3):274–81.

69. Littleford J. Effects on the fetus and newborn of maternal analgesia and anesthesia: a review. *Can J Anaesth* 2004; 51(6):586–609.

70. Aldrich CJ, et al. The effect of maternal posture on fetal cerebral oxygenation during labour. *Br J Obstet Gynaecol* 1995; 102(1):14–9.

71. Lieberman E, et al. Intrapartum maternal fever and neonatal outcome. *Pediatrics* 2000; 105(1 Pt 1):8–13.

72. Impey L, et al. Fever in labour and neonatal encephalopathy: a prospective cohort study. *Br J Obstet Gynaecol* 2001; 108(6):594–7.

73. Vroman S, et al. Elective induction of labor conducted under lumbar epidural block. I. Labor induction by amniotomy and intravenous oxytocin. *Eur J Obstet Gynecol Reprod Biol* 1977; 7(3):159–80.

74. Thiery M, et al. Elective induction of labor conducted under lumbar epidural block. II. Labor induction by amniotomy and intravenous prostaglandin. *Eur J Obstet Gynecol Reprod Biol* 1977; 7(3):181–200.

75. Thorngren-Jerneck K, Herbst A. Low 5-minute Apgar score: a population-based register study of 1 million term births. *Obstet Gynecol* 2001; 98(1):65–70.

76. Kumar M, Paes B. Epidural opioid analgesia and neonatal respiratory depression. *J Perinatol* 2003; 23(5):425–7.

77. Hale T. *Medications and Mother's Milk.* Amarillo TX: Pharmasoft, 1997.

78. Hale, T. The effects on breastfeeding women of anaesthetic medications used during labour. The Passage to Motherhood Conference; 1998; Brisbane Australia. CAPERS.

79. Camann W, Brazelton TB. Use and abuse of neonatal neurobehavioral testing. *Anesthesiology* 2000; 92(1):3–5.

80. Halpern SH, et al. The neurologic and adaptive capacity score is not a reliable method of newborn evaluation. *Anesthesiology* 2001; 94(6): 958–62.

81. Murray AD, et al. Effects of epidural anesthesia on newborns and their mothers. *Child Dev* 1981; 52(1):71–82.

82. Sepkoski CM, et al. The effects of maternal epidural anesthesia on neonatal behavior during the first month. *Dev Med Child Neurol* 1992; 34(12):1072–80.

83. Rosenblatt DB, et al. The influence of maternal analgesia on neonatal behaviour: II. Epidural bupivacaine. *Br J Obstet Gynaecol* 1981; 88(4):407–13.

84. Loftus JR, et al. Placental transfer and neonatal effects of epidural sufentanil and fentanyl administered with bupivacaine during labor. *Anesthesiology* 1995; 83(2):300–8.

85. Murray AD, et al. Effects of epidural anesthesia on newborns and their mothers. *Child Dev* 1981; 52(1):71–82, p 71.

86. Krehbiel D, et al. Peridural anesthesia disturbs maternal behavior in primiparous and multiparous parturient ewes. *Physiol Behav* 1987; 40(4):463–72.

87. Levy F, et al. Intracerebral oxytocin is important for the onset of maternal behavior in inexperienced ewes delivered under peridural anesthesia. *Behav Neurosci* 1992; 106(2):427–32.

88. Golub MS, Germann SL. Perinatal bupivacaine and infant behavior in rhesus monkeys. *Neurotoxicol Teratol* 1998; 20(1):29–41.

89. Righard L, Alade MO. Effect of delivery room routines on success of first breast-feed. *Lancet* 1990; 336(8723):1105–7.

90. Matthews MK. The relationship between maternal labour analgesia and delay in the initiation of breastfeeding in healthy neonates in the early neonatal period. *Midwifery* 1989; 5(1):3–10.

91. Ransjo-Arvidson AB, et al. Maternal analgesia during labor disturbs newborn behavior: effects on breastfeeding, temperature, and crying. *Birth* 2001; 28(1):5–12.

92. Nissen E, et al. Effects of maternal pethidine on infants' developing breast feeding behaviour. *Acta Paediatr* 1995; 84(2):140–5.

93. Rajan L. The impact of obstetric procedures and analgesia/anaesthesia during labour and delivery on breast feeding. *Midwifery* 1994; 10(2): 87–103.

94. Radzyminski S. Neurobehavioral functioning and breastfeeding behavior in the newborn. *J Obstet Gynecol Neonatal Nurs* 2005; 34(3):335–41.

95. Riordan J, et al. The effect of labor pain relief medication on neonatal suckling and breastfeeding duration. *J Hum Lact* 2000; 16(1):7–12.

96. Dewey KG, et al. Risk factors for suboptimal infant breastfeeding behavior, delayed onset of lactation, and excess neonatal weight loss. *Pediatrics* 2003; 112(3 Pt 1):607–19.

97. Radzyminski S. The effect of ultra low dose epidural analgesia on newborn breastfeeding behaviors. *J Obstet Gynecol Neonatal Nurs* 2003; 32(3):322–31.

98. Baumgarder DJ, et al. Effect of labor epidural anesthesia on breast-feeding of healthy full-term newborns delivered vaginally. *J Am Board Fam Pract* 2003; 16(1):7–13.

99. Volmanen P, et al. Breast-feeding problems after epidural analgesia for labour: a retrospective cohort study of pain, obstetrical procedures and breast-feeding practices. *Int J Obstet Anesth* 2004; 13(1):25–9.

100. Henderson JJ, et al. Impact of intrapartum epidural analgesia on breast-feeding duration. *Aust N Z J Obstet Gynaecol* 2003; 43(5):372–7.

101. Kiehl EM, et al. Social status, mother–infant time together, and breast-feeding duration. *J Hum Lact* 1996; 12(3):201–6.

102. Halpern SH, et al. Effect of labor analgesia on breastfeeding success. *Birth* 1999; 26(2):83–8.

103. Kannan S, et al. Maternal satisfaction and pain control in women electing natural childbirth. *Reg Anesth Pain Med* 2001; 26(5): 468–72.

104. Green JM, et al. Expectations, experiences, and psychological outcomes of childbirth: a prospective study of 825 women. *Birth* 1990; 17(1):15–24.

105. Morgan BM, et al. Analgesia and satisfaction in childbirth (the Queen Charlotte's 1000 Mother Survey). *Lancet* 1982; 2(8302):808–10.

106. Morgan BM, et al. Analgesia and satisfaction in childbirth (the Queen Charlotte's 1000 Mother Survey). *Lancet* 1982; 2(8302):808–10, p 809.

107. Klein MC, et al. Epidural analgesia use as a marker for physician approach to birth: implications for maternal and newborn outcomes. *Birth* 2001; 28(4):243–8.

Leaving Well Alone ~
perspectives on a natural third stage

P REGNANCY and birth have become medicalised to an extreme extent in the twenty-first century. This medicalisation has become so ingrained in our culture that we have forgotten the more simple way of birth of our ancestors; a way that has ensured our survival as a species for millennia, and that is genetically encoded in our bodies.

Our genetic code for birth is rich and accurate, and has evolved to reflect the most efficient and effective means of human reproduction, including optimal outcomes for mother and baby in the short, medium and long term. These outcomes are mediated by the mother's hormones and instincts, which influence her emotions and behaviours, from preconception (with her choice of mate) through to pregnancy, birth and mothering. Above all, this code, and the events that it triggers, is directed towards the formation of a secure bond between mother and offspring. This bond ensures optimal nourishment, care, and protection for the growing baby – who is the most immature and incapable of any species – and is, historically and still today, the basis of human survival.

Although well intentioned, modern obstetrics has not honoured this genetic code. In the rush to protect mothers and babies from misfortune and death, obstetrics has ignored the powerful influences of the birthing mother's hormones, emotions, and instinctive behaviours, even as researchers struggle to understand their complexity.

This culturally unprecedented neglect of the emotional and instinctive aspects of pregnancy and birth has major consequences for mothers and babies. During the third stage of labour, when mother and baby meet for the first time, the gap between our instincts and genetic code, and our culture's usual birthing practices, is especially wide.

At a time when Mother Nature prescribes awe and ecstasy, we have injections, examinations, and clamping and pulling on the cord. Instead of body heat, skin-to-skin contact, and the baby's innate instinct to find the breast, we offer separation, wrapping, and outside assistance to "attach" the baby. Where time should stand still for those eternal moments of first contact as mother and baby fall deeply in love, we have haste to deliver the placenta and clean up for the next case.

Medical management of the third stage – the time between the birth of the baby and delivery of the placenta – has been taken even further in recent years with the popularity of "active management of the third stage". While much of the activity is designed to reduce the risk of maternal bleeding (postpartum haemorrhage, PPH), which is certainly a serious event, it seems that, as with the active management of labour, the medical approach to labour and birth may actually lead to many of the problems that active management is designed to address.

Active management also creates specific problems for mother and baby. In particular, active management can lead to the deprivation of up to half of a newborn's expected blood volume. When active management is used, this extra blood, intended to perfuse the newly functioning lungs and other vital organs, is discarded along with the placenta. Possible sequelae include breathing difficulties and anaemia, especially in vulnerable babies; long-term effects on brain development are also very plausible.

The drugs used in active management have well-documented and potentially serious risks for the mother, which are further explored here. Active management poses other risks to the baby, as

185

noted below, and we do not know the long-term effects of the drugs used in third stage, which may cross the placenta and reach the baby at an extremely vulnerable stage of brain development.

Hormones in the third stage

As a mammalian species – defined by our mammary glands and the milk that they produce for our young – we share almost all features of labour and birth with our fellow mammals. We also have in common the complex orchestration of labour hormones, produced deep within our middle (mammalian) brain, which co-ordinate these processes and ultimately ensure the survival and wellbeing of mother and baby.[1]

For example, the hormone oxytocin causes the uterine contractions that signal labour, and helps us to enact our instinctive mothering behaviours. Endorphins, the body's natural opiates, produce an altered state of consciousness and aid in transmuting pain; and the fight or flight hormones adrenaline and noradrenaline (epinephrine and norepinephrine, also known as catecholamines or CAs) give us the burst of energy that we need to push our babies out.[1] These hormones continue to play crucial roles for mother and baby during the third stage.

At this time, the new mother's uterus continues to contract strongly and regularly under the continuing influence of oxytocin. Her uterine muscle fibres shorten (retract) with each contraction, leading to a gradual decrease in uterine size, which helps to shear the baby's placenta away from its attachment site. Efficient uterine contractions are also necessary to slow bleeding from the placental site, which is initially a large and raw surface. These contractions cause a tightening of the interlacing muscle fibres in the new mother's uterus (also called living ligatures), which seal off the maternal blood vessels and stop bleeding. Third stage is complete when the birthing mother delivers her baby's placenta.

For the new mother, the third stage is a time of reaping the rewards of her labour. Mother Nature provides peak levels of oxytocin, the hormone of love, and endorphins, hormones of pleasure, for both mother and baby. Skin-to-skin contact and the baby's first attempts to breastfeed further increase maternal oxytocin levels,[2] strengthening the uterine contractions that will help the baby's placenta to separate and the mother's uterus to contract down. In this way, oxytocin (and the mother–newborn interactions that cause its release) act to prevent haemorrhage, as well as to establish, in concert with the other hormones, the positive first impressions that will help to develop a secure bond between mother and baby.

The fight-or-flight (CA) hormones are also important at this time. These hormones are normally produced under conditions of fear, stress, anxiety, hunger, and cold when they divert blood to skeletal muscles, heart, and lungs to prepare the body for flight or fight. If the mother is fearful or anxious in labour, she will release these hormones, which will reduce the blood supply to her uterus and baby, and also reduce her oxytocin release, slowing or even stopping her contractions.

During an undisturbed birth, however, the mother's CA levels will naturally and substantially increase with the transition from first to second (pushing) stage, giving her the extra strength that she needs to be upright and to push her baby out. This large increase in CA hormones also causes the fetal ejection reflex: high CA and oxytocin levels that create several strong contractions that help her to give birth quickly and easily. High CA levels also ensure that mother and baby are wide-eyed and alert at first contact.

Within minutes of birth, the new mother's CA levels start to decline and, at these lower levels, revert to their original negative influence on oxytocin. A warm and calm atmosphere is needed to keep CAs declining and oxytocin levels unopposed.

If the new mother feels cold or fearful her CA levels will remain elevated, which will oppose her oxytocin release and therefore reduce the ability of her uterus to contract and stop bleeding at this critical time. She may shiver, giving warning of this danger, and requiring urgent action to warm her up. Elevated CA levels at this time have been linked with a higher risk of PPH[3, 4] and, in one small study, women with lower oxytocin levels were more likely to have third-stage problems.[5]

The new baby also enjoys peak hormone levels in the minutes after birth, including oxytocin, beta-endorphin and catecholamines. As with the mother, the reduction of CA hormones post-birth is vital. If these hormones are not soothed by contact with the mother, the baby can go into a state of stress-induced shock, which, according to author Joseph Chilton Pearce, will prevent the activation of the specific brain functions that are Mother Nature's blueprint for this time.[6]

Michel Odent notes that almost every existing culture has rituals that disturb the early postnatal time – most often by separating mother and baby – and he believes that such rituals have predominated because they instill aggressive, and therefore more dominating and successful, traits in the offspring and culture. For example, Spartan warriors-to-be were apparently thrown on the floor after birth.[7] One must wonder about the effects, on the newborn male and on our society, of the postnatal ritual of circumcision.

Animal studies show that separation from the mother in the early postpartum period is associated with abnormal stress responses in adulthood,[8–10] although this has not been scientifically researched in humans. Pearce believes that the separation of mother and baby after birth is "… the most devastating event of life, which leaves us emotionally and psychologically crippled."[11]

One might also wonder whether the modern epidemic of stress (a term that was invented by researchers in the 1950s) and stress-related illness in our culture is a further outcome of current third-stage practices. It is scientifically plausible that our entire hypothalamic-pituitary-adrenal (HPA) axis, which mediates both short-term fight-or-flight reaction as well as long-term stress responses and immune function, could be permanently mis-set by the continuing high stress hormone levels that ensue when newborn babies are routinely separated from their mothers.

Carter comments, "There is increasing evidence for tuning or programming of neuronal [brain/nerve] systems by early experiences, in some cases by endogenous [internal] or exogenous [external] hormones."[12] This concept of vulnerability, in early life, to permanent mis-programming of central nervous system function because of experiences that are outside our genetic blueprint, is supported by Csaba's work on hormonal imprinting (see chapter 13, "Undisturbed Birth").

Other research has suggested that contemporary tragedies such as suicide, drug addiction and violent criminality may be linked to problems in the perinatal period such as exposure to drugs, birth complications and separation from or rejection by the mother.[13-16]

With these understandings, the role of birth attendants in the hours following birth becomes clear. This role is to ensure unhurried and undisturbed contact between mother and baby; to adjust the temperature to ensure warmth for mother and baby; to facilitate skin-to-skin contact, mutual gaze, and early breastfeeding and pre-breastfeeding behaviour, with no other expectations for mother or baby; and to not remove the baby for any reason. These measures can also include sensitively practiced observations, resuscitation (which can be done next to the mother or, for a baby with an intact cord, on the mother's thigh) and other safety measures.

Such priorities are sensible, intuitive and safe, and help to synchronise our hormonal systems with our genetic blueprint, giving maximum success and pleasure for both partners at this critical beginning of child rearing.

Placental transfusion and the baby

Adaptation to life outside the womb is the major physiological task for the baby in the third stage. In the mother's womb, the wondrous placenta fulfils the functions of lungs, kidney, gut, skin, and liver for our babies. Blood flow to these organs is minimal until the baby takes a first breath, at which time huge changes begin in the organisation of the circulatory system.

Within the baby's body, blood becomes diverted away from the umbilical cord and placenta over several minutes and, as the baby's lungs fill with air, blood is sucked into the pulmonary (lung) circulation.[17] Mother Nature ensures a reservoir of blood in the cord and placenta that provides the additional blood necessary for the perfusion of these pulmonary and organ systems; this is known as the placental transfusion.

The transfer of this reservoir (transfusion) of blood from the placenta to the baby happens in a stepwise progression. With each of the mother's third-stage contractions (which are as powerful as those during labour), blood enters the baby, and between contractions, as the mother's uterus relaxes, some blood returns to the placenta. Crying slows the baby's intake of blood, which is also controlled by constriction of the vessels within the cord,[18] both of which imply that the baby can regulate the transfusion according to their individual need.

Gravity will affect the transfer of blood, with optimal transfer occurring when the baby remains at, or slightly below, the level of the uterus, until the cessation of cord pulsation signals that the transfer is complete.[19] This process, sometimes called physiological clamping, typically takes three minutes but it may take longer, or alternatively may be complete in only one minute.[20]

This elegant and time-tested system, which ensures that an optimum, but not a standard, amount of blood is transferred, is rendered inoperable by the current practice of early clamping of the cord, which usually occurs within 30 seconds of birth.

Early clamping and the baby

Early clamping has been widely adopted in western obstetrics as part of the package known as active management of the third stage. Active management includes the use of an oxytocic agent – a drug that, like oxytocin, causes the uterus to contract strongly – usually given by injection into the mother's thigh as the baby is born. Active management also includes early cord clamping and controlled cord traction; that is, pulling on the cord to deliver the placenta as quickly as possible.

Active management proponents have believed that if the cord is not clamped before the oxytocic effect commences, the baby is at risk of having too much blood pumped from the placenta by the stronger uterine contractions. This area has been poorly studied. One older study using the ergot drug methylergometrine has suggested that use of an oxytocic will shorten the baby's placental transfusion from three minutes to one minute, but, in this study, blood and red cell volumes, as measured by radioisotope, were equivalent for babies with and without oxytocic exposure.[21] In contrast, Dunn's research indicated that babies whose mothers received ergometrine, with cord clamping at three minutes, received an average of 37 mL in excess of the normal placental transfusion, as measured by residual placental blood volume.[22] More research is obviously needed in this area.

And while the aim of active management is to reduce the risk of haemorrhage for the mother, "… its widespread acceptance was not preceded by studies evaluating the effects of depriving neonates [newborns] of a significant volume of blood."[23]

Usher estimated that early clamping deprives the baby of 54 to 160 mL of blood,[24] which represents up to half of a baby's total blood volume at birth. Average placental transfusion is 100 mL (3½ oz, or almost half a cup), and an average newborn's total blood volume is around 300 to 350 mL. Morley comments,

> Clamping the cord before the infant's first breath results in blood being sacrificed from other organs to establish pulmonary perfusion [blood supply to the lungs]. Fatality may result if the child is already hypovolemic [low in blood volume].[25]

Peltonen recorded an early-clamped newborn's heart function, as the baby took a first breath.[26] This film showed that, for several cardiac cycles after the first breath, the baby's left heart had insufficient blood. Peltonen concludes:

> It would seem that the closing of the umbilical circulation [cord clamping] before the aeration of the lungs has taken place is a highly unphysiological measure and should be avoided.[27]

Caesarean babies

Where the baby is lifted well above the uterus before clamping – for example during caesarean surgery – the mother's uterus is unable to pump blood against the uphill gradient, and the baby's blood may even flow back to the mother's uterus with gravity. Caesarean babies are therefore especially liable to receive less than their expected blood volume. The consequence of this may be an increased risk of respiratory (breathing) distress. Several studies have shown that respiratory distress can be eliminated in caesarean-born babies when a full placental transfusion is allowed.[26, 28]

UK paediatrician Peter Dunn recommends that the cord of caesarean babies remains unclamped, and that, after removal from the mother's uterus, the baby and conjoined placenta remain level until the cord stops pulsing in five to 10 minutes.[29] The naked baby and (wrapped) placenta could also be placed on the mother's chest. Morley has similar recommendations for caesarean babies.[30] Other researchers have hung cesarean babies' placentas above them like a transfusion bag until the cord stops pulsating.[28]

Reduced iron stores and other early clamping sequelae

The baby whose cord is clamped early also loses the iron contained within that blood; early clamping has been linked with an increased risk of anaemia in infancy. A recent review suggests that delayed cord clamping reduces the risk of anaemia by 15 percent at two to three months for babies in both developing and industrialised countries, with more benefits for infants of anaemic mothers.[31] The 30 to 35 mg of additional iron in an average placental transfusion is equivalent to the amount of iron in 100 litres of breastmilk.[32]

These sequelae of early clamping were recognised as far back as 1801, when Erasmus Darwin wrote:

> Another thing very injurious to the child is the tying and cutting of the navel string too soon; which should always be left till the child has not only repeatedly breathed but till all pulsation in the cord ceases. As otherwise the child is much weaker than it ought to be, a part of the blood being left in the placenta which ought to have been in the child.[33]

In one study, premature babies who experienced a delay in cord clamping of only 30 seconds showed a reduced need for transfusion, less severe breathing problems, better oxygen levels and indications of probable improved long-term outcomes compared with those whose cords were clamped immediately.[34]

Premature babies whose cord clamping is delayed also gain protection from intraventricular haemorrhage (IVH),[35] a form of bleeding in the brain that is not uncommon in this group. The reduced risk with delayed clamping may reflect the fact that early cord clamping causes a sudden (but transient) increase in the baby's blood pressure,[36] which may particularly affect the premature baby's immature brain. As below, the early-clamped baby may subsequently suffer from insufficient blood to supply the brain. Reduced cerebral (brain) blood flow is a further risk factor for IVH.[37]

One must also wonder about the effects of the deprivation of a significant amount of blood on the newborn baby's brain. Some have suggested that some of our children's developmental problems, such as cerebral palsy,[38] autism[39] and learning difficulties,[40] may be related to the practice of early cord clamping, which has only been widespread in the last 50 years or so.[41]

Mercer and Skovgaard also document the elegant unfolding of the newborn's lungs that occurs at birth, and that ensures a safe transition to breathing.[42] This unfolding requires an adequate blood (and red blood cell) volume, which comes from an adequate placental transfusion. Their paradigm also explains the wet lungs that are more likely for caesarean babies, who are deprived of their full placental transfusion, and is another powerful argument for leaving well alone in the third stage.

Polycythemia and jaundice

Some studies have shown an increased risk of polycythemia (more red blood cells in the blood) and jaundice when the cord is clamped later. Research shows that late clamped newborns may have up to 60 percent increased red cell volume (RCV) compared to early clamped babies.[43] Polycythemia may be beneficial because more red cells will be able to carry more oxygen to the newborn's organs and tissues. The higher levels of protein contained in this blood is also advantageous in drawing fluid from the newborn lungs by colloid osmotic pressure (COP), and so preventing wet lungs.[42]

The idea that polycythemia will cause the blood to become too thick (hyperviscosity syndrome), which is often used as an argument against delayed cord clamping, arose from two old and poorly validated trials involving small numbers of babies, some of whom were premature.[44, 45] This finding has not been substantiated in more recent high-quality research.[46] It is also illogical, as a healthy newborn can easily compensate by dilating the blood vessels to accommodate higher viscosity blood.[46, 47] As with all mammalian species, our babies' circulatory systems are designed to balance this normal adjustment to life outside the womb.

Jaundice is almost certain when a baby gets his or her full quota of blood and is caused by the breakdown of red blood cells to produce bilirubin, the pigment that causes the yellow appearance of a jaundiced baby. Physiological jaundice – that is, jaundice due only to the normal breakdown of excess red blood cells – is present in almost all human infants to some extent, and may be prolonged by breastfeeding (breastmilk jaundice).

Our understanding of jaundice has expanded recently, with bilirubin – which has been called a "born-again benignant pigment"[48] – now recognised as an important anti-oxidant, more powerful than vitamin E.[49] Bilirubin may have a critical role in protecting the newborn baby from oxidative stresses associated with adjustment to significantly higher oxygen levels outside the womb. An older study has also found that bilirubin has antibiotic properties sufficient to kill the pneumococcal bacteria.[50]

A recently published 15-year follow-up of babies with severe jaundice – bilirubin levels much higher than would be present in physiological jaundice – concluded:

> Neonatal bilirubin levels seem to have little effect on IQ, definite neurologic abnormalities, or hearing loss. Higher bilirubin levels are associated with minor motor abnormalities, but the clinical importance of this finding is limited by the weakness of the association, the mild nature of the abnormalities, and the lack of evidence that they are prevented by treatment.[51]

Studies do not show an excess of severe jaundice in babies who have had late clamping.

Early cord clamping carries the further disadvantage of depriving the baby of the oxygen contained in the placental blood, which Mother Nature provides to tide the baby over until breathing is well established. In situations of extreme distress – for example, if the baby takes several minutes to breathe – this reservoir of oxygenated blood can be life saving. Standard practice is to cut the cord immediately if resuscitation is needed, but resuscitation can be performed on the mother's thigh with the baby's placental circulation still intact. Garrison, a family physician from Canada, reports resuscitating a newborn who was unable to breathe for seven recorded minutes (due to thick meconium), and who survived without disability with an intact cord and placental circulation.[52]

When the cord is intact and the placenta still in the mother's womb, any drug given to the mother can pass to the baby, even during third stage. Garrison reports a positive use for this conduit.[52] He notes that naloxone (Narcan) – which is sometimes administered to a newborn baby to counteract the sedating effects of opiate drugs such as pethidine (meperidine), given to the mother in labour – can alternatively be administered effectively intravenously (IV) to the mother in third stage, flowing to and waking up the baby in a matter of seconds.

Synthetic oxytocin and the baby

The baby exposed to active management may also be affected by maternal administration of synthetic oxytocin during the third stage. Carter administered a single dose of synthetic oxytocin to prairie voles within 24 hours of birth and found disturbances in adult sexual and parental behaviour. She suggests that small amounts may cross the human placenta, or alternatively there may be indirect effects,[53] and cautions:

> The assumption that perinatal oxytocin manipulations are without effect is largely untested, although the small but growing literature in animals suggests that this may be an invalid assumption.[54]

A final consideration is the possibility that, as Edwards cautions, "… though very rare, injections can be mixed up."[55] There are case reports of oxytocic drugs being accidentally given to newborns instead of Vitamin K.[56, 57]

Cord blood banking

The recent discovery of the amazing properties of cord blood, and in particular the stem cells contained within it, heightens the need to ensure that a newborn baby gets the full quota intended by Mother Nature. Newborn stem cells are unique to this stage of development, and will migrate to the baby's bone marrow soon after birth, transforming themselves into various types of blood cells. (In contrast, stem cells obtained from embryos retain the ability to transform into almost any body cell type.)

Cord blood harvesting, which involves collecting the baby's placental transfusion, requires early clamping – ideally within

30 seconds of birth – so that an adequate number of stem cells is obtained. Delayed cord clamping, which allows this blood to be transferred to the baby, as above, is likely to lead to an inadequate volume of blood harvested.

For example, in one study, the average volume of cord blood was reduced from 75 mL, collected when the cord was clamped at 30 seconds after birth, to 39 mL collected when clamping occurred 30 to 180 seconds. A low-volume collection indicates insufficient stem cells to be usable for transfusion.[58] Public cord blood banks usually discard collections below 40 mL,[59] with overall one-third to one-half of collections discarded, mostly because of low volume.[60] Private banks, which are paid by parents to collect and store their baby's blood, do not generally discard the collections, and some may have a policy to accept lower volumes.

Some centres collect residual blood from the baby's placenta after it is delivered, although this is usually less than the blood obtained from the cord straight after birth, and still requires early cord clamping,[58] depriving the baby of the placental transfusion. A cord blood collection of 100 mL is equivalent to the loss of 1.5 litres (2 ½ pints) of adult blood,[61] or two to three times the volume of a usual adult blood donation.

Clinicians have expressed concern about the effects of this loss of haematopoietic (blood-making) stem cells, as well as the effects of early cord clamping, on the newborn.[62] The American Academy of Pediatrics states:

> If cord clamping is done too soon after birth, the infant may be deprived of a placental blood transfusion, resulting in lower blood volume and increased risk of anemia in later life… There may be a temptation to practice immediate cord clamping aggressively to increase the volume of cord blood that can be harvested for cord blood banking. This practice is unethical and should be discouraged.[63]

In many hospitals, altruistic cord blood donation is being promoted to fill public cord blood banks for the future treatment of children with leukaemia. In the US, public cord blood banks sell cord blood for transplantation to matched recipients for US$15,000 to $20,000, which is usually covered by health insurance.

In places, private cord-blood banks are persuading parents to pay large sums of money (US$600 to $1,700 initially plus an annual fee of around $100[64]) to store their baby's blood for future use, although the chance of the blood being useful for the child (or family) is very remote.[65]

For example, the likelihood of low-risk children needing their own stored cells (autologous transfusion) has been estimated at 1 in 20,000,[66] and cord blood donations are likely to be ineffective for the treatment of adults,[67] because the number of stem cells is too small.

Autologous cord blood may be unsuitable for children who develop leukemia because it may contain pre-leukemic changes, and may increase the risk of relapse.[66] Autologous cord blood cannot cure inherited conditions such as thalassemia and bone marrow failure.[66] According to Fisk, autologous cord blood is only suitable for children who develop solid tumours, lymphomas or auto-immune disorders (where the body starts to attack itself): all other uses are speculative.[66]

By one estimate, at least 13,600 cord blood units have been stored in private blood banks since 1998, but only seven autologous units have been used, and another 16 have been used for sibling transplants,[64] some of which may have been specifically set up after an older sibling developed a disorder treatable with cord blood. According to the Boston Globe in 2004, Corcell, one of the largest private cord blood banking companies, had not shipped a single unit in seven years of operation.[68]

Cord blood banks use emotive advertising with very improbable scenarios – for example, implying that banked cord blood may help to treat the child if they develop conditions such as stroke and Alzheimer's disease in old age. This is extremely unlikely, given that cord blood is currently inadequate for adult treatment, and that private companies (who are not regulated at present) may not have the storage standards necessary to ensure prolonged viability of stem cells.[68] Public banks report that cord blood can be stored for 15 to 20 years.[69]

It is also highly likely that other sources of stem cells, and other therapies, will be developed in the coming years. For example,

South Korean researchers were recently able to clone embryonic-type stem cells using adult skin cells, giving a perfect match for transplantation.[70]

Private cord blood banking is not recommended by the American Academy of Pediatrics,[71] has been highlighted as a source of serious ethical concern in the European Union, and has been banned in Italy.[66]

The International Federation of Gynaecology and Obstetrics (FIGO) Committee for the Ethical Aspects of Human Reproduction and Women's Health concluded, in 1998:

> The information mothers currently receive at the time of requesting consent (for the collection of umbilical cord blood) is that blood in the placenta is no longer of use to the baby and this 'waste blood' may help to save another person's life. This information is incomplete and does not permit informed consent. Early clamping of the umbilical cord following vaginal delivery is likely to deprive the newborn infant of at least a third of its normal circulating blood volume, and it will also cause a haemodynamic disturbance. These factors may result in serious morbidity [illness]. For consent to be informed, the harmful effects of early cord clamping should be disclosed and the mother assured that the collection of cord blood will not involve early clamping. In summary, permission to collect blood from the cord for banking should not lead to clamping the cord earlier than 20–30 seconds after delivery of the baby.[72]

In summary, private cord blood banking involves taking the blood that is needed by the baby at birth, and paying thousands of dollars to store it away, with a very remote chance of later use by that child or the family. Public cord blood banking is perhaps more justifiable and more likely to be used, but both involve the loss of up to one-half of the newborn's blood volume, with negative sequelae that may be very significant.

Active management and the mother

Active management (oxytocic, early clamping and controlled cord traction) represents a further development in third-stage interference, which began in the mid-seventeenth century, when male birth attendants began confining women to bed and cord clamping was introduced to spare the bed linen.[73]

Pulling on the cord was first recommended by the Frenchman Mauriceau in 1673, who feared that the uterus might close before the placenta was spontaneously delivered.[73] In fact, the bed-bound horizontal postures increasingly adopted under medical care meant that spontaneous delivery of the placenta was less likely: an upright posture, which women and midwives have traditionally used, encourages the placenta to fall out with the help of gravity.

The first oxytocic to be used medically was ergot, derived from a fungal infection of rye. Ergot was used by seventeenth- and eighteenth-century European midwives; its use was limited, however, by its toxicity. It was refined and revived as ergometrine (ergonovine, US) in the 1930s, and by the late 1940s some doctors were using it preventatively, as well as therapeutically, for postpartum haemorrhage.[73]

Potential side effects from ergot derivatives include a rise in blood pressure, nausea, vomiting, headache, palpitations, cerebral haemorrhage, cardiac arrest, convulsion, and even death. Ergot derivatives should not be administered to any woman who already has high blood pressure.

Ergot derivatives (ergotamine, ergonovine, Ergometrine, Ergotrate) may have other unwanted effects, including suppression of prolactin, the hormone of breastmilk synthesis. According to Jordan,

> … intravenous ergotamine 500 mcgms for management of the third stage gave a statistically significant increase in the number of women supplementing and ceasing breastfeeding by one and four weeks postpartum, mainly because lactation was inadequate for the infants' needs.[74]

She warns, "Midwives need to consider that syntometrine [which combines ergometrine with Syntocinon/Pitocin] may adversely impact on breastfeeding." According to Hale, the ergot derivative methylergonovine (methylergometrine, MEM, Methergine) may not have this effect.[74]

Synthetic oxytocin, known as Syntocinon or Pitocin (US), mimics the effects of natural oxytocin on the uterus, and was first marketed in the 1950s. Synthetic oxytocin has largely replaced ergometrine for use in third stage, although the combination drug syntometrine is still used in the UK and in other places for severe haemorrhage. Syntocinon causes an increase in the strength of contractions, whereas ergometrine causes a large continuous (tonic) contraction, which significantly increases the chance of trapping the placenta. Ergometrine may also interfere with the process of placental separation, increasing the chance of partial separation.[75]

In recent years misoprostol, a synthetic prostaglandin, has also been researched for use in the third stage. Misoprostol is cheap and can be given orally, which makes it attractive for low-resource settings. Evidence suggests that it is less effective as a preventative than other oxytocic drugs, with more side effects such as nausea, vomiting, diarrhoea, fever and shivering.[76] However, it may be a useful drug for emergency treatment of PPH, and less misoprostol is transferred to breast milk compared to ergot derivatives.[77] More research is obviously needed before this new drug is recommended for widespread use.

Active management trials

Active management has been proclaimed "… the routine management of choice for women expecting a single baby by vaginal delivery in a maternity hospital",[78] largely because of the results of the 1998 Hinchingbrooke trial[79] comparing active and expectant (non-active, or physiological) management.

In this trial, which involved only women at low risk of bleeding, active management was associated with a rate of postpartum haemorrhage (blood loss greater than 500 mL or around 17 fl oz) of 6.8 percent, compared with 16.5 percent for expectant management. Rates of severe PPH (blood loss greater than 1,000 mL) were low in both groups: 1.7 percent active and 2.6 percent expectant.

The authors note that, based on these figures, 10 women would need to receive active management to prevent one PPH. They comment,

> Some women … may rate a small personal risk of PPH of little importance compared with intervention in an otherwise straightforward labour, whereas others may wish to take all measures to reduce the risk of PPH.[80]

Reading this paper, one must wonder how it is that almost one in six women bled after physiological management, and whether one or more components of western obstetric practices might actually increase the rate of haemorrhage.

Botha, who attended more than 26,000 Bantu women over the course of 10 years, reports, "... a retained placenta was seldom seen ... Blood transfusion for postpartum haemorrhage was never necessary."[81] Bantu women deliver both baby and placenta while upright and squatting, and the cord is not attended to until the placenta is delivered by gravity.

PPH and the mother

Some evidence shows that clamping the cord, which is not practised by indigenous cultures (or obviously by other mammals), contributes both to PPH and retained placenta by trapping extra blood within the placenta. This increases placental bulk, which the mother's uterus cannot contract (and retract) efficiently against, and which can lead to increased blood loss.[82] The maternal effects of cord clamping are the subject of a forthcoming Cochrane Collaboration review.[83]

Other western practices that may contribute to PPH include the use of oxytocin for induction and augmentation of labour,[84–87] epidural pain relief,[88–91] episiotomy, perineal trauma, forceps delivery, caesarean and previous caesarean, which increases the risks of placental problems such as placental abruption, and placenta accreta.[92–94]

Gilbert notes that PPH rates in her UK hospital more than doubled, from five percent in 1969–70 to 11 percent in 1983–5, and concludes,

> Changes in labour ward practice over the last 20 years have resulted in the re-emergence of PPH as a significant problem.[91]

In particular, she links an increased risk of bleeding to the following: induction using oxytocin; forceps delivery; long first and second stages (but not prolonged pushing); and epidurals, which increase the chances of a long second stage and forceps, as well as reducing the oxytocin peak at birth.[95] The prolonged use of synthetic oxytocin during labour (for induction or augmentation) has been shown to desensitise the labouring mother's uterus to the effects of oxytocin by reducing her oxytocin receptor numbers.[96]

As noted, western practices neither facilitate the production of a mother's own oxytocin, nor pay attention to reducing catecholamine levels in the minutes after birth, both of which can be expected to physiologically improve the new mother's contractions and therefore reduce her blood loss. The routine practice of separating mother and baby deprives the mother of important opportunities to increase her natural oxytocin release.

It is also interesting to note Logue's finding of a significant difference in PPH rates according to the practitioner.[97] In the hospital that she surveyed, PPH rates varied between 1–16% for midwives and 1–31% for registrars. She notes that doctors and midwives who were considered to be "heavy handed" had much higher rates.

Early clamping and the mother

Clamping the cord can have other detrimental effects. Immediate clamping traps the placental transfusion – around 100 mL of blood – in the baby's placenta, which is then squeezed by the mother's uterus during third stage contractions. With this extra volume, even the pressure of a normal contraction may force a significant amount of blood back through the placental barrier (which usually keeps mother's and baby's blood separate) and into the mother's blood supply.[98, 99] This is called a fetomaternal haemorrhage (FMH).

A fetomaternal haemorrhage allows the baby's blood, which is immunologically different to the mother's, into her bloodstream, where her immune system can recognise it as foreign and form antibodies to destroy it. This occurs mainly when an Rh-negative mother (a mother whose blood does not contain the RhD factor) is exposed to the blood of her Rh-positive baby (whose blood has the RhD factor) via FMH. This will cause the mother to make antibodies against the RhD factor (sensitisation).

If this FMH occurs in third stage, this will not harm the newborn baby. However, these antibodies can be reactivated if the mother has a subsequent pregnancy with an Rh-positive baby.

These antibodies can pass through the placenta to her Rh-positive baby, destroying blood cells and causing anaemia or even death.

Major blood group reactions between Rh-negative mothers and their Rh-positive babies can be very effectively prevented by the routine use of anti-D products such as Rhogam but, because they are pooled blood products, these products carry the potential risk of transmitting as yet unrecognised infections.

The use of oxytocic drugs, either during labour or in third stage, has also been linked to an increased risk of FMH and blood group incompatibility problems,[100, 101] because the stronger uterine contractions can cause microfractures in the placental barrier.[100] Cord traction has been shown to damage the delicate placental vessels, producing an increased FMH risk.[102] Recent case reports have noted fetomaternal haemorrhage during pregnancy (which can cause significant harm to the baby) with the use of oxytocin stress test[103] and with oxytocin induction.[104]

Avoiding active management is therefore likely to reduce the risk of FMH and Rh sensitisation. Rh sensitisation is also less likely if mother and baby are incompatible in ABO blood groups[105] (for example, mother O, baby A, B or AB; Mother A, baby B; mother B, baby A) because the mother has preformed antibodies and her immune system may destroy the baby's cells that enter her circulation. However, a moderate risk of sensitisation exists (possibly around 10 percent[106]) and probably even under ideal circumstances. For a more detailed discussion, see Sara Wickham's excellent writing.[106, 107] Note that mechanisms of FMH at delivery have been poorly researched since the widespread use of anti-D after birth.

Cord traction carries other potential hazards. When the baby's placenta is not yet separated, strong cord traction can actually pull off the cord, making placental delivery more difficult and surgery for removal more likely. Cord traction is also a painful procedure for the new mother. Strong cord traction can also rarely cause an inversion of the new mother's uterus, producing a state of profound maternal shock.

The World Health Organization, in its 1996 publication *Care in Normal Birth: A practical guide*, considers these risks and concludes:

In a healthy population (as is the case in most developed countries), postpartum blood loss up to 1,000 mL may be considered as physiological and does not necessitate treatment other than oxytocics... [108]

In relation to routine oxytocics and controlled cord traction, WHO cautions:

Recommendation of such a policy would imply that the benefits of such management would offset and even exceed the risks, including potentially rare but serious risks that might become manifest in the future.[109]

Recent developments in third stage management

In the last five years there have been some welcome developments in the thinking and practice of third stage. US authors Morley,[30] Mercer[42, 46] and others have published papers that have deepened our understanding of neonatal physiology during third stage, and of the risks of early clamping for the baby.

In the UK, the influential Cochrane Collaboration, the best source of evidence-based medicine, has reviewed the literature on early versus delayed umbilical cord clamping in preterm infants, and concluded:

Delaying cord clamping by 30 to 120 seconds, rather than early clamping, seems to be associated with less need for transfusion and less intraventricular haemorrhage.[35]

The Canadian Pediatric Society has also recently recommended delayed cord clamping to reduce the need for blood transfusions in premature babies.[110]

The Cochrane Collaboration has published a recent review of the use of oxytocin for prevention of bleeding in the third stage and, although noting a decrease in PPH, has suggested that "... there is not enough evidence about adverse effects. More research is needed."[111] A Cochrane review of maternal and neonatal outcomes in relation to the timing of umbilical cord clamping in full-term infants is pending.

It is also heartening to read the recent joint statement by the International Confederation of Midwives and the International

Federation of Gynaecologists and Obstetricians, as part of the Safe Motherhood project.[112] This statement advocates routine active management, but, in a major shift for ICM/FIGO, now recommends that the baby's cord should not be clamped until pulsation has ceased.

Choosing a natural third stage

A woman's choice to forego preventative oxytocics, to clamp late (if at all), and to deliver the placenta by her own effort, all require forethought, commitment and the selection of birth attendants who are comfortable and experienced with these choices.

A natural third stage is more than this, however. We must ensure respect for the emotional and hormonal processes of both mother and baby, remembering how unique this time is. Odent stresses the importance of not interrupting, even with words, and believes that the new mother should feel unobserved and uninhibited in the first encounter with her baby.[4]

This level of non-interference requires skill, experience, and confidence, as well as support from mentors and institutions. However, as I argue, attention to these non-medical elements is essential for a safe natural third stage.

Lotus birth, in which the placenta remains attached to the baby until the cord separates naturally, gives us another way to "slow the fire drill" after birth, as Canadian midwife Gloria Lemay puts it,[113] and allows our babies the full metaphysical, as well as physical, benefit of prolonged contact with the placenta. Like a good midwife, lotus birth secludes mother and baby in the early hours and days, ensuring rest and keeping visitors to a minimum.[114] (For more about lotus birth, see chapter 5, "Lotus Birth – a ritual for our times".)

Third stage represents the first meeting between mother and baby, creating a powerful imprint upon their relationship. When both are undrugged and quiet, fully present and alert, new potentials for love and trust are invoked for mother, baby, family and the world we share.

Previous versions of this article have been published in Rachana S (ed), Lotus Birth *(Yarra Glen, Australia: Greenwood Press, 2000), and in* Medical Veritas *2005, 2(2), 492–9. This version updated May 2005.*

Suggestions for a natural third stage

For the mother

- Choose carers who have skills, confidence, and trust in the natural processes of birth and third stage
- Enjoy an undisturbed birth (see chapter 13)
- Ensure a warm (even hot) room immediately after birth
- Follow suggestions for the carer as below

For the carer

- Arrange resuscitation facilities that can be brought close to the mother after birth
- Delay cord clamping, ideally until the baby's placenta is delivered (or longer). Or, in order of increasing benefit to baby and mother:
  - until the baby takes a first breath
  - until 30 seconds after birth
  - until 3 minutes or so after birth
  - until the cord stops pulsing
- If the baby does not breathe, or is 'flat' at birth, do not clamp the cord. The baby needs the placental transfusion, which can supply essential oxygen for several minutes, protecting brain and organ systems. The baby can almost always be resuscitated on the mother's thigh.
- Facilitate uninterrupted skin-to-skin contact between mother and baby, ideally for the first hour after birth. An undrugged baby can find the mother's nipple and attach in this time.
- Allow at least half to one hour for the mother to deliver her baby's placenta. A longer interval is likely to be safe, if there is no bleeding.
- Allow the mother to deliver the placenta by her own effort. The mother can squat, cough, and/or blow into the neck of a bottle, if necessary.
- The cord can be cut after placental delivery, if desired. Clamping is likely to be unnecessary at this stage. Parents may wish to observe their baby's reaction to handling the cord in making this decision.
- If necessary, and a delay is safe, oxytocics are better given after delivery of the baby's placenta.
- If a caesarean is necessary, keep the newborn baby's body close to, or slightly below, the level of the mother's uterus immediately after delivery. Keep the cord unclamped; baby and joined placenta can be cared for on the same level (mother's chest, resuscitation trolley) until pulsation stops. Support skin-to-skin contact between mother and baby.

References

1. Buckley SJ. Undisturbed birth: Nature's blueprint for ease and ecstasy. *Journal of Prenatal and Perinatal Psychology and Health* 2003; 17(4):261–288 See also chapter 13, Undisturbed Birth.

2. Matthiesen AS, et al. Postpartum maternal oxytocin release by newborns: effects of infant hand massage and sucking. *Birth* 2001; 28(1):13–9.

3. Saito M, et al. Plasma catecholamines and microvibration as labour progresses. *Shinshin-Thaku* 1991; 31:381–89.

4. Odent M. Don't manage the third stage of labour! *Pract Midwife* 1998; 1(9):31–3.

5. Thornton S, et al. Plasma oxytocin during third stage of labour: comparison of natural and active management. *Br Med J* 1988; 297(6642):167–9.

6. Pearce JC. *Evolution's End: Claiming the Potential of Our Intelligence*. San Francisco: HarperSanFrancisco, 1995.

7. Odent M. *The Scientification of Love*. Revised edn. London: Free Association Books, 2001.

8. Dettling AC, et al. Repeated parental deprivation in the infant common marmoset (Callithrix jacchus, primates) and analysis of its effects on early development. *Biol Psychiatry* 2002; 52(11):1037–46.

9. Kalinichev M, et al. Long-lasting changes in stress-induced corticosterone response and anxiety-like behaviors as a consequence of neonatal maternal separation in Long-Evans rats. *Pharmacol Biochem Behav* 2002; 73(1):131–40.

10. Daniels WM, et al. Maternal separation in rats leads to anxiety-like behavior and a blunted ACTH response and altered neurotransmitter levels in response to a subsequent stressor. *Metab Brain Dis* 2004; 19(1–2):3–14.

11. Pearce JC. *Evolution's End: Claiming the Potential of Our Intelligence*. San Francisco: Harper San Francisco, 1992 p 124.

12. Carter CS. Developmental consequences of oxytocin. *Physiol Behav* 2003; 79(3):383–97, p 386.

13. Jacobson B, et al. Perinatal origin of adult self-destructive behavior. *Acta Psychiatr Scand* 1987; 76(4):364–71.

14. Jacobson B, et al. Opiate addiction in adult offspring through possible imprinting after obstetric treatment. *Br Med J* 1990; 301(6760):1067–70.

15. Jacobson B, Bygdeman M. Obstetric care and proneness of offspring to suicide as adults: case-control study. *Br Med J* 1998; 317(7169): 1346–9.

16. Raine A, et al. Birth complications combined with early maternal rejection at age 1 year predispose to violent crime at age 18 years. *Arch Gen Psychiatry* 1994; 51(12):984–8.

17. Redmond A, et al. Relation of Onset of Respiration to Placental Transfusion. *Lancet* 1965; 17:283–5.

18. Gunther M. The transfer of blood between baby and placenta in the minutes after birth. *Lancet* 1957; 272(6982):1277–80.

19. Yao AC, Lind J. Effect of gravity on placental transfusion. *Lancet* 1969; 2(7619):505–8.

20. Linderkamp O. Placental transfusion: determinants and effects. *Clin Perinatol* 1982; 9(3):559–92.

21. Yao AC, et al. Placental transfusion-rate and uterine contraction. *Lancet* 1968; 1(7539):380–3.

22. Dunn P. Reservations about the Methods of Assessing at Birth the Predictive Value of Intrapartum Fetal Monitoring including premature interruption of the feto-placental circulation. In: Rolfe P, ed. *Proceedings of the 2nd International Conference on Fetal and Neonatal Physiological Measurements*, Oxford, 2–4 April 1984. London: Butterworths, 1986:130–7.

23. Pisacane A. Neonatal prevention of iron deficiency. *Br Med J* 1996; 312(7024):136–7, p 136.

24. Usher R, et al. The Blood Volume of the Newborn Infant and Placental Transfusion. *Acta Paediatr* 1963; 52:497–512.

25. Morley GM. Cord Closure: Can Hasty Clamping Injure the Newborn? *OBG Management* July 1998; 29–36, p 33.

26. Peltonen T. Placental transfusion – advantage and disadvantage. *Eur J Pediatr* 1981; 137(2):141–6.

27. Peltonen T. Placental transfusion – advantage and disadvantage. *Eur J Pediatr* 1981; 137(2):141–6, p 142.

28. Landau DB. Hyaline membrane formation in the newborn; hematogenic shock as a possible etiologic factor. *Mo Med* 1953; 50(3):183–5.

29. Caesarean section and the prevention of respiratory distress syndrome of the newborn. Third European Congress of Perinatal Medicine; 1972; Lausanne. Hans Huber.

30. Morley G. To Clamp or not to Clamp: This is the Answer. 2002. www.cordclamping.com/clamp.htm

31. van Rheenen P, Brabin BJ. Late umbilical cord-clamping as an intervention for reducing iron deficiency anaemia in term infants in developing and industrialised countries: a systematic review. *Ann Trop Paediatr* 2004; 24(1):3–16.

32. Zlotkin S. Current issues for the prevention and treatment of iron deficiency anemia. *Indian Pediatr* 2002; 39(2):125–9.

33. Darwin E. *Zoonomia or The Laws of Organic Life*. Second edn. London: J Johnson, 1796.

34. Kinmond S, et al. Umbilical cord clamping and preterm infants: a randomised trial. *Br Med J* 1993; 306(6871):172–5.

35. Rabe H, et al. Early versus delayed umbilical cord clamping in preterm infants. *Cochrane Database Syst Rev* 2004(4):CD003248.

36. Hofmeyr GJ, et al. Hasty clamping of the umbilical cord may initiate neonatal intraventricular hemorrhage. *Med Hypotheses* 1989; 29(1):5–6.

37. Meek JH, et al. Low cerebral blood flow is a risk factor for severe intraventricular haemorrhage. *Arch Dis Child Fetal Neonatal Ed* 1999; 81(1): F15–8.

38. Morley G. Neonatal encephalopathy, Hypoxic Ischemic Encephalopathy, and Subsequent Cerebral Palsy: Etiology, Pathology and Prevention. 2003. www.cordclamping.com/Lancet2003analysis.htm

39. Morley G. Autism, ADD/ADHD, and related disorders: Is a common childbirth practice to blame? *Red Flags Weekly enewsletter* 2002. redflagsweekly.com/features/Morley.html

40. Simon E. Developmental Language Disability: One consequence of ischemic brainstem injury? *31st Annual Meeting of the Fetal and Neonatal Physiological Society*. Tuscany, 2004. www.cordclamping.com/poster1.doc.

41. Simon E. The History of Cord Clamping. 2004. www.cordclamping.com/History.htm

42. Mercer JS, Skovgaard RL. Neonatal transitional physiology: a new paradigm. *J Perinat Neonatal Nurs* 2002; 15(4):56–75.

43. Yao AC, et al. Distribution of blood between infant and placenta after birth. *Lancet* 1969; 2(7626):871–3.

44. Saigal S, et al. Placental transfusion and hyperbilirubinemia in the premature. *Pediatrics* 1972; 49(3):406–19.

45. Saigal S, Usher RH. Symptomatic neonatal plethora. *Biol Neonate* 1977; 32(1–2):62–72.

46. Mercer JS. Current best evidence: a review of the literature on umbilical cord clamping. *J Midwifery Womens Health* 2001; 46(6):402–14.

47. Morley GM. Cord Closure: Can Hasty Clamping Injure the Newborn? *OBG Management* July 1998; 29–36.

48. McDonagh A. Bilirubin the beneficent. *Pediatrics* 2004; 114(6):1741–2; author reply 1742–3.

49. Sedlak TW, Snyder SH. Bilirubin benefits: cellular protection by a biliverdin reductase antioxidant cycle. *Pediatrics* 2004; 113(6):1776–82.

50. Najib-Farah. Defensive role of bilirubinemia in pneumococcal infection. *Lancet* 1937; 1:505–6.

51. Newman TB, Klebanoff MA. Neonatal hyperbilirubinemia and long-term outcome: another look at the Collaborative Perinatal Project. *Pediatrics* 1993; 92(5):651–7.

52. Garrison L. www.gentlebirth.org/archives/cordIssues.html, 1999.

53. Carter CS. Developmental consequences of oxytocin. *Physiol Behav* 2003; 79(3):383–97.

54. Carter CS. Developmental consequences of oxytocin. *Physiol Behav* 2003; 79(3):383–97, p 392.

55. Edwards NP. *Delivering Your Placenta: The Third Stage.* AIMS for British Maternity Trust, 1999.

56. Hoff DS, Maynard RC. Accidental administration of oxytocin to a premature infant. *Neonatal Netw* 2002; 21(1):27–9.

57. Brereteon-Stiles GG, et al. Accidental administration of syntometrine to a neonate. *S Afr Med J* 1972; 46(52):2052.

58. Donaldson C, et al. Impact of obstetric factors on cord blood donation for transplantation. *Br J Haematol* 1999; 106(1):128–32.

59. Smith FO, Thomson BG. Umbilical cord blood collection, banking, and transplantation: current status and issues relevant to perinatal caregivers. *Birth* 2000; 27(2):127–35.

60. Lasky LC, et al. In utero or ex utero cord blood collection: which is better? *Transfusion* 2002; 42(10):1261–7.

61. Dunn P. Clamping the umbilical cord. *AIMS Journal (UK)* 2004/5; 16(4):8–9.

62. Wardrop CA, Holland BM. The roles and vital importance of placental blood to the newborn infant. *J Perinat Med* 1995; 23(1–2):139–43.

63. Cord blood banking for potential future transplantation: subject review. American Academy of Pediatrics. Work Group on Cord Blood Banking. *Pediatrics* 1999; 104(1 Pt 1):116–8, p 117.

64. Private cord blood banks. *Med Lett Drugs Ther* 2004; 46(1178):21–2.

65. Steinbrook R. The cord-blood-bank controversies. *N Engl J Med* 2004; 351(22):2255–7.

66. Fisk NM, et al. Can routine commercial cord blood banking be scientifically and ethically justified? *PLoS Med* 2005; 2(2):e44.

67. Laughlin MJ, et al. Outcomes After Transplantation of Cord Blood or Bone Marrow From Unrelated Donors in Adults With Leukemia. *Obstet Gynecol Surv* 2005; 60(5):295–296.

68. Agovino T. As business grows, umbilical cord blood storage prompts debate. *Boston Globe* 2004, 4 Oct 2004; A4.

69. Woodhouse D. Cord Blood banking movement grows. *O&G: the Royal Australian and New Zealand College of Obstetricians and Gynaecologists* 1999; 1(1):35–8

70. Hwang WS, et al. Patient-Specific Embryonic Stem Cells Derived from Human SCNT Blastocysts. *Science* 2005; 2038(17 June):1777–83.

71. Cord blood banking for potential future transplantation: subject review. American Academy of Pediatrics. Work Group on Cord Blood Banking. *Pediatrics* 1999; 104(1 Pt 1):116–8.

72. International Federation of Gynaecologists and Obstetricians (FIGO) Committee for the Ethical Aspects of Human Reproduction. Ethical guidelines regarding the procedure of collection of cord blood (1998). *Recommendations on Ethical Issues in Obstetrics and Gynecology.* London: FIGO, 2000:42–3.

73. Inch S. *Birth Rights: What Every Parent Should Know About Childbirth in Hospital.* New York: Random House, 1984.

74. Jordan S. *Pharmacology for Midwives.* Hampshire UK: Palgrave, 2002.

75. Sorbe B. Active pharmacologic management of the third stage of labor. A comparison of oxytocin and ergometrine. *Obstet Gynecol* 1978; 52(6):694–7.

76. Gulmezoglu AM, et al. Prostaglandins for prevention of postpartum haemorrhage. *Cochrane Database Syst Rev* 2004(1):CD000494.

77. Vogel D, et al. Misoprostol versus methylergometrine: pharmacokinetics in human milk. *Am J Obstet Gynecol* 2004; 191(6):2168–73.

78. Prendiville WJ, et al. Active versus expectant management in the third stage of labour. *Cochrane Database Syst Rev* 2000(3):CD000007.

79. Rogers J, et al. Active versus expectant management of third stage of labour: the Hinchingbrooke randomised controlled trial. *Lancet* 1998; 351(9104):693–9.

80. Rogers J, et al. Active versus expectant management of third stage of labour: the Hinchingbrooke randomised controlled trial. *Lancet* 1998; 351(9104):693–9, p 698.

81. Botha M. Management of the Umbilical Cord During Labour. *South African Journal of Obstetrics and Gynecology* 1968; 6:30–33. p 30.

82. Walsh SZ. Maternal effects of early and late clamping of the umbilical cord. *Lancet* 1968; 1(7550):996–7.

83. Soltani H, et al. Placental cord drainage after spontaneous vaginal delivery as part of the management of the third stage of labour. *The Cochrane Database of Systematic Reviews* 2004; (1):CD004665.

84. Phillip H, et al. The impact of induced labour on postpartum blood loss. *J Obstet Gynaecol* 2004; 24(1):12–5.

85. Stones RW, et al. Risk factors for major obstetric haemorrhage. *Eur J Obstet Gynecol Reprod Biol* 1993; 48(1):15–8.

86. MacKenzie IZ. Induction of labour and postpartum haemorrhage. *Br Med J* 1979; 1(6165):750.

87. Brinsden PR, Clark AD. Postpartum haemorrhage after induced and spontaneous labour. *Br Med J* 1978; 2(6141):855–6.

88. St George L, Crandon AJ. Immediate postpartum complications. *Aust N Z J Obstet Gynaecol* 1990; 30(1):52–6.

89. Magann EF, et al. Postpartum hemorrhage after vaginal birth: an analysis of risk factors. *South Med J* 2005; 98(4):419–22.

90. Ploeckinger B, et al. Epidural anaesthesia in labour: influence on surgical delivery rates, intrapartum fever and blood loss. *Gynecol Obstet Invest* 1995; 39(1):24–7.

91. Gilbert L, et al. Postpartum haemorrhage – a continuing problem. *Br J Obstet Gynaecol* 1987; 94(1):67–71.

92. Chattopadhyay SK, et al. Placenta praevia and accreta after previous caesarean section. *Eur J Obstet Gynecol Reprod Biol* 1993; 52(3):151–6.

93. Hemminki E, Merilainen J. Long-term effects of cesarean sections: ectopic pregnancies and placental problems. *Am J Obstet Gynecol* 1996; 174(5):1569–74.

94. Lydon-Rochelle M, et al. First-birth cesarean and placental abruption or previa at second birth(1). *Obstet Gynecol* 2001; 97(5 Pt 1):765–9.

95. Goodfellow CF, et al. Oxytocin deficiency at delivery with epidural analgesia. *Br J Obstet Gynaecol* 1983; 90(3):214–9.

96. Phaneuf S, et al. Loss of myometrial oxytocin receptors during oxytocin-induced and oxytocin-augmented labour. *J Reprod Fertil* 2000; 120(1):91–7.

97. Logue M. The management of the third stage of labour: a midwife's view. *J Obstet Gynaecol* 1990; 10(Suppl 2):10–12.

98. Ladipo OA. Management of third stage of labour, with particular reference to reduction of feto–maternal transfusion. *Br Med J* 1972; 1(5802):721–3.

99. Doolittle JE, Moritz CR. Prevention of erythroblastosis by an obstetric technic. *Obstet Gynecol* 1966; 27(4):529–31.

100. Beer AE. Fetal erythrocytes in maternal circulation of 155 Rh-negative women. *Obstet Gynecol* 1969; 34(2):143–50.

101. Weinstein L, et al. Third stage of labor and transplacental hemorrhage. *Obstet Gynecol* 1971; 37(1):90–3.

102. Doolittle JE. Placental Vascular Integrity Related to Third-Stage Management. *Obstet Gynecol* 1963; 22:468–72.

103. Bakas P, et al. Massive fetomaternal hemorrhage and oxytocin contraction test: case report and review. *Arch Gynecol Obstet* 2004; 269(2):149–51.

104. Valdes V, et al. [Massive fetomaternal transfusion after induction of labor by oxytocin]. *Arch Pediatr* 2002; 9(8):818–21.

105. David M, et al. Risk factors for fetal-to-maternal transfusion in Rh D-negative women – results of a prospective study on 942 pregnant women. *J Perinat Med* 2004; 32(3):254–7.

106. Wickham S. *Anti-D in Midwifery: Panacea or Paradox?* Oxford: Books for Midwives, 2001.

107. Wickham S. Anti-D: Exploring midwifery knowledge. *MIDIRS Midwifery Digest* 2000; 9(4):450–55 www.withwoman.co.uk/contents/info/antid.html

108. World Health Organization. *Care in Normal Birth: a Practical Guide. Report of a Technical Working Group.* Geneva: World Health Organization, 1996, p 31.

109. World Health Organization. *Care in Normal Birth: a Practical Guide. Report of a Technical Working Group.* Geneva: World Health Organization, 1996, p 32.

110. Fetus and Newborn Committee Canadian Paediatric Society. Red blood cell transfusions in newborn infants: Revised guidelines. *Paediatrics & Child Health* 2002; 7(8):553–8.

111. Elbourne DR, et al. Prophylactic use of oxytocin in the third stage of labour. *Cochrane Database Syst Rev* 2001(4):CD001808.

112. International Confederation of Midwives and International Federation of Gynaecologists and Obstetricians. Joint statement: management of the third stage of labour to prevent post-partum haemorrhage. *J Midwifery Womens Health* 2004; 49(1):76–7.

113. Lemay G. Leaving the umbilical cord to pulse. *Online birth centre news* 1999(14.8).

114. Rachana S, ed. *Lotus Birth*. Yarra Glen Australia: Greenwood Press, 2000.

Breech Choices

In 2002, a pregnant woman in Brisbane, Australia – a mother of three, including naturally born twins – was refused the option of a vaginal breech birth in hospital, and told she could only have her baby by caesarean. She sought a midwife to assist her and gave birth successfully at home. Her picture – glowing with new motherhood, holding her healthy, happy baby – appeared in the Brisbane Courier Mail newspaper a few days later.

In the media furor that followed this event, I was interviewed for television and I also wrote this article, which I have updated with new research findings. My interest in natural breech is personal as well as political, as my fourth baby was born easily and unexpectedly breech at home (see chapter 8, "Maia's Birth").

As a GP (family physician) I am aware that breech birth is more complicated than for head-down babies, but I do not believe that this justifies coercing all women with breech babies into major abdominal surgery. The opinion that vaginal breech birth is "as dangerous as giving a child a ball to play with in a busy street", as suggested by one Brisbane obstetrician, is not only inaccurate in terms of risk but ignores the complexity of the decision. In this situation, as in much of pregnancy and birth, there are risks on both sides and no obstetrician or midwife can guarantee a perfect outcome for any mother or baby.

Doctors have justified their refusal to offer this mother a vaginal breech birth with reference to the Term Breech Trial (TBT), a large international study that showed increased risks for women birthing breech babies vaginally under study conditions, compared to women having a planned caesarean.[1]

Conditions in this study were highly medicalised – for example, almost two-thirds of women were administered drugs to induce or speed up their labours. Many practitioners experienced with breech birth would see this as dangerous, putting the baby at extra risk of fetal distress. Around half of the participants who planned to give birth vaginally had an epidural or spinal. As the World Health Organization notes, an epidural transforms labour from a physiological event into a medical procedure.[2]

Women in this study were also disadvantaged by a lack of the most basic physiological requirements for successful birth. For example, neither privacy nor choice of position for labour and birth were considered important in this study, and women were not offered continuity of carer (having the same care giver during pregnancy, birth, and postnatal), which is associated with better condition of babies at birth, among other benefits.[3]

The TBT has also been criticised for including, in the final analysis, several babies whose poor outcome was unrelated to vaginal breech birth. These included two babies who probably died before being involved in the study (one of whom was a twin – twins were supposed to be excluded – and one of whom was actually head-down) and one baby who possibly died from a congenital abnormality (babies with lethal congenital abnormalities were supposed to be excluded). Two healthy babies who died at home after hospital discharge were also included. Although inclusion of these babies is scientifically correct, a further analysis excluding these babies would have been important.

Even with these provisos, however, the TBT actually shows that the risk of a poor outcome for this Brisbane mother and her baby were very low. With a well-positioned baby – frank breech, with straight legs – a skilful attendant, and a smooth and drug-free labour and birth, she had over 97 percent chance of a good outcome for herself and her baby. (In the TBT, good outcome means mother and baby are alive and well for the first four to six weeks after birth.) If she had chosen a caesarean, her chance of this outcome would have been a little higher – 98.5 percent – but in weighing up this risk, this experienced mother no doubt considered other factors about caesarean birth.

For example, recovering from major abdominal surgery is not easy while caring for a new baby – and this mother had three other young children as well. After a caesarean, she would have had a one-in-five chance of an infection, which could have delayed her recovery even more. She would also have been likely to lose more blood, and to have more ongoing fatigue – up to four years later, according to some research – than after a vaginal birth.[4] Some mothers have reported difficulty in bonding with their baby after a caesarean, with comments such as: "I wasn't even sure if it was my baby." The risk of postnatal depression is increased, and the chance of successful breastfeeding is decreased after a caesarean, both of which can impact long-term on the mother–baby relationship, as well as on the health of both.[4]

This mother would also have had a small, but statistically significant, increase in her risk of dying after a caesarean compared to a vaginal birth[5] and, once her uterus had been cut, she would have been labelled "high risk" in every subsequent pregnancy because of an increased risk of death for herself and her baby – even with another elective caesarean. (See also chapter 17, "Caesareans – the risks".)

In contrast, in choosing a natural birth, she gave her baby the advantage of initiating her own labour at the time when she was ready – as research has shown, even with ultrasound dating, a significant number of caesarean babies are delivered prematurely.[6] During labour, her birth hormones helped her baby's lungs to prepare for breathing – caesarean babies have an increased risk of breathing difficulties partly because they lack this hormonal preparation. These same hormones also naturally protected her baby from low oxygen levels and fetal distress as her labour progressed. Her baby was no doubt alert and in good health at birth; thanks again to the hormones and processes of natural birth.[7]

This mother would also have been thinking of long-term implications when she made this decision, an aspect that is not often considered in the medical context, where the outcome of birth is usually assessed by how many babies are alive (and, in the TBT, healthy) for the first week, or weeks, after birth. There are very few studies of the long-term health outcome for children born by caesarean. However, several studies show an increased risk of asthma in adulthood[8-10] – in one study by three times[10] – highlighting that caesarean birth is a major deviation from the natural process for babies as well as for mothers.

Ironically, 18 months after this mother's home breech birth, the TBT researchers published their two-year follow-up study, which showed no difference between the caesarean and vaginally born children, in terms of death and delayed development, at two years of age.[11] This turn-around in outcome was mainly because most of those vaginally born babies who had appeared very unwell after birth had recovered, with no lasting disabilities. As Kotaska has highlighted, the use of a short-term combined end point (death or apparent compromise at four weeks of age) seems to have been misleading in this study.[12]

Unfortunately by 2004, when this follow-up study was published, many hospitals around the world had already adopted a policy of routine caesarean delivery for breech birth,[13] and there has not been, in most places, a review of policy. This is despite much international criticism of the study, and of the impact that it has had on women carrying breech babies.[14, 15]

While the baby's breech position made this situation unusual, this woman's story is familiar to many pregnant women and their carers, in countries where doctors are using the evidence from scientific studies to give advice on birth choices. This is a welcome development when the information given is accurate and unbiased, and when both mother and caregivers are applying the principles of informed choice, well stated by Grose:

> Informed choice is a process involving the provision of accurate and understandable information about treatment alternatives. The woman should then be given the time she needs to make her own decisions. Informed choice is not interchangeable with "informed consent", nor does it mean that consumers should comply with hospital policy because well-qualified people laid down these policies.[16]

The woman can then take her rightful place at the centre of the decision-making process, also taking her rightful share of responsibility. This also benefits medical and other carers, who are currently shouldering an excessive responsibility for birth outcomes.

However, it appears, from women's reports, and from the sequelae of research such as the TBT, that the process of informed choice is poorly understood or implemented in many parts of the world. For example, most women carrying breech babies are now told that they must have a caesarean, and are given very limited information about the risks and benefits of caesarean versus vaginal breech birth.

In other situations, women have felt coerced into accepting interventions such as induction and epidurals without being advised that these procedures carry risks. Like the mother in this story, many women who question their doctor's advice receive an exaggerated and emotive response such as being told, "Your baby will die if you don't accept my advice."

This mother eventually found the care that she wanted and her good outcome – a happy mother and a healthy, happy baby – was not accidental. It is shameful, however, that her choice for vaginal birth was not respected in the hospital system, where she originally preferred to birth her baby.

I encourage mothers with breech babies to research all of their options; there are still many birth attendants (mostly older obstetricians and midwives who practised in the low-caesarean era) who are skilled in assisting with vaginal breech birth, and there are many resources available to help with decision-making.[17–20]

I believe that it is every woman's right to choose the birth she wants for her baby and herself – whether vaginal or caesarean; high-technology or low-technology – and that no-one can make a decision that is as trustworthy and far-sighted as that of a well-informed mother.

This article was submitted to the Courier Mail, *June 2003 but not published. This version updated May 2005.*

References

1. Hannah ME, et al. Planned caesarean section versus planned vaginal birth for breech presentation at term: a randomised multicentre trial. Term Breech Trial Collaborative Group. *Lancet* 2000; 356(9239):1375–83.

2. World Health Organization. *Care in Normal Birth: a Practical Guide. Report of a Technical Working Group*. Geneva: World Health Organization, 1996.

3. Hodnett ED. Continuity of caregivers for care during pregnancy and childbirth. *Cochrane Database Syst Rev* 2000(2):CD000062.

4. DiMatteo MR, et. al. Cesarean childbirth and psychosocial outcomes: a meta-analysis. *Health Psychol* 1996; 15(4):303–14.

5. Enkin M, et al. *Effective Care in Pregnancy and Childbirth*. 3rd edn. Oxford: Oxford University Press, 2000.

6. Hook B, et al. Neonatal morbidity after elective repeat cesarean section and trial of labor. *Pediatrics* 1997; 100(3 Pt 1):348–53.

7. Buckley SJ. Undisturbed birth: Nature's blueprint for ease and ecstasy. *Journal of Prenatal and Perinatal Psychology and Health* 2003; 17(4):261–288. See also chapter 13, Undisturbed Birth.

8. Hakansson S, Kallen K. Caesarean section increases the risk of hospital care in childhood for asthma and gastroenteritis. *Clin Exp Allergy* 2003; 33(6):757–64.

9. Kero J, et al. Mode of delivery and asthma – is there a connection? *Pediatr Res* 2002; 52(1):6–11.

10. Xu B, et al. Caesarean section and risk of asthma and allergy in adulthood. *J Allergy Clin Immunol* 2001; 107(4):732–3.

11. Whyte H, et al. Outcomes of children at 2 years after planned cesarean birth versus planned vaginal birth for breech presentation at term: the International Randomized Term Breech Trial. *Am J Obstet Gynecol* 2004; 191(3):864–71.

12. Kotaska A. Inappropriate use of randomised trials to evaluate complex phenomena: case study of vaginal breech delivery. *Br Med J* 2004; 329(7473):1039–42.

13. Hogle KL, et al. Impact of the international term breech trial on clinical practice and concerns: a survey of centre collaborators. *J Obstet Gynaecol Can* 2003; 25(1):14–6.

14. Banks M. Commentary on the Term Breech Trial. *UK midwifery archives* 2001. www.radmid.demon.co.uk/breechbanks.htm

15. Bernstein P. Who Will Deliver Breech Babies Vaginally? *Medscape* 2004. www.medscape.com/viewarticle/481402

16. Grose C. Consumer framework for maternity service provision. *AIMS Australia Quarterly Journal* 1998; 6(1):8–10.

17. Banks M. *Breech Birth, Woman Wise*. Hamilton New Zealand: Birthspirit Books, 1998.

18. Bloome P. Heads Up: All about breech babies. www.breechbabies.com

19. Gaskin IM. The undervalued art of vaginal breech birth. *Mothering* July–August 2004; 125:52–58.

20. Waites B. *Breech Birth*. London: Free Association Books, 2003.

Caesareans ~ the risks

C AESAREAN SURGERY is very new in human history. This operation can be a necessary and life-saving intervention for mother and baby, but its current overuse is of major concern. This information was written to dispel the myth that caesarean birth is safer than normal birth, and to balance the arguments for routine caesareans in, for example, vaginal birth after caesarean (VBAC) and breech pregnancies.

Worldwide increases in caesarean rates

Worldwide, caesarean rates have been increasing substantially in the last decades.

- The 2002 Australian rates are 27 percent overall, compared to 19 percent in 1993.[1]
- The US figures for 2003 are 27.6 percent,[2] UK 23 percent in 2003–4,[3] and Canada 22.5 percent in 2001–2.[4]
- "There is no justification for any region to have a higher rate [of caesareans] than 10–15 percent." (World Health Organization)[5]
- The full cost of a caesarean in Australia is approximately A$4,500 compared to A$1,700 for a normal birth.[6]
- The estimated cost for a caesarean in the US is US$3,000 more than vaginal birth, by 1986 figures.[7]

Risks to the mother

High caesarean rates make birth more dangerous, not safer, for the following reasons:

- The risk of the mother dying after caesarean surgery is four times higher than after vaginal birth, even considering maternal health conditions.[8, 9]
- The risk of the mother dying after elective (non-emergency) caesarean is two in 10,000 – four times higher than normal vaginal birth.[9]
- Twenty to 40 percent of women have complications post-operatively – uterine, wound, or urine infections are most common.[10–13]
- "Serious infections such as pelvic abscess, septic shock and pelvic thromboembolism [blood clot] are not rare."[14]
- Up to one in 10 women have a surgical laceration (cut) to their uterus.[13]
- An Australian study showed a six times increased risk of postnatal depression three months after an emergency caesarean.[15] This may be due to early separation of mother and baby.[16]
- After a caesarean, women are less satisfied with their birth experience; less confident with their babies; more fatigued (up to four years after); more likely to be re-hospitalised, and less likely to breastfeed.[17–19]
- Short-term pelvic floor function is mildly affected by normal birth but significantly affected by forceps or vacuum delivery.[20] Pelvic floor training during or after birth can significantly improve this in the short and medium term.[21]
- Large population studies have shown that caesareans do not significantly protect the mother's pelvic floor in the long term.[22]

Risks for future pregnancies

The mother also suffers significant risks in all her future pregnancies, including:

- Reduced fertility.[23–25]

- Increased risk of ectopic (outside the uterus) pregnancy.[26, 27]
- Increased risk of unexplained stillbirth: around twice as common in the pregnancy following a caesarean first birth.[28]
- Increased risk of rupture of the uterus before or during labour (around one in 200, or 42 times normal[29, 30]), and two to four times higher when labour is induced or augmented.[29]
- Risk of placental problems (placenta praevia or low-lying placenta; placental abruption where placenta separates early; placenta accreta, where placenta won't separate) all increased by two to four times.[31, 32] All are potentially life threatening and also increase the risk of the baby dying.
- Seven to 15 times increased risk of emergency hysterectomy after birth, for the above reasons.[33, 34]
- Increased risk of bleeding after birth, severe anaemia, blood transfusion, repeat caesarean, and infection, for all the reasons mentioned.

Risks to the baby

"Non-emergency" babies born by caesarean are exposed to a number of risks and unnecessary interventions:

- Caesarean babies miss the labour-induced activation of organ and hormone systems, including thyroid,[35, 36] adrenal,[37] kidney,[38] lung,[39] gut,[40] blood[41] and immune system.[42, 43]
- Changes in the immune system last at least six months,[44] and changes to the gut flora (friendly bowel bacteria) are permanent.[45]
- Loss of placental transfusion, which may contribute to breathing difficulties and other problems after birth. (See chapter 15, "Leaving Well Alone".)
- Five times increased risk of needing intensive care treatment after birth.[39]
- Increased risk of prematurity; even with ultrasound scans, around 10 percent of babies are born more than two weeks early.[46]
- Increased risk of breathing difficulties after birth: minor problems around six percent compared to three percent vaginal delivery, even when born at term.[46, 47]

- With caesareans, 1.6 percent of babies require a machine for severe breathing difficulties compared to 0.3 percent vaginal births.[39]
- Persistent pulmonary hypertension, of which 40 to 60 percent of affected babies die, can affect up to three to four per 1,000 elective caesarean babies, compared to 0.8 per 1,000 vaginal births.[48]
- One to two percent risk of surgical laceration (cut) during the operation.[49, 50]
- Risks to the baby in all pregnancies following a caesarean include: increased risk of prematurity, low birth weight, poor condition at birth, and death, for the reasons mentioned above.

Better outcomes?

A number of studies question whether caesareans provide better outcomes.

- Over-use of obstetricians at birth. "Having a highly trained obstetrician surgeon attend a normal birth is analogous to having a pediatric surgeon baby-sit a healthy two-year-old."[51]
- Countries with high numbers of obstetricians caring for healthy women have high caesarean rates, but no better outcomes (Australia, Canada, US, Greece).[7]
- Low-technology models of care (midwifery, birth centre, homebirth) are at least as safe, involve fewer interventions and have lower caesarean rates, typically below 10 percent.[52-55]

Reasons for unnecessary caesareans

- Maternal request is a very uncommon reason for caesareans. Surveys internationally find that one to two percent of pregnant women request a caesarean without medical reason.[56]
- Women preferring caesarean typically have had a caesarean or an "awful" or "unpleasant" prior birth, and nominated "safety for the baby" as a major reason.[57]

Psychological outcomes

- Vaginal delivery is associated with peak levels of at least four feel-good hormones, which contribute to mother–infant bonding as well as safety for mother and baby.[58]
- In animal studies, these hormones catalyse instinctive mothering behaviours.
- Caesarean mothers have a different hormonal pattern three days after birth, which implies longer-term effects on this delicate system.[59]
- An Australian study shows that after a vaginal birth, women generally experience an elevation in self-esteem. After a caesarean, women are more likely to have a loss of self-esteem.[60]
- "We do not yet know the subtle but long-term effects of depriving the baby of the full processes of labour."[61]

This information was written as a background briefing for Queensland Members of Parliament on behalf of the Maternity Coalition. This version updated May 2005.

References

1. Laws P, Sullivan E. *Australia's mothers and babies 2001*. Sydney: Australian Institute of Health and Welfare/National Perinatal Statistics Unit, 2004.

2. Hamilton B, et al. Births: Preliminary data for 2003. *National vital statistics reports* 2004; 53(9).

3. Department of Health. *NHS maternity statistics, England: 2003–4*. London: DoH, 2005.

4. Canadian Institute for Health Information. *Giving Birth in Canada*. Ontario: CIHI, 2004.

5. World Health Organization. Appropriate technology for birth. *Lancet* 1985; 2(8452):436–7.

6. Tracy SK, Tracy MB. Costing the cascade: estimating the cost of increased obstetric intervention in childbirth using population data. *Br J Obstet Gynaecol* 2003; 110(8):717–24.

7. Wagner M. *Pursuing the Birth Machine*. Sydney: ACE Graphics, 1993.

8. Harper MA, et al. Pregnancy-related death and health care services. *Obstet Gynecol* 2003; 102(2):273–8.

9. Enkin M, et al. *Effective Care in Pregnancy and Childbirth*. 3rd edn. Oxford: Oxford University Press, 2000.

10. Allen VM, et al. Maternal morbidity associated with cesarean delivery without labor compared with spontaneous onset of labor at term. *Obstet Gynecol* 2003; 102(3):477–82.

11. Hager RM, et al. Complications of cesarean deliveries: rates and risk factors. *Am J Obstet Gynecol* 2004; 190(2):428–34.

12. Henderson E, Love EJ. Incidence of hospital-acquired infections associated with caesarean section. *J Hosp Infect* 1995; 29(4):245–55.

13. van Ham MA, et al. Maternal consequences of caesarean section. A retrospective study of intra-operative and postoperative maternal complications of caesarean section during a 10-year period. *Eur J Obstet Gynecol Reprod Biol* 1997; 74(1):1–6.

14. Enkin M, et al. *Effective Care in Pregnancy and Childbirth*. 3rd edn. Oxford: Oxford University Press, 2000, p 409.

15. Boyce PM, Todd AL. Increased risk of postnatal depression after emergency caesarean section. *Med J Aust* 1992; 157(3):172–4.

16. Rowe-Murray HJ, Fisher JR. Operative intervention in delivery is associated with compromised early mother–infant interaction. *Br J Obstet Gynaecol* 2001; 108(10):1068–75.

17. DiMatteo MR, et al. Cesarean childbirth and psychosocial outcomes: a meta-analysis. *Health Psychol* 1996; 15(4):303–14.

18. Lydon-Rochelle MT, et al. Delivery method and self-reported postpartum general health status among primiparous women. *Paediatr Perinat Epidemiol* 2001; 15(3):232–40.

19. Thompson JF, et al. Prevalence and persistence of health problems after childbirth: associations with parity and method of birth. *Birth* 2002; 29(2):83–94.

20. Rortveit G, et al. Urinary incontinence after vaginal delivery or cesarean section. *N Engl J Med* 2003; 348(10):900–7.

21. Harvey MA. Pelvic floor exercises during and after pregnancy: a systematic review of their role in preventing pelvic floor dysfunction. *J Obstet Gynaecol Can* 2003; 25(6):487–98.

22. MacLennan AH, et al. The prevalence of pelvic floor disorders and their relationship to gender, age, parity and mode of delivery. *Br J Obstet Gynaecol* 2000; 107(12):1460–70.

23. Mollison J, et al. Primary mode of delivery and subsequent pregnancy. *Br J Obstet Gynaecol* 2005; 112(8):1061–5.

24. Hemminki E. Impact of caesarean section on future pregnancy – a review of cohort studies. *Paediatr Perinat Epidemiol* 1996; 10(4):366–79.

25. Murphy DJ, et al. The relationship between Caesarean section and subfertility in a population-based sample of 14,541 pregnancies. *Hum Reprod* 2002; 17(7):1914–7.

26. Maymon R, et al. Ectopic pregnancies in Caesarean section scars: the 8-year experience of one medical centre. *Hum Reprod* 2004; 19(2):278–84.

27. Hemminki E, Merilainen J. Long-term effects of cesarean sections: ectopic pregnancies and placental problems. *Am J Obstet Gynecol* 1996; 174(5):1569–74.

28. Smith GC, et al. Caesarean section and risk of unexplained stillbirth in subsequent pregnancy. *Lancet* 2003; 362(9398):1779–84.

29. Landon MB, et al. Maternal and perinatal outcomes associated with a trial of labor after prior cesarean delivery. *N Engl J Med* 2004; 351(25):2581–9.

30. Lydon-Rochelle M, et al. Risk of uterine rupture during labor among women with a prior cesarean delivery. *N Engl J Med* 2001; 345(1):3–8.

31. Chattopadhyay SK, et al. Placenta praevia and accreta after previous caesarean section. *Eur J Obstet Gynecol Reprod Biol* 1993; 52(3):151–6.

32. Lydon-Rochelle M, et al. First-birth cesarean and placental abruption or previa at second birth(1). *Obstet Gynecol* 2001; 97(5 Pt 1):765–9.

33. Kacmar J, et al. Route of delivery as a risk factor for emergent peripartum hysterectomy: a case-control study. *Obstet Gynecol* 2003; 102(1):141–5.

34. Sheiner E, et al. Identifying risk factors for peripartum cesarean hysterectomy. A population-based study. *J Reprod Med* 2003; 48(8):622–6.

35. Lao TT, Panesar NS. Neonatal thyrotrophin and mode of delivery. *Br J Obstet Gynaecol* 1989; 96(10):1224–7.

36. Franklin RC, et al. Neonatal thyroid function: influence of perinatal factors. *Arch Dis Child* 1985; 60(2):141–4.

37. Hagnevik K, et al. Catecholamine surge and metabolic adaptation in the newborn after vaginal delivery and caesarean section. *Acta Paediatr Scand* 1984; 73(5):602–9.

38. Fujimura A, et al. The influence of delivery mode on biological inactive renin level in umbilical cord blood. *Am J Hypertens* 1990; 3(1):23–6.

39. Annibale DJ, et al. Comparative neonatal morbidity of abdominal and vaginal deliveries after uncomplicated pregnancies. *Arch Pediatr Adolesc Med* 1995; 149(8):862–7.

40. Sangild PT, et al. Vaginal birth versus elective caesarean section: effects on gastric function in the neonate. *Exp Physiol* 1995; 80(1):147–57.

41. Franzoi M, et al. Effect of delivery modalities on the physiologic inhibition system of coagulation of the neonate. *Thromb Res* 2002; 105(1):15–8.

42. Agrawal S, et al. Comparative study of immunoglobulin G and immunoglobulin M among neonates in caesarean section and vaginal delivery. *J Indian Med Assoc* 1996; 94(2):43–4.

43. Thilaganathan B, et al. Labor: an immunologically beneficial process for the neonate. *Am J Obstet Gynecol* 1994; 171(5):1271–2.

44. Gronlund MM, et al. Mode of delivery directs the phagocyte functions of infants for the first 6 months of life. *Clin Exp Immunol* 1999; 116(3):521–6.

45. Gronlund MM, et al. Fecal microflora in healthy infants born by different methods of delivery: permanent changes in intestinal flora after cesarean delivery. *J Pediatr Gastroenterol Nutr* 1999; 28(1):19–25.

46. Hook B, et al. Neonatal morbidity after elective repeat cesarean section and trial of labor. *Pediatrics* 1997; 100(3 Pt 1):348–53.

47. Richardson BS, et al. The impact of labor at term on measures of neonatal outcome. *Am J Obstet Gynecol* 2005; 192(1):219–26.

48. Levine EM, et al. Mode of delivery and risk of respiratory diseases in newborns. *Obstet Gynecol* 2001; 97(3):439–42.

49. Smith JF, et al. Fetal laceration injury at cesarean delivery. *Obstet Gynecol* 1997; 90(3):344–6.

50. Wiener JJ, Westwood J. Fetal lacerations at caesarean section. *J Obstet Gynaecol* 2002; 22(1):23–4.

51. Wagner M. Choosing caesarean section. *Lancet* 2000; 356(9242): 1677–80.

52. Parratt J, Johnston J. Planned homebirths in Victoria, 1995–1998. *Aust J Midwifery* 2002; 15(2):16–25.

53. Rooks JP, et al. Outcomes of care in birth centers. The National Birth Center Study. *N Engl J Med* 1989; 321(26):1804–11.

54. Lydon-Rochelle M. Cesarean delivery rates in women cared for by certified nurse-midwives in the United States: a review. *Birth* 1995; 22(4):211–9.

55. Johnson KC, Daviss BA. Outcomes of planned home births with certified professional midwives: large prospective study in North America. *Br Med J* 2005; 330(7505):1416.

56. Gamble JA, Creedy DK. Women's request for a cesarean section: a critique of the literature. *Birth* 2000; 27(4):256–63.

57. Gamble JA, Creedy DK. Women's preference for a cesarean section: incidence and associated factors. *Birth* 2001; 28(2):101–10.

58. Buckley SJ. Undisturbed birth: Nature's hormonal blueprint for safety, ease and ecstasy. *MIDIRS Midwifery Digest* 2004; 14(2):203–9. (See also chapter 13.)

59. Nissen E, et al. Different patterns of oxytocin, prolactin but not cortisol release during breastfeeding in women delivered by caesarean section or by the vaginal route. *Early Hum Dev* 1996; 45(1–2):103–18.

60. Fisher J, et al. Adverse psychological impact of operative obstetric interventions: a prospective longitudinal study. *Aust N Z J Psychiatry* 1997; 31(5):728–38.

61. Arms S. *Immaculate Deception II: Myth, Magic and Birth*. Berkeley CA: Celestial Arts, 1996, p 92.

Choosing Homebirth

THROUGHOUT human history, women have always given birth in a familiar place, with familiar and trusted companions. Globally most babies are still born at home, and even in westernised countries, homebirth was the norm until 50 years ago. Many of our grandparents would have been born at home, and even some of our parents – including my own father.

A brief history of hospital birth

The move from home to hospital began in the eighteenth century, when male midwives – the equivalent of today's obstetricians – needed a captive population to practise their skills in childbirth, and began offering free hospital care for poor (and sometimes homeless) women. The first lying-in hospital was established in Dublin in 1745, and lying-in hospitals were subsequently established in other parts of Europe and the US.

Hospital birth under the care of the male midwives was initially exceedingly dangerous. As Da Costa records,

> … the crowding of patients, frequent vaginal examinations and the use of contaminated instruments, dressings and bed linen spread infection in an era when there was no knowledge of antisepsis.[1]

This new disease – "childbed fever" – killed, for example, 13 percent of women under the care of doctors in the Vienna Ly-ing-In Hospital in 1846, compared to two percent of women under the care of midwives.[2] Its contagious nature was identified by Ig-naz Semmelweis in Vienna, Thomas Watson in London and Oliver Wendall Holmes in Boston, but there was strong resistance to the idea that childbirth fever could be due to doctor's negligence of hygiene. It was not until the end of the nineteenth century that the need for attention to basic antisepsis was appreciated, and became part of routine care.[1]

Although the mortality for women giving birth in hospital is now equivalent to home birth, there remain increased risks of infection – especially antibiotic-resistant infection – for mothers and babies in hospital. In addition, there are other major iatro-genic (doctor-caused) risks in hospital that can make homebirth a good choice.

Birth interventions and homebirth safety

Perhaps the major risk of birth in hospital is the risk of unnec-essary intervention. As described in chapter 13, "Undisturbed Birth", medical interventions have been shown to interfere with the delicate hormonal orchestration of birth for mother and baby, with unknown long-term sequelae. Caesareans increase the risk of maternal death, even among healthy mothers (see chapter 17, "Caesareans – the risks"), and a traumatic birth can make the transition to motherhood more difficult and painful for mother and baby.

In the US, the 2002 *Listening to Mother* survey by the Maternity Center Association found "virtually no natural childbirth" among the 1,583 mothers surveyed.[3] Around one-half were induced, two-thirds of women had an epidural administered and one-quarter gave birth by caesarean. In Australia a 1997 survey of first-time mothers giving birth in hospital found that only nine out of 237 had no medical procedures during labour and birth.[4]

In comparison, women who plan homebirth have, in most reported studies, around 70 to 80 percent chance of giving birth without intervention. Caesarean rates for women who plan to give birth at home are generally five to 10 percent.[5-8] Because of the low use of drugs (most homebirth practitioners do not carry any pain-relieving drugs), home-born babies are generally born more alert and in better condition than those born in hospital. Official US figures give the out-of-hospital birth rate (including birth at home and in freestanding birth centers) as one percent.[9]

In terms of outcomes for mothers and babies, most studies of planned homebirth show perinatal mortality figures (the numbers of babies dying around the time of birth) that are as least as good as hospital, with lower rates of complications and interventions.

For example, Johnson and Daviss' recent landmark study of over 5,000 US women intending to deliver at home under the care of certified professional midwives (CPMs, also called direct entry midwives) showed equivalent perinatal mortality, with rates of intervention that were up to 10 times lower, compared to low-risk women birthing in hospital. Rates of induction, intravenous drip (IV), rupture of membranes, fetal monitoring, epidural, augmentation, episiotomy, and forceps were each less than 10 percent, and 3.7 percent of women required a caesarean.[8]

In a Cochrane review of the safety of homebirth, the best evidence states:

> There is no strong evidence to favour either home or hospital birth for selected low-risk pregnant women. In countries where it is possible to establish a home birth service backed up by a modern hospital system, all low-risk women should be offered the possibility of considering a planned home birth...[10]

In the Netherlands, where around one-third of babies are born at home under the care of a midwife, outcomes for first babies have been shown to be equivalent to, and outcomes for second or subsequent babies have been shown to be better than, those of babies born to low-risk women in hospital.[11]

UK statistician Marjory Tew has analysed some of the largest data sets of home and hospital birth in the Netherlands[12] and the UK (before the advent of hospitalisation).[13] Her conclusion, accepted by UK Government policy makers, is that birth at home or in small GP units is safer than birth in obstetric hospitals for mothers and babies in all categories of risk.[14] She also concludes that modern obstetric interventions, applied to the whole birthing population, have made birth more dangerous, not safer.[15] Her book, *Safer Childbirth? A critical history of maternity care*, documents the mistruths that were used to promote a shift from home to hospital birth in the UK in the 1950s to 1980s.[14]

Why homebirth?

Homebirth is often an instinctive choice, although this instinct may also be backed up by good-quality information and research.

Some women choose homebirth because of a previous negative experience in hospital, or because they have witnessed (or heard stories of) bad experiences.

Others come to homebirth because they have heard positive homebirth stories or even, like my partner and me, have had the privilege of supporting their friends birthing at home.

Others may want to make choices that are very difficult to implement in hospital, such as vaginal birth after caesarean or natural breech birth, and some families want their children, or other family members, to be more involved than is possible in a hospital birth room. Some homebirthers have been born at home themselves.

Women who choose homebirth tend to be older and better educated than the general population and include many health professionals – including midwives and a few doctors, such as my partner and myself.

Homebirthers are generally trusting of their bodies and of the natural processes of birth, and tend to be self-reliant and self-responsible in other aspects of their lives. The experience of giving birth in one's own time, in one's own space, also reinforces these attitudes, giving the new mother a solid confidence in her abilities and those of her baby, and laying a firm foundation for pleasurable mothering.

For the homebirth father, being fully present and involved at the birth of his child can be a life-changing event. The father's experience is usually very different at a hospital birth, where he may be treated as peripheral, or may be conscripted by hospital staff to persuade his wife to agree to interventions.

Making an uncommon choice

Homebirth is still a minority choice in western countries. Couples who choose homebirth may encounter negative attitudes from friends, family, doctors, and media, many of whom are unaware of the good outcomes associated with homebirth. It may also be difficult to find a carer, especially outside metropolitan areas, and in some places, including here in Australia, homebirth may be an expensive choice, with all costs borne by the family.

However, the one-on-one midwifery care that most women will receive through choosing homebirth is – as the Chief Medical Officer of Health in Brisbane told us – the "Rolls Royce" of maternity care, shown to give as good or better outcomes and higher rates of satisfaction than care from a doctor or obstetrician.[16] A midwife who provides this type of care becomes intimate and knowledgeable about the woman and her family, building a trusting relationship that will provide real support through labour, birth, and early parenting. Many midwives create their own birthing community, formally or informally, where expectant and new mothers can meet and socialise.

Outside such supportive circles, however, homebirthers may encounter negative attitudes towards their informed choice. It may be useful to remember that these anxieties are often expressed by people who have a genuine and appropriate concern for the family's welfare, such as prospective grandparents. Sometimes it may be useful to engage in dialogue and education to counter these anxieties, and at other times it may be better to save energy and remain confident internally. Sometimes keeping plans undisclosed may be the best option, especially around people who are likely to share their horror stories of birth.

Homebirth in other countries

The Netherlands has the highest rate of homebirth in the western world, which is consistent with its philosophy of protecting low-risk women from unnecessary interventions.[17] In the Netherlands, specialist obstetric care is only provided by the state to women who need it, whereas midwifery care (for home or hospital birth) is free to every pregnant woman. The Netherlands has some of the lowest rates of intervention (especially caesareans and epidurals) in the western world, with good outcomes for mothers and babies.

Midwifery care for homebirth is also provided free in the UK, although, in the public system, women are not able to choose their own midwife and may not have the same carer in pregnancy and birth. Some mothers report that there are biases against homebirth within the system, although homebirth has been recognised at a governmental level (by the Changing Childbirth Report) as a valid option. One UK survey found that, given a free choice, 22 percent of women would opt for homebirth.[18]

In New Zealand, there has been a renaissance of midwifery care in the last 15 years, which increased the homebirth rate to an estimated 13 percent in 1998,[19] although rates vary widely between regions. Women can choose their own midwife, who will care for them at home or in hospital and is paid by the government. Nationwide, outcomes for mothers and babies have continued to improve with this model of care.

There has also been a resurgence of midwifery care and homebirth in Canada, with the first training and recognition of midwives, whose practice was previously illegal, in 1999. Midwifery care is also increasing in the US, with the number of births attended by midwives (mostly in hospital) increasing from one percent in 1975 to 8.1 percent in 2002.[9]

Setting up a homebirth

How do you go about organising a homebirth? This varies from country to country, but generally your first task will be to find a midwife.

In some places, midwives may work with obstetricians (Ob/Gyns) or GPs (family physicians), and in other places, they will work independently. To find an independent midwife, you can look in the phone book under medical, birth or childbirth services. Also search the Internet and look at the websites listed

(your midwife

experience do you have?

philosophy of birth care?

do you provide?

you work with other midwives? Am I likely to meet them or to have them care for me during labour?

- What back-up arrangements do you have?
- What care and observations will you do during labour?
- What equipment do you carry?
- What assistance can you give if labour is difficult or prolonged?
- Are you experienced and trained in resuscitation of mother and baby?
- Can you suture (stitch) tears at home?
- What happens if I need to transfer to hospital?
- What postnatal care do you provide?
- What are your rates of transfer to hospital, of interventions and of complications such as perineal tears and postpartum haemorrhage?
- Do you have children yourself and, if so, what was your experience of birth?
- Do you offer any alternative skills such as herbs, homeopathy, and/or acupuncture?

Consider, too, how flexible and accommodating your interviewees seem: your situation may change or you may change your mind about various aspects of your care later in pregnancy, and it is good, in any planning for birth, to keep your options as open as possible.

You can get a sense of how calm, confident and non-judgmental the midwife is, and how much she allows the interview to focus on you and your needs. This tells you that she will stand back during labour, allowing you and your labour to take centre stage, although she will be observing you and attending to your care. Some of the best midwives may seem quiet and unassuming at first meeting.

at www.sarahjbuckley.com. Even better, ask around for personal recommendations or look for a local homebirth group who can give you more advice and a list of names.

In places like the UK, you usually need to go through a doctor, or the supervisor of midwives at your local health care trust, to book for a homebirth, unless you are engaging your own independent midwife. It may be useful to take your partner or a friend with you to the interview, if this feels a little intimidating.

When you find a prospective midwife – or hopefully a list of prospective midwives – consider asking the questions on the previous page by phone or, ideally, in person. Your gut feeling about the midwives you interview may be as important as the information they give you.

A homebirth support group

Attending a homebirth support group, or just getting together with a few experienced homebirth mothers, is one of the best ways to prepare for homebirth. You can share stories of birth, ask questions and, most importantly, have the experience of being with mothers and babies, which has sadly become uncommon in our culture.

If there is no local group, you could consider starting up a homebirth support group yourself. Choose one day per month that suits you, and ask local midwives to get the word out for you. Our local (Brisbane, Australia) homebirth support group always begins with an introduction around the circle, then we ask one mother to share her birth story. After this, we have a general discussion, especially inviting questions from new members, and we finish with a short evaluation from everyone. After the meeting we enjoy a shared lunch, with plenty of time to chat and pass the babies around!

Homebirth and the sacred cycle

Birth is not an isolated event in our lives, but rather a part of our feminine sexual cycle. As mothers, we move from menstruation to conception, pregnancy, birth, postnatal, and breastfeeding, and then back to menstruation. When this cycle is honoured as a life-giving continuum, each of these experiences can be deep and satisfying.[20]

Homebirth ensures that these sacred events stay within our own space, keeping the circle whole and inviolate. Homebirth can bless our homes and our families many times over, creating a wondrous atmosphere in the early weeks and months, and giving us memories and experiences that can sustain us – mothers, babies, fathers, and children – for a lifetime.

This article is adapted from the Homebirth Fact Sheet, *first published as a brochure by the Home Midwifery Association, Queensland (Australia) 2003.*

References

1. De Costa CM. "The contagiousness of childbed fever": a short history of puerperal sepsis and its treatment. *Med J Aust* 2002; 177(11–12): 668–71.
2. whonamedit.com. Ignaz Philipp Semmelweis. www.whonamedit.com/doctor.cfm/354.html; n.d.
3. Dedera E. *Listening to Mothers: Report of the First National U.S. Survey of Women's Childbearing Experiences.* New York: Maternity Center Association, 2002.
4. Fisher J, et al. Adverse psychological impact of operative obstetric interventions: a prospective longitudinal study. *Aust N Z J Psychiatry* 1997; 31(5):728–38.
5. Lydon-Rochelle M. Cesarean delivery rates in women cared for by certified nurse-midwives in the United States: a review. *Birth* 1995; 22(4):211–9.
6. Parratt J, Johnston J. Planned homebirths in Victoria, 1995–1998. *Aust J Midwifery* 2002; 15(2):16–25.
7. Rooks JP, et al. Outcomes of care in birth centers. The National Birth Center Study. *N Engl J Med* 1989; 321(26):1804–11.
8. Johnson KC, Daviss BA. Outcomes of planned home births with certified professional midwives: large prospective study in North America. *Br Med J* 2005; 330(7505):1416.
9. Martin J, et al. *Births: Final data for 2002. National vital statistics reports.* Hyattsville MD: National Center for Health Statistics, 2003.
10. Olsen O, Jewell MD. Home versus hospital birth. *Cochrane Database Syst Rev* 2000(2):CD000352.
11. Wiegers TA, et al. Outcome of planned home and planned hospital births in low risk pregnancies: prospective study in midwifery practices in The Netherlands. *Br Med J* 1996; 313(7068):1309–13.

12. Tew M, Damstra-Wijmenga SM. Safest birth attendants: recent Dutch evidence. *Midwifery* 1991; 7(2):55–63.

13. Tew M. Place of birth and perinatal mortality. *J R Coll Gen Pract* 1985; 35(277):390–4.

14. Tew M. *Safer Childbirth? A critical history of maternity care*. 3rd edn. London: Free Association Books, 1998.

15. Tew M. Do obstetric intranatal interventions make birth safer? *Br J Obstet Gynaecol* 1986; 93(7):659–74.

16. Hodnett ED. Continuity of caregivers for care during pregnancy and childbirth. *Cochrane Database Syst Rev* 2000(2):CD000062.

17. Smulders B. The Place of Birth: Its impact on midwives and mothers. *Future Birth Conference*. Brisbane, Australia: Birth International, 1999.

18. Department of Health. Changing Childbirth, Part 1: the Report of the Expert Maternity Group. London: HMSO, 1993, p 23.

19. Guilliland K. The Place of Birth: Managing change in midwifery practice. *Future Birth Conference*. Brisbane, Australia: Birth International, 1999.

20. Wickham S. *Sacred Cycles. The Spiral of Women's Well-Being*. London: Free Association Books, 2004.

Gentle Mothering

Attachment Parenting ~ an introduction

THE day you bring your baby home from hospital is momentous. She's fallen asleep in the car, and you carry her into the nursery. It's freshly painted with a beautiful new bassinet, and a rocking chair for nighttime feeding. You put her down ever so gently, breathing a sigh of relief; it's been a big day and you're dying for a cuppa. Her eyes open a little. By the time you're at the door she's whimpering and, before you even get the kettle on, she's crying.

You pick her up. Maybe she's hungry? She falls asleep as you feed her, and the scene is replayed. You can't figure it out. Maybe you're not wrapping her up enough? (But then there's the fear of SIDS.) Maybe you're not burping her properly? Maybe she's having the wrong sort of milk, or not enough, or too much...?

In a few days' time you begin to worry that you might be spoiling her, as you've been warned, by picking her up straight away, but when you delay it takes hours of pacing the floor at night to settle her and you're desperate for some peace and quiet. Your partner is sleeping in the spare room because he's back at work by now, and needs a bit of sleep. She still wants to feed all the time, and you haven't even had time to hang out yesterday's washing.

But it's a strange thing. After a few weeks you find yourself becoming adept at housekeeping – or at least putting on the kettle – one-handed. And the hours in the rocking chair are a dreamy and increasingly delicious time, when there's only you and her, and the bliss on her face as she falls asleep, drunk with milk, makes you ignore the perils of feeding her to sleep. You've even had her in bed a few times, though you haven't told anyone, and you managed to catch up on some sleep as well; and your parenting manual, which warns against these things, is gathering dust under the bed somewhere.

You're not living in a cave, but you're discovering the wisdom of stone-age parenting.

Since humans have been on this earth, we have reared our babies in this way, and it has worked because it is what babies, and their mothers, are adapted to; hormonally, physiologically, and developmentally. We are not a "caching" species, designed for long absences from our mothers in nests and burrows; such animals do not cry (or they would attract predators) and their milk is extremely high in protein and fat to sustain the young for long periods. We are in every way much closer to the continuous-feeding, carrying mammals,[1] as were our stone-age ancestors, and our babies remind us of this when they cry to be carried, to be fed frequently, and to be nestled up against our bodies in sleep.

In fact continuous carrying (usually in specially designed slings and carriers), frequent and extended breastfeeding, and mothers co-sleeping with their babies are the norm in most non-western cultures, as they were in our culture 150 years ago.[2, 3] US paediatrician and author Dr William Sears has coined the phrase "attachment parenting",[4] which describes both the style and the outcome, when babies are cared for in this way. Attachment, for a baby, means security and love. In attachment parenting we trust the messages that our babies give us, and attend to their needs until they are settled. Contrary to ideas of spoiling, research has shown that babies whose cries are quickly attended to are more contented and cry less as they grow older.[5]

In a society that is obsessed with individualism and independence, ideas that are completely foreign to small babies, it is reassuring to know that developing a secure attachment with your baby in infancy leads to emotional security and independence in later years. And those years arrive sooner than you'd dream of, as you're feeding your baby to sleep, again, at four am.

An edited version of this article was published in the Courier Mail, *Brisbane as 'Don't be fooled by the manual', 17 June 1998. This version updated May 2005.*

References

1. McClure V. Crying – Good for you, good for baby. *Mothering* 1996; 84:22–30.
2. Thevenin T. In Support of the Family Bed. *Mothering* 1996; 84:69–72.
3. Thevenin T. *The Family Bed*: Perigree Trade, 2002.
4. Sears W, Sears M. *The Baby Book: Birth to Two Years*. Boston: Little, Brown and Company, 2003.
5. Bell SM, Ainsworth MD. Infant crying and maternal responsiveness. *Child Dev* 1972; 43(4):1171–90.

Extended Breastfeeding ~
the gift of a lifetime

E MMA, my first-born, was 14 months old. I had enrolled in a course, and, with the feeling of my life opening up again, had begun to wean. It was at that time, a junction between two worlds, that I read a book called *Mothering Your Nursing Toddler*.[1]

Starting with the assumption that extended breastfeeding is satisfying for both mother and child, the author, Norma Jane Bumgarner, writes of the security, confidence, and self-esteem that we can give our children when we allow them to nurse and wean according to their own schedule. With this new information, and a glad and open heart, I recommitted to breastfeeding and I went on to nurse Emma for three more years. The ease and pleasure of extended breastfeeding continued with Emma's three younger siblings, who also breastfed to around four years of age.

These four unique but overlapping experiences have shown me the benefits of an extended nursing relationship; my children have displayed a physical resilience and emotional independence that comes, I believe, from the access to loving arms and the secure base that breastfeeding provided. Over the years, I have also learned about the more tangible advantages of extended breastfeeding, which is becoming more commonplace as women rediscover the pleasures of devoted mothering in their children's early years.

Breastfeeding is well accepted in Australia, with around 80 percent of babies starting out on the breast. By three months, 54 percent are still feeding and this has dropped to 32 percent by six months,[2] and 23 percent by 12 months.[3] In the US, 70 percent of mothers initiate breastfeeding, 33 percent of babies are still breastfed at six months and 20 percent at 12 months.[4] In the UK, 61 percent of mothers initiate nursing, 21 percent are nursing at six months, and 19 percent at nine months.[5]

As these figures show, breastfeeding a toddler is still uncommon in most western countries, but there has also been a recent increase in community awareness and professional support for prolonged breastfeeding. The American Academy of Pediatrics now recommends breastfeeding for at least 12 months,[6] and the World Health Organization recommends that, for optimal growth, development, and health, breastfeeding should continue for up to two years or beyond.[7] The American Academy of Family Physicians states, "Breastfeeding beyond the first year offers considerable benefits to both mother and child, and should continue as long as mutually desired."[8]

Extended breastfeeding also has strong historical and cross-cultural support. Mothers in most traditional cultures breastfeed their babies into at least the second year, as did most mothers in western Europe until this century.[9] Even in medieval times, the dangers of early weaning were understood, and sickly infants, twins, and males were breastfed longer than the usual one to two years.[10] Katherine A Dettwyler, associate professor of anthropology and nutrition at Texas A&M University, estimates (from anthropological data) that the natural age for weaning is between four and six years.[9]

Extended breastfeeding continues to offer significant benefits for modern mothers and babies. Babies who are breastfed through the first year of life have fewer illnesses, both minor and major,[11, 12] and a lower chance of death,[13] which extends to at least three years of age.[14] Breastfeeding gives young children protection from deaths due to SIDS and injuries, as well as infections.[13] The American Academy of Family Physicians states, "If the child is younger than two years of age, the child is at increased risk of illness if weaned."[8]

The benefits of breastfeeding increase with duration,[13] and the disease-protective effects actually increase as weaning approaches. Some have called this increased concentration of antibodies, as breastfeeding declines, the "parting gift" to the baby, ensuring ongoing good health and strong immunity.[15, 16]

Breastfeeding into the second year also gives a strong benefit in terms of nutrition. Research from Kenya, where the nursing mother's nutrition was judged to be marginal, has estimated that breastmilk can supply up to one-third of a toddler's daily energy needs, as well as two-thirds of fat requirements, 58 percent of vitamin A requirements, and almost a third of calcium needs.[17] A US study shows that breastfeeding through the first year has an ongoing dietary benefit, giving a better food intake, and less need for maternal persuasion to eat well, in the second year.[18]

Extended breastfeeding also has physical benefits for mothers, partly through the release of hormones in her body as she nurses. Prolactin, sometimes known as the mothering hormone, has been shown in humans and animals to have a relaxing effect on the mother, and to enhance her mothering abilities and desire for contact with her young.[19] Oxytocin, which is responsible for the let-down reflex during breastfeeding, has been called the love hormone because it brings feelings of calm and connectedness.[20, 21] Breastfeeding also releases beta-endorphin, a hormone of pleasure, for both mother and baby, and this hormone may be important in delaying the return of fertility in breastfeeding mothers.[22]

As well as these immediate benefits, the nursing mother also receives protection against pre-menopausal breast cancer (more so with prolonged nursing);[23] ovarian cancer; and osteoporosis.[24] One study estimated that our current high rates of breast cancer in western countries would be reduced by almost half if we increased our lifetime duration of breastfeeding.[23]

As a GP (family physician), all of these benefits impress me, but as a breastfeeding mother, the best aspects of extended breastfeeding have been the relationships with my nurslings. Breastfeeding has helped me to stay connected and in love; relaxed and open, and reminded me that, as big as my nurslings may sometimes seem, they are in reality still young, with strong needs for nurture.

Through extended breastfeeding, we can promote health and happiness in our families, and give our children the gift of a lifetime.

An edited version of this article was first published in the Courier Mail *(Brisbane, Australia), 7 May 1998, as "Breastfeeding and Bonding". This version updated March 2005.*

References

1. Bumgarner N. *Mothering Your Nursing Toddler*. Schaumburg IL: La Leche League International, 2000. www.myntoddler.com
2. Australian Breastfeeding Association. *Australian Breastfeeding Leadership Plan*. Melbourne: Australian Breastfeeding Association, 2004. www.breastfeeding.asn.au/advocacy/030804abastrategy.pdf
3. Australian Bureau of Statistics. *Breastfeeding in Australia*, Publication No. 4810.0.55.001, 2003.
4. Abbott Laboratories. *Mothers Survey*, Ross Products Division, Abbott Laboratories: Abbott Laboratories, 2003. www.ross.com/images/library/BF_Trends_2002.pdf
5. Hamlyn B, et al. *Infant Feeding 2000: A survey conducted on behalf of the Department of Health, the Scottish Executive, the National Assembly for Wales and the Department of Health, Social Services and Public Safety in Northern Ireland*. London: Crown Copyright, 2003. www.dh.gov.uk/assetRoot/04/05/97/62/04059762.pdf
6. Gartner LM, et al. Breastfeeding and the use of human milk. *Pediatrics* 2005; 115(2):496–506.
7. World Health Organization. *Global Strategy for Infant and Young Child Feeding*. Geneva: World Health Organization, 2003. www.who.int/child-adolescent-health/New_Publications/NUTRITION/gs_iycf.pdf
8. American Academy of Family Physicians. *AAFP Policy Statement on Breastfeeding*. 2005. www.aafp.org/x6633.xml
9. Dettwyler K. A Time to Wean: the hominid blueprint for the natural age of weaning in modern human populations. In: Stuart-Macadam P, Dettwyler K, eds. *Breastfeeding; Biocultural Perspectives*. New York: Aldine de Gruyter, 1995.
10. Filds V. The Culture and Biology of Breastfeeding: an historical review of Western Europe. In: Stuart-Macadam P, Dettwyler K, eds. *Breastfeeding; Biocultural Perspectives*. New York: Aldine de Gruyter, 1995.
11. Cunningham AS. Morbidity in breast-fed and artificially fed infants. *J Pediatr* 1977; 90(5):726–9.
12. Dewey KG, et al. Differences in morbidity between breast-fed and formula-fed infants. *J Pediatr* 1995; 126(5 Pt 1):696–702.
13. Chen A, Rogan WJ. Breastfeeding and the risk of postneonatal death in the United States. *Pediatrics* 2004; 113(5):e435–9.

14. van den Bogaard C, et al. The relationship between breast-feeding and early childhood morbidity in a general population. *Fam Med* 1991; 23(7):510–5.

15. Lawrence R, Lawrence R. *Breastfeeding: A guide for the medical profession.* 5th edn. Sydney: Mosby, 1999.

16. Hatherley P. *The Homeopathic Physician's Guide to Lactation.* Brisbane: Luminoz, 2004.

17. Onyango AW, et al. The contribution of breast milk to toddler diets in western Kenya. *Bull World Health Organ* 2002; 80(4):292–9.

18. Fisher JO, et al. Breast-feeding through the first year predicts maternal control in feeding and subsequent toddler energy intakes. *J Am Diet Assoc* 2000; 100(6):641–6.

19. Grattan DR. The actions of prolactin in the brain during pregnancy and lactation. *Prog Brain Res* 2001; 133:153–71.

20. Uvnas-Moberg K. *The Oxytocin Factor.* Cambridge MA: Da Capo Press, 2003.

21. Uvnas-Moberg K. Oxytocin linked antistress effects – the relaxation and growth response. *Acta Physiol Scand Suppl* 1997; 640:38–42.

22. Tay CC. Mechanisms controlling lactational infertility. *J Hum Lact* 1991; 7(1):15–8.

23. Collaborative Group on Hormonal Factors in Breast Cancer. Breast cancer and breastfeeding: collaborative reanalysis of individual data from 47 epidemiological studies in 30 countries, including 50302 women with breast cancer and 96973 women without the disease. *Lancet* 2002; 360(9328):187–95.

24. Labbok MH. Effects of breastfeeding on the mother. *Pediatr Clin North Am* 2001; 48(1):143–58.

21

Bees, Baboo, Boobies ~ my breastfeeding career

Bees, baboo, boobies
These are the words that my four children have used for my breasts, and for their experiences of breastfeeding.

Blissful, breast-full, intense, addictive
These are some of my experiences during my 14 years of breastfeeding.

Healthy, holistic, healing
These are just some properties of the liquid love that my breasts have generously produced, day in, day out, for my nurslings, and that every breastfeeding mother and baby enjoy.

MY FIRST CHILD, Emma, was born in 1990, and my youngest child, Maia, is now almost weaned. Over this time – my "breastfeeding career" – I have discovered more about breast-feeding, and learned that it is actually designed to be blissful and addictive, and to reward both partners, through the flow of the hormones of love, pleasure, and tender mothering, with each nursing episode.

First nursling

My story of breastfeeding begins with my birth in New Zealand in 1960. This era was a very low point for breastfeeding, and neither my three siblings nor I were breastfed. My mother was told that her ample breasts couldn't make enough milk, although I am sure that, given the right support, she could have breastfeed as easily as her own mother, my grandmother, who nursed each of her three children for nine months.

When I became pregnant for the first time (then living in Melbourne, Australia), I had few concerns about breastfeeding; I simply presumed that it would be smooth and easy for me. Later in my pregnancy, I had a vivid dream that my baby was skinny in my womb but fattened up quickly on my breast. This was an accurate premonition; Emma was born at home after a short and sweet labour, one month early and weighing only 5 lb 1 oz (2,250 g). (See "Emma's Birth", chapter 7.) Her prematurity and low birth weight gave my partner Nicholas (also a GP/family physician) and myself a beautiful opportunity to devote ourselves to her wellbeing, and she filled out within a few weeks, just as I dreamed.

Breastfeeding Emma was an unexpected pleasure for me; holding her close by day and snuggling up with her for those long, milky nights. I returned to work part-time when she was four months, leaving her in Nicholas's care. I learned the art of expressing, and of building up my milk to make it easy. For example, I would feed from one breast all night and express the other side in the morning. After a few months, Emma decided that she preferred to wait for my return, which I appreciated, being heavy with milk after a five-hour separation. I found expressing my milk to be rather a chore – luckily I was able to avoid it with my subsequent babies, who came to work with me.

Emma's first year came and went, and my contemporaries were weaning their babies. I enrolled in a women's health course and felt my focus begin to shift, all the while slowly cutting down Emma's feeds. At this time, the idea of feeding a two-year-old was strange to me, and Nicholas thought it was absolutely warped (although his mother had breastfed him until he was 18 months, in 1958!).

However, my revelation was soon to come. When Emma was 14 months old, I came across a book, *Mothering Your Nursing Toddler*[1] at our local breastfeeding group. Here was one of the clearest expressions of what I wanted for my child – an inner sense of security, loving relationships, and good health – and it was as simple as continuing to breastfeed. Enthusiastically, I opened myself back up to Emma, and breastfed her right through my next pregnancy. When Zoe was born, I tandem fed and I finally weaned Emma when she was just over four – around the same time that I conceived my third child.

Second and third nurslings

Breastfeeding Emma through my second pregnancy was not always easy. My nipples were very sensitive, although this eased around 20 weeks. It was difficult, but necessary, to cut down on Emma's feeds, and I noticed how much more solid food she ate; obviously she had still been substantially nourished through her five or six daily breastfeeds.

Zoe's birth was my most difficult. Like Emma, she was born posterior (facing up) and I had several challenging hours at the end of my labour. (Zoe later told me that she hadn't wanted to come out!) Zoe was a very easy and content baby who lived in my front carrier – her outside womb – for quite a few months. Breastfeeding was again easy; Emma, at two years and 10 months, was old enough to wait her turn, and I appreciated her help with my overabundant supply in the early days. I noticed with surprise that my toddler was gentler in her feeding than my chomping newborn.

When Zoe was just 14 months, I unexpectedly conceived again, while on a family holiday in Tasmania. It took me a while to realise that I was pregnant – I was sure that my delayed period was due to intensively breastfeeding Zoe, who had been sick with ear infections, fevers, and vomiting for the whole holiday.

I continued to nurse Zoe throughout this third pregnancy, supporting my body with traditional Chinese medicine and good nutrition. Towards the end of my pregnancy, when I really needed some space, I stopped nursing Zoe at night and she moved to sleeping in another bed with Nicholas and Emma. Zoe had just celebrated her second birthday, and Emma was not yet five, when they saw their brother born – a beautiful waterbirth in the sunshine of our back room, overlooking the garden. (See chapter 6.)

Having three babies close together, and breastfeeding so intensely, was a big challenge for my body, and I learned a lot about looking after myself through this experience. One of the most nourishing rituals that I began was taking an afternoon rest. This hour or two in bed (or at least with my feet up) has given me a physical rest, and sometimes sleep too, and has also quietened the house down. My children, if too old to sleep, could play with special toys, listen to tapes, or read books in bed with me. My afternoon rest kept my life simple by ensuring that major outings were confined to mornings, and also gave me the energy that I needed to get through the evening shift.

Having a regular massage also became a habit, and a wonderful way of thanking my body for the intense hands-on mothering that I have given to my children.

Jacob was another easy-going and delightful baby, who was adored by his big sisters. Feeding him was pleasurable, but I was stretched in feeding Zoe as well, and often had to refuse her requests for "bees". When Jacob was around five months, Zoe stopped asking for regular breastfeeding, although I still nursed her occasionally until she was about four. This was sad for me, but I really needed to look after myself at this time.

I had an ideal job to go back to, working with a homebirth GP (family physician) and his wife: I was able to choose my own hours, I could bring Jacob to work with me, and I was blessed with a wonderful carer for Zoe. However, work became less and less attractive because of the organisation and shift in consciousness that I needed to make to be a good medical practitioner. I eventually went back to one half-day per fortnight when Jacob was nine months old, taking him with me, and I was relieved when our plan to move interstate allowed me to stop working altogether when he was around 20 months.

In transit

We moved from Melbourne to Brisbane just before Jacob turned two, taking a month's camping holiday in the process. I spent most of the transition time feeding and carrying him, and it wasn't until we settled into our new home that I could prise him off my breast.

After this I also stopped feeding him overnight (when he understood "no baboo until morning"), and later he moved in to sleep in a double bed with his sisters.

The next year was one of the most difficult times for me as a mother. We settled on the outskirts of Brisbane, where I had no friends or acquaintances, and I was at low ebb physically, after eight years of continual breastfeeding (and three pregnancies as well). I was lucky to find some wonderful natural health practitioners, who helped me to rebuild my body with good nutrition and well-chosen remedies. (I took a lot of homeopathic sepia – the remedy for worn-out bodies!) Slowly I found my community of like-minded mothers and families, and regained my vitality.

Jacob's late toddler age was replete with negotiation around "baboo", and my rule was "Baboo in the morning, baboo at rest time, baboo at sleep time" – a theme that I later repeated with Maia. Breastfeeding has, for me, naturally subsided as my nurslings have grown, due partly to their increasing interest in the outside world and partly to my own need to reclaim my space (and my breasts).

I was committed to breastfeeding Jacob until he was four, and continued to nurse him happily twice a day or so. Going away for a day or two wasn't difficult, as we were both easy and flexible about it. A few months before his fourth birthday, Jacob announced, "You can stop giving me baboo now, Mummy."

"Ok," I said, "but what if you change your mind?"

"Just say no," he advised me.

So the next time he asked, I did this, to which he replied, "I didn't mean it, Mummy!"

His fourth birthday was my limit, although there were maybe one or two breastfeeds afterwards. I was also turning my attention to having another baby. One month after Jacob's weaning, I conceived my fourth child, Maia Rose, which delighted the children, especially Jacob, who told me: "Good mummy for having another baby."

Fourth nursling

Maia's was a very enjoyable pregnancy. We were all in a blissful state; the only tensions arose from negotiations between Nicholas and me about my desire for an unassisted birth. (See "Maia's birth", chapter 8.) I enjoyed having a break from breastfeeding and began to wonder if I really wanted to go back to it. But after an ecstatic birth and beautiful baby, of course I loved every minute.

The early weeks with Maia were also blissful. I rested a lot – in fact, I didn't leave the bedroom for a week, or the house for a whole six weeks. I was blessed with a lot of household support, and I allowed myself to be fully nourished. I knew, from experience, that this nourishment and rest would keep me centred for the whole of the following year.

I did have some challenges at this time with baby Maia, who was unsettled at irregular times. I finally figured out, with some help, that I had an oversupply problem; that is, my milk was letting down too quickly and in too big volumes for Maia's newborn digestive system. Once I adjusted my feeding techniques – feeding her in an upright position was especially effective – it settled down.

After this, breastfeeding was easy and enjoyable. I began practising elimination communication (not using nappies/diapers) with Maia, which added another dimension to our relationship, and increased my intuitive connection with her. (For more about this, see chapter 24, "Mothering, Mindfulness and a Baby's Bottom".) She was very much an "in-arms" baby, and I barely put her down for the first six months. I carried her in my traditional Asian front carrier in the day, and nestled up with her for daytime and nighttime sleeps.

I stopped feeding Maia overnight at around two years of age, as I had with Jacob, and began to limit her daytime feeds to three or four. Our afternoon rests were simple, as she was usually keen to "have boobies, go sleep" after lunch. Her nighttimes have also been easy because our family members have all gone to bed together at around 8.30 pm.

Now, at four and a half, Maia continues to nurse occasionally, usually at sleep times, when she often has her hand on my breast. We still co-sleep and Maia has an acute awareness of my presence (or absence) at night, as she did as a baby. Our ongoing connection continues to nourish me, and keep me in a heartful space, echoing the bliss I felt carrying and nursing her in the early months.

For me, breastfeeding has been meditative as well as pleasurable, and has contributed immensely to the mindfulness of my mothering. Breastfeeding has kept me soft, present, and surrendered, and at times of stillness I have consciously experienced the dissolution of my self, as "my heart melts, and flows into my baby as breast milk", as Jeannine Parvati Baker so eloquently says.[2]

My breasts have been all kinds of shapes and sizes over the years, and now, towards the end of my breastfeeding career, they are different again. They are softer and stretchier – more relaxed, as Emma kindly observed, especially my well-loved nipples. My breasts have been a source of pleasure and nourishment for my children, and through them I have also been pleasured and nourished.

Breastfeeding reminds us of the universal truth of abundance: the more we give out, the more we are filled up, and that divine nourishment – the source from which we all draw – is, like a mother's breast, ever full and ever flowing.

This article was first published as "My Breastfeeding Career" in The Mother *(UK) 2004, No 10, pp 48–9. This version updated May 2005.*

References

1. Bumgarner N. *Mothering Your Nursing Toddler*: La Leche League International, 2000. www.myntoddler.com
2. Baker JP. Personal communication.

The Cosiness of Co-sleeping

IMAGINE this. Your baby is two weeks old, and you have finally settled her to sleep for the night in her cot, in the nursery next to your room. You are awakened from a short but deep sleep by distressed crying, and you stagger out of bed. You turn on the lamp and pick her up. She is red-faced and too loud for that time of the morning, and her crying has awoken your partner, whom you can hear sighing loudly next door.

After a few minutes, you calm her and persuade her to breast-feed. Eventually, just as you are about to nod off yourself, she falls off the breast contentedly. Slowly and carefully – you are more awake now, appreciating the delicacy of this manoeuvre – you slide her into the cot. Only two steps away from the door – and she bleats. As you turn the door handle, she cries softly, and then increasingly loudly. Your partner, angel that he is, comes in bleary eyed and offers to walk the corridor with her, which he does for 15 minutes before putting her gently back in her cot.

"Welcome to parenthood", your friends say, but you can't accept that, or the bone-aching tiredness. Then one day you discover that you can actually nurse her lying down. The next day, as you feel her nestling up against you on the sofa, you begin to wonder if you could feed her like this in bed at night. Your partner is sceptical, and you don't tell anyone else. After a few nights, you realise that, if your baby starts the night with you, you don't actually need to get out of bed at all. Your partner is pleased to be hardly disturbed, because you attend to her before she cries, and you feel decidedly brighter in the morning too.

Congratulations. You have rediscovered co-sleeping.

For millions of years of human evolution, mothers and babies have slept together. For our ancestors, who lived outside in the wild, co-sleeping was essential for survival. In modern times, co-sleeping continues to provide a perfect nighttime environment for our babies, through the warmth of our bodies; our vigilance even in deep sleep (actually, a breastfeeding, co-sleeping mother spends less time in deep sleep); the easy access to our breast; and the synchronising of sleep cycles.

These benefits are confirmed by the elegant research done by James McKenna, professor of anthropology at University of Notre Dame, Indiana. McKenna and colleagues invited 35 mother–baby pairs into a sleep research laboratory and monitored their overnight sleep patterns as they slept together or in separate rooms.[1] They found that, not only did co-sleeping pairs get into the same sleep cycles, but that babies who co-slept experienced more frequent low-level arousals, triggered by the mother's movements, and spent less time in deep sleep.

As a researcher in SIDS, Prof McKenna believes that these low-level arousals, which do not actually awaken either partner, give the baby practice in arousing and may lessen a baby's susceptibility to some forms of SIDS, which are thought to be caused when a baby fails to arouse from deep sleep to re-establish breathing patterns.

Professor McKenna speculates that our young are not developmentally prepared to sleep through the night in a solitary bed, involving, as this does, long periods of deep sleep, which is not a normal pattern for young babies.

Videos taken during the study showed that co-sleeping mothers, even in deep sleep, were obviously aware of their baby's position, and moved when necessary to avoid over-laying. At no time in the study did co-sleeping mothers impede the breathing of their babies, who had higher average oxygen levels than solitary sleepers.

Professor McKenna's theories, which support the evolution-ary wisdom of co-sleeping, are supported by international studies, as well as by research in western countries. For example, studies show that some of the lowest rates of SIDS are found in cultures where co-sleeping is predominant.

On a world-wide basis, co-sleeping is still very much the norm.[2] Even in western cultures, bed sharing between mother and nursing baby (usually up to two years old) was standard practice up until around 150 years ago. Older children would co-sleep with siblings, with a member of the extended family or, for the upper classes, with a servant or nursemaid.[3]

The 1800s saw the rise of the child-rearing expert, usually male, who emphasised self-reliance from an early age, with strict guidelines for breastfeeding, toilet training, and sleep. Newborns were expected to sleep with their mother, but they were to be re-moved to an unshared room before the age of one.[3]

With the industrial revolution in the late 1800s, the extended family began to splinter. The mother became solely responsible for the house and children, and this was easier if her children required less of her time. The rise of the germ theory, where the public were warned not to breathe the air of another, led to a further emphasis on separate sleeping.[3]

Later this century, smaller and increasingly affluent families began to build houses with separate sleeping quarters, so that each child could sleep alone. The myth arose that "cot-death" was caused by mothers over-laying and smothering their babies; this misinformation further frightened mothers away from co-sleeping.[3]

Thankfully, there has been a recent turn-around, and many parents now feel more comfortable about sleeping with their babies. Books such as Tine Thevenin's classic, *The Family Bed*[3] have helped to dispel some of the myths around co-sleeping. The most stubborn concern, that of safety, has also been addressed, with recent western studies showing that co-sleeping does not increase SIDS risk unless co-sleeping parents smoke or use alcohol or drugs.[4]

However, our soft western bedding may offer more hazards than sleeping surfaces in other cultures. Co-sleeping parents need to ensure that their baby's face or head does not become covered by bedding (pillows or quilts can cause problems); that the baby cannot sink into an overly soft mattress (water beds are not recommended); and that the baby does not become entrapped, especially in a face-down position.[4-6] (See also "Ten tips for safe sleeping" on the following pages.)

Co-sleeping is safe, satisfying and pleasurable; and it is fun to wake up to a cute smile in the mornings. Co-sleeping does not guarantee unbroken sleep, but co-sleeping mothers in McKenna's studies slept as many hours, in total, as solitary sleepers. Personally, I have found that waking several times from light sleep, in synchrony with my baby, is less tiring than the panic of being woken, even once, from deep sleep, by my baby crying in another room.

I have particularly enjoyed the nighttime intimacy with my second and subsequent babies, for whom daytimes are shared with siblings. I have also made a conscious effort to relax and to stop counting the night wakings, knowing that it passes in its own time. Through watching my children, all now happy, confident and independent people, I have learned that satisfying my babies' needs is an investment that pays rich dividends in the years to come.

This article was first published in the Newsletter of Nursing Mothers of Australia, *vol 35, no 3, winter 1999, as "Cosleeping". This version updated May 2005.*

References

1. McKenna J. Breastfeeding and Mother–Infant Cosleeping in Relation to SIDS Prevention. In: Trevathan WR, Smith E, McKenna JJ, eds. *Evolutionary Medicine.* New York: Oxford University Press, 1999.

2. Small M. *Our Babies, Ourselves.* New York: Random House, 1998.

3. Thevenin T. *The Family Bed*: Perigree Trade, 2002.

4. SIDS and Kids safe Sleeping Programme Development Committee. Frequently asked questions about SIDS and Kids safe sleeping, 2002. www.sidsandkids.org/pdf/faq_21jun02.pdf

5. American Academy of Pediatrics. Task Force on Infant Sleep Position and Sudden Infant Death Syndrome. Changing concepts of sudden infant death syndrome: implications for infant sleeping environment and sleep position. *Pediatrics* 2000; 105(3 Pt 1):650–6.

6. Buckley SJ. Ten Tips for Safe Sleeping. *Natural Parenting* 2003(4):39–40.

Ten Tips for Safe Sleeping

Whether your baby sleeps in a cot, bassinet, crib, "side car", or co-sleeps next to you in bed – there are some general principles that will make your baby's sleep as safe as possible. These apply to all babies under one.

1. Put your baby on the back or side to sleep

Babies are more at risk of sudden infant death syndrome (SIDS) when they sleep prone, or face down. A baby in the prone position can't get rid of body heat as efficiently, and can't kick off excess bedding. Both factors can contribute to overheating, a risk factor for SIDS. "Back to back" campaigns in many countries have reduced the number of babies dying of SIDS by up to 60 to 70 percent.

If you choose the less-advised side position, make sure your baby's lower arm is well forward, because you want to prevent your baby from rolling onto the tummy. A co-sleeping baby will almost always sleep on their side or back, facing the mother.

2. Keep your baby's head uncovered during sleep

Babies are safest without soft bedding items around them. This includes pillows (no child under one needs a pillow), quilts/doonas/duvets/comforters (blankets are safer), cot/crib bumpers (not recommended) and soft toys, all of which can end up over the baby's head.

Sheets need to be tucked in firmly, or fitted snugly so that they can't come loose.

Babies in a cot/crib are safest tucked in firmly with their feet at the very bottom. Co-sleeping babies also need to be kept from slipping under the bedding.

Waterbeds and beanbags are not safe places for sleeping babies, who can slip into a soft pocket of bedding. Firm mattresses are recommended wherever your baby sleeps.

3. Avoid entrapment hazards

A small baby can become wedged in a gap and suffocate. This hazard applies to the gap

- between a mattress and the side of a cot/crib (Australian standards allow a gap no greater than 25 mm (one inch))
- between the mattress of an adult bed and the wall or adjoining furniture
- between the mattress and head or foot boards and railings

- between a mattress and bed guard rail (bed guard rails are not recommended for children under one, but I highly recommend the simple "Humanity Family Bed co-sleeper" for a safe guard system – see references).

An adult mattress may be safer on the floor well away from walls, but always ensure that the baby cannot become trapped or injured if they roll off.

Also ensure that bedding is fitted firmly, and unable to come loose. Loose bedding can cover and suffocate.

4. Avoid strangulation hazards

Check your baby's sleep environment for long strings or ties. This also applies to mobiles hung over cots. It is recommended that co-sleeping adults prevent entanglement and/or strangulation by tying up their hair if it is longer than waist-length. As above, cot/crib bumpers (with or without ties) are not recommended.

5. Dress your baby appropriately for the room temperature

It is important to avoid both over- and under-heating.

In winter, your baby does not need both very warm clothing and very warm bedding. A solitary sleeping baby can be dressed in a one-layer "blanket sleeper", and securely tucked into bedding appropriate to the season.

A co-sleeping baby will be kept warm by body contact and also does not need more than one layer of clothing. A cotton singlet or T-shirt, long or short sleeved according to the climate, and a nappy/diaper, is usually sufficient. Natural fibre (cotton, wool, hemp, silk) clothing and bedding is recommended.

Also ensure that the room is not over-heated or too cool. Consider whether the heating, bedding and clothing would add up to a comfortable sleeping temperature for you.

6. Keep your baby smoke and drug free

This means avoiding smoking during pregnancy as well as after birth. Studies show that babies born to mothers who smoked in pregnancy have an increased risk of SIDS, and it is recommended that these mothers do not co-sleep with their babies.

After birth, keep cigarette smoke away from your baby at all times. For mothers who cannot quit, cutting down will reduce the risk to some extent. Babies are also generally safer from SIDS if the father does not smoke, but co-sleeping next to the mother, with a smoking father in the same bed, has not been shown to increase the risk of SIDS.

It is also important that co-sleeping parents are not under the influence of drugs or alcohol. These can make them sleep too deeply, and increase the risks of overlaying.

7. Do not put your baby to sleep alone in an adult bed

Adult beds have entrapment hazards, as noted above, as well as the danger of suffocation from soft bedding. Your baby is safer sleeping alone in a cot/crib or in a secure place on the floor, away from pets and small children. It is also considered dangerous to sleep a baby next to a sibling or young child who might roll onto them.

Cultures with low SIDS rates incorporate baby sleep-time into family life, for example sleeping babies in a family room, rather than isolating them at sleep-time. Most babies will sleep happily with a large amount of noise and activity around them. (Consider how noisy and active it was in your belly!)

8. Ensure that older babies in cots/cribs cannot climb or fall out

Once your baby can sit, lower the mattress if adjustable. Once they can stand, put the mattress at the lowest level and ensure that there are no aids to escape – that is, items they can stand on or pull down into the cot/crib.

Measure your child standing against the side rail – when they are taller than three-quarters of the height, they have outgrown the cot/crib.

9. Do not put your baby to sleep on a sofa or chair

Not only is this dangerous in terms of falling off, but babies can become entrapped in the gaps of a sofa or chair.

Also check your baby's pushchair, carriage, or stroller if they are sleeping without adult supervision. Babies can become entrapped or suffocated while sleeping in these, which are not designed for unsupervised sleep.

10. Breastfeed your baby

In some studies, breastfeeding has been shown to give added protection against SIDS. Breastfed babies are more easily roused from active sleep (when pauses in breathing, which can lead to SIDS, are common). Breastfed babies also have more mature brain development, possibly because of the beneficial fats in breastmilk.

Breastfeeding and co-sleeping are also an ideal combination, because co-sleeping babies nurse more often but with less effort on the mother's part. This extra breastfeeding provides more nourishment for the baby and benefits the mother by delaying the return of her fertility, acting as a natural birth control mechanism.

First published in Natural Parenting *no 4, Spring 2003. This version updated May 2005.*

References

Information for this article is drawn from the following sources:
Sleeping with your baby – the world's top scientists speak out. *Mothering* no 114, Sept–Oct 2002, special edition, especially the following articles:
- Safe Environment Safety Checklist – Patricia Donohue-Carey, pp 44–7
- The New Zealand Experience – how smoking affects SIDS rates. Taylor B, Baddock S, Mitchell E, Ford R, Tipene-Leach D, Galland B. pp 62–7
- Breastfeeding and Bedsharing – Still Useful (and Important) after All these Years. McKenna J. pp 28–37

All on-line at: www.mothering.com/articles/new_baby/sleep/sleep.html
Sharing a bed with your baby (brochure) UNICEF/UK Baby Friendly Hospital Initiative. www.babyfriendly.org.uk/parents/sharingbed.asp
Humanity Family Bed Co-sleeper.
www.humanityinfantandherbal.com/humanityfamilybed.html
Australian SIDS Recommendations. Reducing the Risk of Sudden Infant Death Syndrome (SIDS). (Brochure published by SIDS), Melbourne 1997. www.sidsandkids.org/resources.html
Australian standards and recommendations for cots.
www.consumer.gov.au/html/babysafe/housecots.html

Getting a Good Night's Sleep ~
gentle approaches to night waking

A s a GP (family physician), writer on pregnancy, birth, and parenting, and currently full-time mother of four, I have many concerns about the standard advice that many parents are being given about young children and sleep.

I was particularly concerned by the suggestions in the article "How Does Your Child Sleep?" endorsed by Queensland Health and published in *Playtimes*, the official newspaper of Playgroup Queensland (Australia).[1] Similar advice can be found in Richard Ferber's book *Solve Your Child's Sleep Problems*,[2] and in *Toddler Taming*, written by Australian paediatrician Christopher Green.[3]

These controversial methods, designed to make babies and young children sleep through the night, advise parents to leave children alone to cry for increasing periods, sometimes called "controlled crying". Both Ferber and the *Playtimes* article also suggest shutting crying children in their bedrooms for prolonged periods, so that they learn to go to sleep alone.

There are many aspects to consider when we are offered such advice.

First, while sleep can be a very difficult issue for families with small children, I would caution parents to think carefully before adopting a regimen that involves ignoring the cries of a distressed child, for however long. This does not produce a loving and trustful parent–child relationship, and I wonder how many of us would want our partners or friends to treat us this way if we were alone at night and feeling upset and frightened. We can also consider that, as adults, very few of us sleep alone, and that being left alone at night can feel life threatening for a baby or small child, as outlined below.

Second, we can ask: Is this approach fundamentally gentle for our night-waking children and ourselves? Parenting in western countries is not easy – most of us are living in nuclear families and are rearing children in isolation, but we have enormous expectations of our children and ourselves. As well, the child-rearing responsibilities borne by parents, especially mothers, are often overwhelming. Parents now also need to perform daily tasks that require us to be alert, such as driving a car or working in technical areas. Being fatigued from night waking can be difficult for all these reasons, and so we may feel that the answer to our problems is to use methods such as controlled crying to manipulate our babies' sleep, so that we ourselves can sleep through the night.

However, a more gentle approach would involve adapting to our baby's needs, rather than expecting our baby to fit into our (rather hectic and over-scheduled) western lifestyle. We can choose to simplify our lives for the brief time that our children are young, reducing our outside commitments and ensuring that we take the opportunity to rest when our baby sleeps.

Another advantage of choosing to rest with our babies is that young babies, who wake the most frequently at night, will usually also sleep the most during the day. Generally our children's daytime sleeps decrease in parallel with their night wakings, so that we need less rest ourselves as our children become older. I remember sleeping for most of the morning with my first baby; with subsequent children I would rest (and sometimes sleep) in the afternoons while my toddler and baby slept next to me.

I also believe that night waking with our babies may be beneficial to us as mothers. I find that, if my life is not too full, being a little tired can make me pleasantly dreamy, and can keep me more right brained – that is, not analytic or logical, but more grounded in my emotions – which is the space that my children also inhabit.

In this state, my focus stays within my family, on our common needs and interests, and I am less likely to attempt tasks or make major commitments that will take me away from my children.

Third, we can consider why methods such as controlled crying are attractive to stressed families. Many babies (and older children) are still wound up and tense at sleep-time, and this may be compounded by their parents' attempts to get them to sleep independently. Allowing a child to cry at sleep-time, which most parents are reluctant to do during the day, may allow the child to release tension, although with the real risk of losing trust if the child is left isolated and alone. Certainly these approaches are preferable to dangerous practices such as shaking or hitting a baby or child, which can happen when families are desperate or in crisis.

An alternative approach, however, and one that circumvents controlled crying, as well as the rocking, walking, patting and so on that some parents find themselves committed to, is to allow our child to release tension with crying, but in our arms rather than alone in a room. As an adult I know that a good cry, with loving support, clears my feelings and relaxes me, and this is true for our children. For more about this approach, see the work of Aletha Solter and Aware Parenting[4-6] – her work is a perfect and heartful adjunct to attachment-style parenting, and very useful when sleep, and difficulties falling asleep, are issues. (For more about this approach, see chapter 26, "Gentle Discipline".)

Fourth, we may notice, as parents, how strong and influential our own memories and experiences of childhood are. We can use these memories to deepen our understanding of and commitment to gentle parenting. For example, as children many of us may have been locked in our rooms when we were upset, angry, or crying, and this experience can revisit us when we try to do things differently with our children. I remember that one of my first responses to Emma's rages was to shut her in her bedroom but when I realised how bad that felt for me, I locked myself in there with her!

Later I realised that my urge to shut away my angry child reflected my own discomfort with anger, and I also connected this with my parents' difficulty with my anger. I realised that I could use these times, with awareness, to learn to connect with my child, even when angry, and, more profoundly, I could begin to love myself, even when I am angry. To be with anger, and remain open hearted and loving, is an incredible skill, which I am still learning. As Aletha Solter wisely writes, "Children are most in need of loving attention when they act least deserving of it",[7] and I would add, "adults too"!

Fifth, when we consider our options around sleep, we need to consider the intrinsic needs of our babies, who require our constant care and attention, day and night, because of their extreme immaturity. Unlike other mammals, they cannot keep themselves warm, move about, or feed themselves until relatively late in life. This makes the mother–infant relationship crucial to our offspring's survival, and our children have developed behaviours and expectations to ensure that they get the special care they need in babyhood and beyond.

The safest place for a baby is in its mother's arms. This has been the time-tested way of mothers looking after their offspring, and it is still true today, with sudden infant death syndrome (SIDS) being the leading cause of death in young babies. It applies equally at night, when sleeping with the mother, also called co-sleeping, gives the baby protection, temperature regulation, emotional reassurance, and breastmilk. It's a perfect system, and what babies are born to expect.

The mother also receives rewards – nature always supplies rewards to encourage us. Co-sleeping gives us less disturbed sleep, because our sleep cycles become synchronised, and our babies will wake to feed when we are both in light sleep. We can do more breastfeeding for less effort, and therefore maximise the contraceptive effect.

We will also benefit from the extra doses of two breastfeeding hormones. Oxytocin, the hormone of love, is stimulated by both breastfeeding and skin-to-skin contact, and keeps mother and baby soft and loving with each other. Endorphins are the hormones of pleasure, making mother and baby relaxed and sleepy – just right for night feeding. No wonder co-sleeping mothers and babies wake up with a smile!

Worldwide research confirms the safety of co-sleeping, as long as parents are not smokers, very overweight, or under the influence of drugs or alcohol, and attention is given to avoiding the suffocation hazards that go with our soft western bedding.[8]

Finally, we can consider that our standard approaches to sleep – expecting our children to sleep alone from a very early age – are very specific to our western culture, and reflect our cultural belief that children will not become independent unless we force them. In fact, research shows that the exact opposite is true. According to clinical psychologist Paul Klein, "Research… confirms that indulgence of early dependency needs leads to independence",[9] and "A mother's reliability and receptivity promote trust and emotional stability in her child."[10] In other words, when we treat our children with love and respect for their needs, day and night, we plant the seeds for a lifetime of happiness – and relaxed sleep.

Co-sleeping arrangements

Our family has found co-sleeping to be a perfect solution for nighttime parenting. We have co-slept with our four babies from birth, but, in my experience, the benefits of co-sleeping do not end with babyhood.

My older children are equally sweet and cuddly at night, and sharing sleep into the pre-school and school years has its own rewards. For example, sleep becomes a time to share intimacy and loving feelings, especially when the day has been gruelling or conflict has arisen. There is nothing as sweet as lying next to my child as he or she drops into dreams (and often we do this at the same time). We have never had the bedtime battles or night terrors that are considered normal in our culture – remember that, in global terms, our culture is totally abnormal in not sharing sleep between family members.

Every co-sleeping family that I have met has their own unique arrangement. When I first wrote this article in 2001, our middle children were sleeping together in a double bed. Our eldest child Emma (aged ten), who had previously slept with her siblings, had graduated to her own bed and bedroom. We continued to lie down to settle Zoe (eight) and Jacob (five) in their double bed, although Zoe told us that she could put herself to sleep, and Jacob often joined us in the dark hours. My youngest child Maia, at 15 months, was still falling asleep most nights with Mother Nature's best toddy, breastmilk.

The years since then have brought some changes. At around age ten, Zoe decided that she wanted her own bed and bedroom, and so Jacob came back to join us in our king-sized bed. At this point, we turned it around to make it six-foot-six wide and six feet long. With four, and sometimes five, in our family-sized bed, we also added another single bed alongside, giving us a reasonable amount of space each, especially with little Maia sleeping very close to me. Some nights, though, Nicholas (who is a big man) would move away in the night to a double bed in the guest room. (Extra beds are useful for many purposes in a co-sleeping household!)

Recently Jacob has reclaimed his room, moving in a single bed and even sleeping there occasionally. I have to say that we miss having him sleep with us. Maia, age four and a half, is still co-sleeping, and occasionally breastfeeding at sleep-time. In my experience, co-sleeping is even more enjoyable when my children sleep soundly all night!

My older children, who are very confident and sociable, have never had problems with different routines when they sleep over with their friends. Why would they, when sleep has always been easy and pleasurable for them?

Since my first baby, I have also gained more confidence and experience with co-sleeping. From our family's experience I can say that some of the things that are put forward to discourage co-sleeping strike me as ludicrous. For example, it has been said (including in the earlier mentioned article) that if we cuddle or nurse our baby to sleep, they may awaken later and "... may not be able to go back to sleep because their environment has changed."[1]

Ferber makes a similar statement about falling asleep with a pillow.[2] As an adult, I seldom remember how I got to sleep, but I would certainly awaken if I were alone and afraid, or uncomfortable because I had lost my pillow. It seems to me that our babies simply want to be close to us at sleep-time because it is pleasurable, comfortable, and biologically adaptive, and it works.

More gentle approaches to sleep

A family bed might not suit everyone, but I feel that it is important to consider that, through millions of years of human evolution, our children have been hard-wired to protest when left alone at night. A child who was left alone at night in the wild, and who was not successful in attracting parental attention and care, would probably not have survived until the morning. Our babies and small children therefore feel, at a deep instinctive level, that to sleep alone is life threatening, and their cries reflect this. (To put it another way, the monsters that our children see under their beds are real, although possibly extinct by now!)

When we expect our children to sleep alone all night, therefore, we are stretching their biological capabilities and there is a good chance they will not comply. If this happens, we can choose not to shut them away in their bedrooms, but to take their fears seriously and work to find loving, gentle, and co-operative solutions. There are many different possibilities.

Some families have invited an older child back into their bedroom, and found that a dose of co-sleeping, or even sleeping on the floor (in what Emma called a "nest") is all that is needed. In many families, as in ours, one parent lies down with the younger child or children until they fall asleep, giving reassurance at the time when it is most needed. Sitting quietly or meditating next to them also works well at this time, and I am less likely to fall asleep myself.

When one of our children awakes in the dark hours, we have often gone into the child's bed – double beds work best for obvious reasons – and fallen asleep until morning. When I have been busy with a young baby, Nicholas has taken on this role. If a child is sick or needs extra care, having him or her in our bed, an arm's length away, feels good. Needing an extra dose of Mummy or Daddy is a good enough reason most of the time, and I notice that sleeping together promotes family harmony in a subtle and beautiful way.

As parents, we are in it for the long haul. Ferberizing, controlled crying and the like are short-term solutions that can, I believe, be detrimental in the long term. Our children will outgrow their dependency needs – including the need for company at sleep-time – in their own time, and our job is to provide the love, reassurance, and guidance that maximises growth and happiness in both the short and long term.

As one !Kung mother from the African desert responded, upon hearing that Dr Spock advocated ignoring our children's cries:

> Doesn't he understand that he's only a baby and that's why he cries? You pick him up and comfort him. When he's older, he will have sense and he won't cry any more.[11]

I hope that we as a culture can come to our senses and treat our children lovingly day and night.

This article was first published in Playtimes, *the magazine of the Queensland Playgroup Association (Australia), May 2002, in response to a previous article on children's sleep, and also published in* Natural Parenting, *no 2, autumn 2003. This version updated May 2005.*

References

1. Dolton I. How Does Your Child Sleep? *Playtimes: The Official Newspaper of the Playgroup Association of Queensland*. October 2001:4.
2. Ferber R. *Solve Your Child's Sleep Problems: the complete practical guide for parents*. Middlesex England: Penguin, 1985.
3. Green C. *Toddler Taming: The guide to your child from one to four*. Sydney: Doubleday, 1990.
4. Solter A. *Helping Young Children Flourish*. Goleta CA: Shining Star Press, 1989. www.awareparenting.com
5. Solter A. *Tears and Tantrums*. Goleta CA: Shining Star Press, 1998. www.awareparenting.com
6. Solter A. *The Aware Baby: A New Approach to Parenting*. Goleta CA: Shining Star Press, 2001. www.awareparenting.com
7. Solter A. Twenty alternatives to punishment. *Mothering* 1992(65):42. www.awareparenting.com/twenty.htm.
8. Buckley S. Ten tips for safe sleeping. *Natural Parenting* 2003(4):39–40. See also chapter 22.
9. Klein P. The needs of children. *Mothering* 1995(74):39–45, p 41.
10. Klein P. The needs of children. *Mothering* 1995(74):39–45, p 40.
11. Konner M. *Childhood: A Multicultural View*. Boston: Little Brown, 1991.

24

Mothering, Mindfulness and a Baby's Bottom ~
an introduction to raising your baby without nappies/diapers

I S IT REALLY possible to raise a baby without nappies/diapers? Can our babies actually communicate their elimination needs?

Well, how do you know when your baby needs to breastfeed?

Perhaps you recognise a certain gesture or cry. Perhaps your baby is restless, fist or finger sucking, or has a newborn's blind rooting behaviour. Maybe you also consider when your baby last fed, and whether they might have a special need for the breast because of tiredness, teething, or being in an unfamiliar environment. As well, you might think about your infant's activity level, the weather, his or her routine, your routine, and many other factors that you instinctively take into account when you interpret your baby's signals.

And when you offer your breast, you will usually get a "Yes" from your baby, but sometimes they will decline, or be only half interested, whether or not you are reading the signals correctly.

However, gradually and gently, you and your baby learn to fit together, communicating with each other and having a mutually satisfying breastfeeding relationship – not to mention saving on all the cost and activity that formula feeding can imply.

Now imagine the same process, but with a focus on what your baby produces, rather than what they take in. This is elimination communication (EC) – also known as elimination timing

(ET), natural infant hygiene (NIH), and infant potty training (IPT), among other names – in which we learn to communicate with our babies about their elimination: peeing and pooing (pooping).

Just as our babies know their own bodies, and their needs for food and breast, they also know the bodily sensations that go with the need to pee and poo, and they can, and usually do, communicate these needs. They tell us through body language, noises (from the bottom end as well as the top), fussiness, and also by the subtler, psychic communications that result from the intimate sharing of body space between mother and baby.

And if we pick up these signals, we can process them just as we do with breastfeeding, taking into account other factors and arriving at our interpretation of whether baby needs to eliminate. Then we have the opportunity to respond, and to offer a solution matched exactly to this baby's need. We can hold our babies in a position, and in a place, that facilitates their act of elimination. We can also feel, as with breastfeeding, the satisfaction of consciously fulfilling our babies' needs from our own resources.

Sometimes we will misinterpret the signals, or may not be getting a clear message, just as with breastfeeding. And our babies will sometimes generously allow us to feed them – and toilet them – according to our needs, if we are going out, going to sleep, etc.

Like breastfeeding, EC has a powerful impact on our relationships with our babies, opening up new levels of communication and understanding, as well as keeping us finely tuned to their wavelength. EC highlights the mutuality that is, I believe, what our babies most need from us as mothers, and which can be lost or diluted in modern child-rearing practices.

This is not a method of early toilet (potty) training, as some have misinterpreted. Rather, it is an enlightening process for baby and mother (and possibly other carers) that makes conventional toilet training unnecessary, because our babies have never learned to ignore their body's signals. Neither is EC a way of making babies control their bladder or bowels prematurely, coercively, or traumatically. It does, however, dissolve the illusion that children have no control over elimination until the toddler years.

273

EC is also what the global majority of mothers and babies regard as normal. Very few women worldwide have the resources, facilities, or need for nappies/diapers. EC parallels the activities of other mammalian mothers, and seems to be as close to our genetic imprint as we can get.

Why elimination communication?

I came to choose EC with Maia Rose, my fourth baby, after learning about the possibility through several sources. I had read a letter to *Mothering* magazine in 1998 written by Rosie Wilde (who set up the first EC website) describing her positive experiences using elimination timing with her son.[1] Elsewhere, I had read that African women cue their babies by making a "psss" noise when they pee, and I started doing this with Maia when she was newborn. A friend pointed me towards the website when Maia was three months, and, inspired, I held her over the laundry sink for the first time. I made the familiar "psss" noise, and, to my amazement, she peed straight away.

In my daily practice of EC, I had a lot of support from Emma (then ten), Zoe (seven) and Jacob (five) who told me how much they disliked sitting in wet or soiled nappies/diapers as babies. Some believe that we set up our society for sexual problems by encouraging our babies to dissociate, or switch off, from unpleasant sensations in their genital areas.

EC has also made a beautiful contribution to my experience of mindfulness in my mothering. Like breastfeeding, EC has kept me close to my baby, physically and psychologically, ensuring that I remained present to my baby's needs, and providing very immediate and practical feedback when I was not tuned in!

As well as these advantages, EC has given us less washing and less waste, and a better time for Mother Earth. And it's been fun! After three babies in nappies/diapers, I have been constantly delighted at Maia's ability to communicate her needs, and to keep telling me until I understood. I was also blessed with more of her skin to stroke, especially at sleep time, and of course – no nappy/diaper rash.

How does it work?

I've come to the conclusion that probably all babies signal their elimination needs from an early age, but because we're not listening for it, we can misinterpret it as tiredness, needing to feed, or just crankiness – especially if our baby is in a nappy/diaper, and we don't observe the connection with eliminating.

In the first few months, I learnt Maia's signals by carrying her around bare-bottomed (usually with a cloth under her), and observing her closely. This was fairly easy for me, as it was summer and she was very much in arms in her early months. I discovered that she would squirm and become unsettled when she needed to eliminate, sometimes with low-level crying, especially if it took me a while to "get it".

At other times, it was more psychic, and I found myself heading for the laundry sink, where she usually eliminated, without really thinking. When I was distracted, or delayed acting on my hunch, I sometimes got peed on. (However, she almost never peed on me when I carried her in a sling.) Her signal for poo was usually noisy wind, and sometimes she'd pull off the breast as a means of signalling that she needed to go. She didn't want to sit in her own poo!

Learning Maia's daily pattern was also useful. She usually pooed first thing in the morning, and, as a baby, tended to pee frequently (about every 10 minutes) in the first few hours after arising. (Nicholas found this really tricky when he was caring for her in the morning.) I noticed that she would also pee about 10 minutes (that's mama minutes, not clock minutes) after breast-feeding or drinking. She would almost always pee on awaking, which seems true of older children too; I think it is the need to eliminate that actually wakened her.

In her first year, we used the laundry sink by preference. I'd hold her upright by her thighs, with her back resting on my belly. A small plastic bucket with a conveniently concave lip was also useful from the early days;[2] I'd sit down and hold it between my thighs, holding Maia above it. The "blue bucket" – now a family icon – has been very well travelled, and was also invaluable for nighttime eliminating in the later months. As she got older and heavier, I found that sitting her on the toilet in front of me worked well – sometimes we'd have a "double pee", which was always successful if nothing else worked! Along with the position, I cued her with my "psss" noise; and sometimes at the sink, when I thought she had a need but was slow to start, I'd run some water as well.

After three months or so of doing this, I became more certain of my interpretation and I would sometimes gently persist, even when she seemed reluctant. Usually I was on track, but it's a fine line; with EC it's vital to have cooperation, and not a battle of wills, which can sometimes develop around toileting issues. EC is more a dance of togetherness that develops, as with breastfeeding, from love and respect for each other.

On a practical level

I used cloth nappies/diapers when we were out and about, and peed her as much as I could. Mostly the nappies/diapers stayed dry, but I didn't expect to be perfect in these, or any, circumstances. We used toilets or took the bucket (or another plastic container with a tight lid) in the car. When we missed a pee, my reaction was, "Oh well, missed that one." On hot days, I just laid a nappy/diaper on the car seat; if it wasn't convenient to stop, I'd say to her, "Sorry Maia, you'll have to pee on the nappy, and I'll change it as soon as we stop."

Maia didn't like to be disturbed at night in the early months, so I'd lay her on a thick cotton blanket and just let her pee. I changed this whenever I woke up. Or I'd wrap a cloth nappy/diaper loosely around her bottom and change it when wet. I found that, as with naps, she usually peed on awaking and then would want to nurse.

Around six to seven months, Maia went "on strike" (a well-recognised phenomenon in EC) coinciding with teething and beginning to crawl. She stopped signalling clearly and at times actively resisted being peed. I took it gently; offering opportunities to eliminate when it felt right and not getting upset even when, after refusing to go in the laundry sink, she peed on the floor. Even on bad days, though, we still had most poos in the bucket or the toilet.

At nearly ten months, we were back on track. I noticed that as she became more independent and engrossed in her activity, she was not keen to be removed to eliminate, so I started to bring a receptacle to her. She preferred a bowl or bucket on my lap, and later we began to use a potty: I initially held her while she used it. At nighttime, I started sitting her on the blue bucket (and attached to my breast at the same time – tricky to lie down afterwards and not spill the bucket!). When I was less alert, she peed on a nappy/diaper or blanket underneath her.

Nappy/diaper free!

There was a marked shift soon after she began walking at 12 months, and by 14 months, to my amazement, Maia was out of nappies/diapers completely. She now was able to communicate her needs very clearly, both verbally and non-verbally, and her ability to hold on was also enhanced. When she needed to eliminate, she said, "pee" or headed for the potty – we had several around the house.

Nicholas was so delighted when she first did this that he clapped, and so she would stand up and applaud herself afterwards. She began to be very interested in the fate of her body products, and joined me as we tipped it onto the garden or into the toilet. She even began to get a cloth and wipe up after herself!

With this change, I stopped using nappies/diapers altogether, and switched to trainer pants for going out.[2] Dresses are great too, for outings with bare-bottomed girls in warm summer months. By around 16 months, Maia was totally autonomous in her day-time elimination. She could tell us her needs in plenty of time to get to the toilet, or could take herself to the potty.

I did find that when we were out of our usual situation – for example, visiting my family overseas – that she needed more help with her elimination, and it felt good to be able to use EC to tune in more deeply with each other. I also found that I was more alert to her needs when we were travelling, so our flight (about four hours from Australia to New Zealand) involved many trips to the toilet, but we arrived with a dry nappy/diaper!

Nighttimes

Nights continued to be busy through Maia's second year, with lots of nursing and peeing but, unless she was unwell or I was very tired, we had very few misses, and sitting up at night to pee her seemed to me a small effort in return for the benefits we were reaping.

I used a hot-washed (and therefore shrunken and felted) woollen blanket with a towel on top under the sheets to protect the mattress, and if we had a mishap, I just covered the wet patch with a cotton blanket until the morning. Some EC mothers report that their babies stop peeing at night, even in the first year, or have a predictable pattern (for example not peeing after midnight). Knowing that this was around the corner for us was heartening. Some EC babies are happy to be in nappies/diapers at night, but this wasn't right for Maia and me.

When Maia turned two, I began to wean her from night feeds, and so her overnight peeing diminished significantly. By two and a half, we would get through most nights without the blue bucket. Nappy/diaper-free days were very easy, and it was delightful to see her peeing her dollies with the "psss" noise!

Learning more

Throughout my EC time with Maia, I learned a lot from talking with other mothers, from the EC email list and from reading and re-reading the beautiful book *Diaper Free! The Gentle Wisdom of Natural Infant Hygiene* by Ingrid Bauer.[3] It seems that our 14-month shift is a usual pattern, and that at some time in the second year, things fall into place and the baby becomes fully continent, albeit with possible lapses now and again due to changes, illnesses etc.

Ingrid Bauer writes of four tools that we can use to practise EC (a term she coined) with our babies. The first is timing – that is, guessing when your baby needs to pee or poo according to feeding, sleeping, interval since last pee, their usual routine etc. Second, we can learn our baby's signals, noises, and body language, realising also that whatever signal we respond to will be reinforced, thus creating a unique language for each mother and baby pair. Third, we can be open and trusting of our intuition and our psychic connection to our baby. EC is a particularly beautiful way to tune into, and develop trust in, this level of communication, and our babies will respond happily when we follow our intuition. Alternatively, when we fail to act on our hunches, we can get very tangible consequences!

Fourth – and this was the point I learned about first – we can cue our baby through position, sound, and movement so that our baby learns to release their pee and poo in the appropriate place – bucket, sink, toilet, nappy/diaper, garden etc. Different cultures use some or all of these cues; we used a "psss" noise and a supported squat.

I have also learned from *Diaper Free* some of the physiology of EC, which is totally counter to what I was taught at medical school, where it was asserted that babies do not have sphincter control until close to the second birthday. Obviously the paediatricians didn't consult the global majority of mothers and babies! What interests me is that with EC, which must be our evolutionary norm, babies begin with releasing their bladder and bowel before they learn to hold on. This makes EC very convenient because, when co-operative, a baby can empty even a small amount from their bladder and, for example, I could know that we were starting a car-trip with minimal chance of Maia needing to pee for at least half an hour or so.

Wider perspectives

I wonder also about the mind-body implications of this subtle difference to conventional toilet training. I have witnessed the ease with which Maia can let go of her pee and poo, and I feel that this process may help her in letting go on an emotional level as well. I can also feel, in my mothering, the beauty of supporting her in her eliminative functions, which many of us feel shameful about and would prefer to deny – hence nappies/diapers, which hide the eliminating act itself.

For me, the beauty of elimination communication has been in the process, not in the outcome, however remarkable or convenient. (Although it's been great to do less than a full load of washing each day for a family of six!) Using EC has taught me that mothers and babies are connected very deeply – at a gut level – and that babies (and their mothers) are much more capable and smart than our society credits.

I have experienced EC with only one baby, starting at a young age. Many women in many places have done it differently; starting from birth or with an older baby; making less or more use of nappies/diapers; taking a long time or a short time to catch on; doing EC part-time or full-time; having their babies naked or wearing snow-suits; and some women have even begun work outside the home and trained their baby's caregivers in EC. (This is actually not so radical; in many cultures the baby's grandmother teaches EC, as part of caring for the baby while the mother works.)

If you feel drawn to EC, I encourage you to have a go. Look on the Internet[4] – it's all I needed to get started, and is also a great source of ongoing support. Consider also Ingrid Bauer's comprehensive book, as well as talking to other mothers, especially women from countries such as India and China. Laurie Boucke's excellent book, *Infant Potty Training*,[5] has an extensive section on EC-type practices in other cultures. Although it can be more complex for older babies, some of whom may have already learned to ignore their body's signals, others may welcome the chance to communicate their elimination needs.

In our society, mothering is often seen as a chore – a time in our lives when we are unintellectual, and unproductive. Dealing with our children's elimination products is perceived as particularly onerous, and big business has capitalised on this, making millions of dollars and tonnes of waste, by manufacturing disposable nappies/diapers. These attitudes sadden me – how awful for our children to be seen as the cause of bad feelings and unsanitary waste.

There is, however, a radically different point of view, shared by many in other cultures, that sees mothering as a women's spiritual practice, and our babies as our teachers. We have the opportunity in mothering, as never before, to practise devotion, awareness, selflessness, and unconditional love through our daily mothering tasks. Our intellectual capacities may (or may not) be diminished, but our hearts and instincts can bloom, and we can practise the mindfulness that allows us to be totally in the present – in love with our babies and children – which is where they are.

Blessed be the babies!

Previous versions of this article have been published in byronchild *no 4, December 2003, pp 23–5;* The Mother *(UK) issue 3, autumn 2002, pp 32–3; and* Natural Parenting *no 1, summer 2002, pp 20–22. This version updated May 2005 for www.mothering.com.*

References

1. Wilde R. Cloth Diapers (letter). *Mothering*, 1998:11–12.
2. For small EC receptacles and Australian-brand Bright Bots trainer pants, which come in small sizes, see www.theecstore.com
3. Bauer I. *Diaper Free! The Gentle Wisdom of Natural Infant Hygiene*. Salt Spring Island BC: Natural Wisdom Press, 2001.
4. Internet EC sites include:
    www.diaperfreebabies.com
    groups.yahoo.com/group/eliminationcommunication/
    www.natural-wisdom.com
    www.timl.com/ipt
    and EC discussions are also posted at:
    www.mothering.com
    www.parentsplace.com
    www.naturalparenting.com.au
5. Boucke L. *Infant Potty Training – A gentle and primeval method adapted to modern living*. 2nd edn. Lafayette: White-Boucke Publishing, 2002.

Yoga and Motherhood ~ a personal perspective

I HAD BEEN practising yoga for almost ten years when I gave birth to my first child, and I was never more grateful for the gifts that yoga had brought me.

During Emma's birth I was able to ride the waves of labour with grace, and to sink into total relaxation in between. The softness and openness of my body – another gift from my dedicated pregnancy practice – also contributed to a sweet and oceanic labour and a joyful birth. (See chapter 7 for Emma's birth story.) My recovery after Emma's birth was amazingly swift, and I was back on my yoga mat within a few weeks. Again, I credit yoga, at least in part, for this welcome bonus.

My gratitude for yoga continues, fourteen years and three more babies later. I see yoga as a wonderful blessing for women, especially during our years of childbearing and intense mothering. For me, yoga and motherhood are complementary spiritual practices, both of which have required – but also have deepened my experiences of – devotion, discipline, detachment, surrender, peacefulness, and of course, love.

My story

My interest in yoga began when I took a year's break from medical school in my early twenties. I was fortunate to learn Iyengar yoga as my first practice. Initially yoga was a physical experience for me, and very much complementary to my other physical activities; running, swimming, and cycling. In the following years, as I worked as an intern, and then GP (family physician), yoga (of many styles) continued to nourish and relax me.

I was living in Melbourne when I became pregnant with Emma, and I continued my regular classes with my teacher Barbara Brian, whose balanced and satisfying teaching style was easily adapted for my pregnancy. At home, I constructed my own practice based on Barbara's Gita-style routine[1], with input from books on pregnancy yoga and active birth. Yoga gave me the opportunity to sink deeply into my pregnant body, and was a perfect balance to the more intellectual birth preparation that I was doing through my reading. After Emma's beautiful birth, I returned to classes with renewed enthusiasm, and with support from my loving partner Nicholas.

During my second pregnancy, two years later, I developed problems with my sacro-iliac joint. Following the advice of a chiropractor, I agreed to stop my yoga practice, which seemed to be aggravating my problem. (In retrospect, I probably only needed to modify my practice, avoiding twists and strong back bends). Although I did not practise beyond four months, my yoga training was still invaluable in Zoe's birth, which was my most challenging. Through several hours of intense pain, my faith in my body remained strong, and I was eventually rewarded with the joy of another natural birth at home.

With two young children, my physical *asana* practice was on hold, but I was fully engaged in *bhakti* yoga – the yoga of devotion – with my little ones. For me, new motherhood is an exquisite as well as a busy time. I see that my babies, and all babies, hold divine light and love in a very pure way, and are very generous in sharing their bliss, if we can tune into it. My most simple mothering acts – holding, breastfeeding, and settling my baby to sleep – can be filled with grace, keeping me in love, which is where my children are.

Zoe was only 14 months, and I was still totally mothering – breastfeeding, carrying, and sleeping with her – when I conceived my third child. With some mixed emotions, including fear, I was very grateful to come back to yoga, which gave me the space and time to sink deeper, to find my surrender to what is, and to tune in to my growing baby.

The pregnancy yoga class that I attended at Mangala studios in Melbourne, where my girls were enjoying children's dance classes, was exquisite. Our time began with a long meditation, often silent, and we did our postures by candlelight. My home practice – which often included a toddler – was also important in helping me to nourish and connect with my body, and my growing baby.

Again, my yoga practice bore fruit with Jacob's labour and birth. As I went one, and then two weeks overdue, my yoga kept me calm and tuned in to my baby, and I knew, in a very bodily way, that he was fine. My labour was slow and gentle this time, teaching me to go with the flow and to trust my own timing, and that of my baby. Jacob had taught me these same lessons with his unexpected conception, and they were ongoing themes for me in the next few years. After ten hours of labour, Jacob was born gently into the water, surrounded by love, and witnessed by his amazed sisters, Emma (four) and Zoe (two). (See chapter 6, "Jacob's Waterbirth".)

Life was very intense with three small children, but my household tasks – my *karma* yoga – kept me centered and focused on the family. The joy of Jacob's birth, and of all my babies' births, continued to nourish me through the first year and beyond, and I was also fortunate to find a gentle Satyananda yoga class in my neighbourhood. The breathing (*pranayama*) and relaxation (*yoga nidra*), which were emphasised equally with the postures (*asana*), suited my postnatal body perfectly.

The gifts of yoga

After each of my births, my body has been transformed: less armoured and able to hold more softness and more love, which is a perfect state for new motherhood. These changes have been long lasting, and I have naturally softened my yoga practice to honour this shift.

I also found spiritual nourishment during this time through the work of Jeannine Parvati Baker, a US-based yogini, midwife, and mother of six. Jeannine describes her own path as "householding" – practising yoga and family life as a pathway to enlightenment

– and she writes (and speaks) eloquently about the spiritual work of parenting. Jeannine also wrote the first-ever book on pregnancy yoga, *Prenatal Yoga and Natural Childbirth,* published in 1974.[2] From her work as mother and traditional midwife, Jeannine has a beautiful understanding of the spiritual and ecstatic dimensions of birth and mothering, which has matched my experiences exactly.

Over the next few years, Nicholas changed jobs and we moved north to Brisbane, where I took a break from my work in medical practice. I was blessed to find Yoga in Daily Life (YIDL), with their welcome approach to families. It was beautiful to take Jacob, then three, and his sisters to the Saturday morning classes, and later on retreats with Swamiji (Paramhans Swami Maheshwarananda), the YIDL founder and guru. I also recommitted myself to vegetarianism, from which I had lapsed for some years, feeling that my body needed intense nutrition to provide for my babies.

My spiritual path expanded again when I consciously conceived my fourth baby Maia Rose in 2000. My yoga and meditation practices were at the core of my preparation for her birth, and I was very much guided from within. Yoga became an exquisite experience, as I worked deeply with my body to find the surrender, the bliss, in the midst of pain and tightness. My daily meditation was also crucial. In the last few months I meditated with a specific phrase at each *chakra* (energy centre), and breathed into the words until I felt bliss rising through my body. My highest words, which became my *sankalpa*, my spiritual vow, for the birth, were "I totally surrender and trust."

Through my preparation, which also included an excellent diet and various natural therapies, I knew that I could birth this baby gracefully, and without outside help. Maia was born at home, ecstatically and easily, and surrounded by her loving family, with the added surprise that her unexpectedly breech birth gave us all. (See chapter 8 for Maia's birth story.) With Maia, we chose lotus birth, as we had for Zoe and Jacob; this involved leaving her cord uncut and allowing her placenta to separate in its own time. (More about lotus birth in chapter 5.) Through this beautiful ritual, we gave her a gentle transition from womb to world and honoured her placenta – her tree of life.

Through motherhood and through yoga, I have come to experience myself less as an individual and more as part of a greater whole. With four children, the yoga that I seek now is very much family yoga. Zoe, my most keen yogi, now aged 11, accompanies me to our occasional Saturday morning YIDL classes or alternatively – and more practically, with a busy family life – my *asana* practice takes place on our back porch, with the birds and trees.

We have also been fortunate to discover the wonderful Ananda Mela, festival of bliss, held each January in Stanthorpe, Queensland (Australia). At the Mela, all of our family is nourished through six days of yoga, meditation, music and *kirtan* (devotional dancing), not to mention the sumptuous vegetarian food![3] The Ananda Marga chant, *Baba nam kevalam* – "love is all there is" – is often chanted around our table at dinner.

Reflections on yoga and motherhood

Motherhood, as I imply in my story, is so much more than the physical acts that I do to care for my children. Similarly, yoga is more than the *asanas*, the physical postures; "Yoga is trying to be the state of yoga," as Yoga master Desikachar tells us.[4] Both yoga and motherhood are essentially spiritual practices, and both can bless us with bliss and fulfilment when we surrender to them. This includes accepting their ongoing challenges, and agreeing to practise on every level with discipline and dedication.

For example, I have noticed that early pregnancy, which has stopped me (rather unwillingly) in my tracks each time, also gives me wonderful teaching about discipline and dedication. When I experience extreme nausea and fatigue, I must become the follower – the root meaning of *disciple* – of my body, feeding my body what I need to eat, resting a lot, and accepting the necessary help. For many of us, especially busy mothers, it can be more difficult to discipline ourselves to rest than to activity, and it can also be challenging to feel our vulnerability and to welcome practical support. The tumult of early pregnancy also gives me an appreciation of the enormity of bearing another child, and the impact that it will have on my life, as well as the opportunity to fully accept and dedicate myself to this task.

For me, birth is also a time of spiritual teaching and awakening, and yoga has been a great ally in this process. Yoga has given me an inner space and an outer practice, as well as a taste of the bliss that is possible when I fully surrender to the elemental (and unpredictable) forces of labour and birth.

Like yoga, birth is about getting out of the way, shedding what needs to be shed, and allowing our selves (and our egos) to dissolve. Sometimes it is an ecstatic dissolution, and sometimes the process is very painful. As with any spiritual path, the more awareness we bring, the more we reap from our experience. Jeannine Parvati Baker describes this beautifully during the birth of her sixth baby:

> By saying "yes" down to the boneseed of my soul, I was opening like the shutter of a camera to let the light in, to give light, to give forth light in the form of this baby.[5]

After birth, as described above, we are invited into the realms of *bhakti* yoga, the yoga of devotion, and again given an opportunity to experience bliss and surrender. I experienced this most exquisitely with my fourth baby, with whom I felt totally in love as I held her in the early months. My constant devotion to my baby, who was literally in arms, day and night, for the first six months, kept my heart "open to the Divine in every moment" and was truly a "heartfulness practice", which is how yoga teacher Shiva Rea describes the yogic practice of *ishvara pranidhana* – surrender to the Divine.[6]

Breastfeeding can be another intense practice in surrender, particularly in the early weeks, when we seem to do little else. Breastfeeding has also taken me into deeply meditative and loving states, especially when I keep my focus inward, on my breath and my baby.

With my older children, again I experience myself as a disciple – a follower – and student of their perfect teaching. Like my yoga practice, my children take me into the tight, inflexible parts of myself and ask me to find the softness and surrender.

For example, Maia, my fieriest child, has brought me beautiful teaching about anger, and about how to be with my own anger. First I learned to be with her as she raged, and to hold her lovingly – this was very challenging for me. (See chapter 26, "Gentle Discipline", for more about supporting Maia's emotional release.) However, now when I get angry or stressed, she looks at me sweetly and says, "I love you, Mummy". Her love for me, and her acceptance of my anger, is an exquisite and profound experience.

I experience my children as my teachers, but I am theirs also, as Guruprem (Swami Gurupremananda Saraswati) reminds us in her wonderful book on yoga and motherhood, *Mother as First Guru*.[7] When she was six, Emma told me this story: "We were all up in the stars together, and we decided that you would go down first and be our mummy." Emma's words have reminded me many times of the equality of spirit and soul between mother and children.

I also appreciate the learning that yoga and motherhood have given me about detachment. Just as I have learned to smile while in the midst of difficult and painful postures (well, at least sometimes!), I have become more easily detached and non-judgmental in my mothering. I find that, from this position, I can be accepting and loving of, yet still unencumbered by, my children's actions and emotions. This is a very sturdy place from which to love and mother, and I pray that my detachment will become even sturdier through my next 14 years of mothering.

Finally, peacefulness is an attribute that we may not naturally associate with mothering. Surely family life is guaranteed to disrupt our peace! Yet it is a quality that we can aspire to, and that our children will naturally seek in us. As one grown child put it, "I think it's really important for the mother to be steady in herself. That makes the kid much safer as he wobbles away."[8]

When we experience ourselves as bringers of steadiness and stillness into the family, we know we are mothering effectively. It is hard to imagine a more effective way to cultivate personal peace and stability, and therefore family peace and stability, than through yoga and meditation.

Zoe's prayer

It is almost 30 years since Jeannine Parvati Baker first wrote about the wonderful gifts that prenatal yoga can bring to birth and mothering. Now we have many, many mothers (and mothers-to-be) who are also keen devotees of yoga. My prayer is that we, as individuals and as a culture, will reap what these mothers are sowing and that the qualities of yoga – the "yoga of yoga" – will reach a critical mass in our culture.

Perhaps then we will be closer to fulfilling the wish that Zoe wrote on a prayer flag when she was five: "I wish that everybody in the whole universe has peace in every way."

First published in Australian Yoga Life, *no 7, November 2003, pp 25–9. This version updated May 2005.*

References

1. Wood L, Lucas D. *Yoga for You: Gita yoga in theory and practice.* Melbourne: Dolphin, 1994.
2. Baker JP. *Prenatal Yoga and Natural Childbirth.* 3rd edn. Berkley: North Atlantic Books, 2001.
3. Ananda Mela. www.anandamela.com.au
4. Thornley J. Kausthub: The third generation. *Australian Yoga Life* 2001(3):77.
5. Baker JP. *Prenatal Yoga and Natural Childbirth.* 3rd edn. Berkeley CA: North Atlantic Books, 2001, p 87.
6. Rea S. The Practice of Surrender. 2002. www.yogajournal.com/wisdom/776_4.cfm
7. Sarasvati SG. *Mother as First Guru:* Swami Gurupremanada Sarasvati, 2001.
8. Lesser E, Rechtschaffen D. Run away Bunny! Parenting Teens as a Spiritual Path. *Mothering* 2003(118):28–35.

Gentle Discipline

E MMA, my sunny, sweet first child, was 20 months old and we were sitting on the sofa together, having tea with our neighbour, who was planning her first pregnancy. Emma had never really used the word before, and I had wishfully thought that we would avoid it altogether: I don't even remember the question that I asked her, but her response was sudden and shocking. It was the biggest "No" I had ever heard. I was visibly shaken and unsure how to respond. My neighbour retreated – although she may have been a bit put off, she did eventually have a baby – leaving me trying to figure out what was wrong, and how I could avert the next "No".

As you may guess, Emma's "No" continued, stronger than ever, and I became concerned, angry, and finally desperate. I consulted my women's circle and my wise teacher Rachana, who had supported many families through the early years of parenting. She reassured me that I wasn't doing anything wrong. Indeed, Emma was just doing what I had allowed her to do thus far, which was to express herself loudly and clearly, except that this time, it was her own will that she was expressing.

Somewhat reassured, although still perturbed when it actually happened, I sought the book that Rachana recommended – *Parent Effectiveness Training* (PET) by Thomas Gordon,[1] and read it cover to cover. Yes! This book excited and inspired me, and I still know many passages off by heart. This was about discipline in the true sense of the word – being a parent that my children would want to follow – and parenting with integrity, sincerity, compassion, and (best of all) inconsistency.

PET remains my all-time favourite parenting book, and its principles are still guiding me as Emma enters her teenage years. This article on gentle discipline is very much influenced by PET, and also by other aspects of parenting and discipline that I have been blessed to learn from my four children, and from other wise parents and writers, over the last 14 years.

What is discipline?

The word discipline comes from the Latin *disciplina*, meaning instruction or teaching. This definition tells us that discipline is much wider than the problems that we might have with certain behaviours, and includes all that we, as parents, are teaching our children.

One way to look at discipline, from this wider perspective, is as the stage setting for family life, in its many facets. Family life can involve exuberant joy; tragedies and tears; zany humour; and roaring rage – and that's even before breakfast! But if we have a stable and loving setting, the ups and downs of family life can pass over us more gracefully, and we can weather the unavoidable storms without long-term damage. When we become skilful at handling conflict, we may also find that, after the storm is over, we can actually emerge with more love and more understanding in our relationships, and in our family.

The teaching that we gain through discipline is not all one-way. We may see ourselves as the authorities in the family (whether because of our physical bulk, our vast life experience, or merely because we are the parents!) but we will often be brought down to size by our children, who will certainly do their share of instructing us. Perhaps the most useful attitude we can take is openness and curiosity, remembering that every situation is new for both of us, and that even the youngest child will have feelings (and perhaps helpful suggestions) that we need to consider.

We can remember too that our children are disciplining us – training us, if you like – so that we can be the parents that they need us to be, for their own beautiful unfolding.

Loving relationships

Loving relationships are, for me, the cornerstone of discipline. When we have a loving relationship, both parent and child will want to give their best to each other. A loving relationship also helps to build resilience when tensions arise, because both child and parent will know that, underneath the conflicts, they do love and care about each other, and that they will eventually be reconnected in a loving way again.

Our relationships involve all that has happened between us, as well as the feelings and actions that are happening right now. My belief is that our relationships with our children begin at conception, and that we can begin to nurture a loving relationship from this time. Allowing ourselves to be well cared for during pregnancy, and giving our babies a gentle birth, will set us gracefully on the road to parenting, and will also help us to respond from our heart during our children's early years.

We can also build loving relationships with our babies through attachment parenting – carrying our babies, breastfeeding, co-sleeping and other practices that allow for a close attachment between mother and baby – because these are the expectations that our babies have developed through evolution. (See chapter 19 for more on attachment parenting). These behaviours also promote security, trust, and emotional wellbeing for both mother and baby. As William and Martha Sears (who coined the phrase "attachment parenting") note, "The deeper the parent–child connection, the easier discipline will be."[2]

If your relationship has been difficult in the past, or there is trauma for either of you in your relationship, please acknowledge this, and trust that healing is possible. There may be a need for some gentle intervention such as homeopathy, osteopathy, or cranio-sacral therapy to help your child heal from trauma (physical or emotional) at birth or in early childhood.

Alternatively, you can use the ideas in Aletha Solter's books[2-5] and give your child the support to clear the trauma him or herself. I believe that we are all essentially self-healing, and that, if we listen with our hearts and instincts, our children will tell us how best to help them through their difficulties. Sometimes the difficulties we experience with our children may be related to our own traumas, past and present. (See "More on difficult behaviours" below for more about healing ourselves as we parent.)

It is also very useful to maintain our relationship awareness when problems arise. When we are having a so-called discipline problem, we may withdraw from our child, either physically or emotionally, because we don't like what they are doing. However, it is more effective to use our loving relationship positively, and to deliberately draw closer when there are problems. This will help our child feel reassured and reconnected, and the situation will be easier to deal with.

I learned this from my fiery youngest child, Maia, and we developed a habit of going onto "the mat" (a large, soft, gym-style mat) together when she was overcome with anger. I would hold her while she raged and cried, and I could see her working through her emotions, and finally coming back to herself and to me. Now that she is four, we don't use the mat very often, but I have learned that moving in closer to an upset or angry child (of any age) and reassuring them with my presence is much more compassionate, as well as more effective, than moving away. (You can read more about this approach in "Emotional expression" below and in Aletha Solter's book, *Tears and Tantrums*.)

Loving relationships with our children also require an ongoing commitment. We may say that we love our children, but, being very practical creatures, our children actually need us to show them our love. This may be easy for us, or it may be very challenging, especially if we did not receive demonstrations of love in our own upbringing. With very young children, the most effective way to show love is to be available physically, and to give lots of hugs and holding. Breastfeeding our babies is also important, as it not only demonstrates love, but actually makes love; both mother and baby get a dose of oxytocin, the hormone of love, with each breastfeed.

For older children, another useful approach is described in the *Five Love Languages* books by Gary Chapman.[6] Chapman has concluded that we do not all feel loved through the same actions. Instead, some people feel loved when they receive compliments; others through physical contact such as hugs; others through receiving gifts; others through having things done for them; and others through spending time with their loved ones. Any of these actions will help to fill up our children's "love tanks" (and our own), but we will be most effective when we use each other's individual love language. On a personal note, I find that I need to make an extra effort when my children's love languages are different from my own.

Last not least, remember that relationships, even with the smallest of children, involve a two-way reciprocity. We can build up our relationships through supporting our children to show their love and appreciation, and by accepting their gifts – whether verbal, physical, material etc – with grace. For example, when I need help, I often ask my children, "Will you do something nice for me?" They may respond negatively (which I can usually accept) but more often they are keen to help me, and I then tell them what I need. This interaction keeps the love flowing between us, and ensures that I don't get to feel resentful about the things I do for them. (Perhaps you can tell that my primary love language is having people do things for me!)

Setting an (imperfect) example

No matter what we say, or the values we talk about, our children will always be most influenced by what we actually do. To be an effective parent, we really need to walk our talk. This is perhaps the scariest part of being a parent, and we are reminded of this every time we see our worst habits mirrored back to us, sometimes by children who can't even talk!

Setting an example means being the best that we can be at the time, and using our role as parents to consciously teach our children some of our values. It also means working to become aware of the more negative attitudes that we may demonstrate unconsciously. Again, we can consider ourselves blessed by our observant children, who will usually remind us when our actions and our stated values are inconsistent. If we can be accepting and open to their feedback, we gain the sort of honest and real discipline (teaching) that comes from a spiritual master, which is what I believe our children essentially are for us.

Setting an example also means recognising when we make mistakes and admitting it to ourselves and to our children. Admitting our mistakes and apologising are very important because, when we admit that we are not perfect, we give our children permission to be imperfect. We are also teaching our children an important aspect of self-esteem: that we actually don't have to be perfect to be worthy of love, from others or from ourselves.

Finally, when we admit our mistakes, we willingly give away some of our power, and we show that we are human after all. We may lose authority, in the strict sense, but we gain authenticity as well as our children's love and true respect. It is also very sweet to be forgiven by our children, who are often so much kinder to us than we are to ourselves.

The wisdom of inconsistency

As parents, we are told that it is important to be consistent. For example, if we allow our children to open up all the puzzle boxes and spread them out on the floor one day, we should allow them to do the same thing the next day. However, if we think about it from our own perspective, we have to admit that some days we are more tolerant to disorder and some days we need more tidiness around us. If we allow our children to do things because of our notions of consistency, we could end up feeling resentful or overwhelmed by what we have allowed our children to do, based on these ideas.

We might also believe that we need to treat our children consistently – that is, all the same – but again, this can be unhelpful. For example, if my children all asked to take something of mine to school, chances are that I would say "Yes" to those who have looked after things that I have loaned them in the past, and "No" to others, who I know haven't taken care of my things. If I try to be consistent, and say, "Yes" to everyone, I am risking damage, as well as missing an opportunity to teach my children about

responsibility. If I say "No" to everyone, I am also not teaching responsibility, nor allowing the rewards of trustworthiness.

Consistency between parents (and other carers) is also artificial and, to my mind, unnecessary. Our children know that we will
respond differently because we are different people. While I think
that it is important to not let our children manipulate our differences, I also believe that we can have different attitudes, thresholds,
and responses, yet still parent together with ease.

Perhaps the most compelling reason to be inconsistent is that
we are more real and honest when we are inconsistent. Personally,
I have even broken prior arrangements with my children because
I value honesty, and because I know that sometimes I need to put
my own needs first. (In other words, "If Mama ain't happy, ain't
no-one happy"!)

When I am inconsistent, or break a prior arrangement, I
always explain my situation, and I ask my children to be understanding and forgiving. Sometimes we will be able to negotiate a
compromise or other solution, and sometimes there will be disappointment and tears. At other times they will say, "Yes, you are
right Mum, it's not the right thing to do." In following my own instincts and needs, I am also teaching my children to follow theirs,
rather than getting caught up in external situations and demands,
and what we think others expect of us (which is often mistaken).

Active listening – the language of acceptance

Listening skillfully and lovingly is a powerful tool for healing. We
have all, hopefully, had the experience of sharing our problems
with another person, and felt relief and healing through simply
being heard. With our children, too, listening may be all that is
required in many situations.

The most powerful and effective listening that we can do
is what has been called "active listening", because this involves
actively communicating love and acceptance to the speaker, as
well as trusting that the person can handle their own feelings
(with support if necessary). Thomas Gordon calls active listening

"the language of acceptance", and says that, when used by a parent, it fosters catharsis (emotional release); helps our children to accept their own feelings; and promotes a warm relationship.[1]

The first thing we can do, as active listeners, is to draw close. For young children, we may need to get down to their level physically, while older children may be more comfortable with a little space around them. Active listening works well with teenagers when travelling in the car. We also need some time and a relaxed attitude so that we can be truly present with our child; it's hard to give our full attention when we are hurried. I find that I can be more available to my children when my own needs are met. (See "Being a self-centred parent" below for more about this aspect of discipline.)

We also need an attitude of acceptance towards our child. This may be difficult at times, but it may help to remember how much you love your child, or to recall a particular time when you felt especially loving towards them. Openness and warmth are important, so that we can accept whatever our child communicates, and accept the feelings behind the communication. Sometimes we may need to remind ourselves that, as adults, we can take a wider perspective, including the knowledge that our child's emotions are transient and, no matter how powerful, they will pass eventually. We also need to remember that our children are separate people to us, with their own experiences and feelings, but with the ability to know what is best for themselves.

At its most simple, active listening may be simply hearing what the child is saying and reflecting it back, with acceptance and compassion. For example, when our children hurt themselves, often all they need is an acknowledgment of the injury ("Oh, that looks really sore.") and a hug. We can't make it better for them but we can trust them to cope with their own feelings, and to ask us for the comfort that they need.

When our children's needs are more complex, we can use the same basic skills – reflecting and acceptance – to draw out the issue that is bothering them, and that may not be obvious. For me, it's a bit like a treasure hunt; we are both seeking the central issue or expression that will bring resolution and at the same time gaining understanding. To find this treasure, we need to suspend our own judgments, preconceptions, and habitual reactions (usually this means working hard to keep our mouths shut and our hearts open), and listening with a minimum of responses. And sometimes the solution (or treasure) may be elusive, yet somehow the process of active listening seems to dissolve the issue, and it may be all that is needed. My interpretation of this is that active listening may start a process for the child, so that they can reach their own resolution at a later time, or in some other way.

On a practical level active listening involves a lot of listening, and some reflecting back. For example, I might say, "So you don't like it when Jacob pulls a face at you?" Active listening also involves using neutral but encouraging words and noises such as "Uh-huh", "Really?" and "Mmm". I find that the more neutral my language is, the more my children will share with me. My favourite word here is "tricky", which can mean difficult or bad, but doesn't have an emotional overtone.

Active listening also involves using feedback, where we check with the speaker whether we have understood their communication. For example, here is a conversation that I recently had with Jacob, aged eight:

J: "I don't want to go to school any more."

Me: "You're not enjoying school at the moment."

J: "No. Jack is sick and James won't play with me, he always plays with the little kids."

Me: "That sounds tricky."

J: "Yes. And I was in the sandpit all by myself for about two hours and no-one came along."

Me: "You were feeling lonely."

J: "Yes. But then Max and Martin came and we talked a bit."

Me: "Hmmm..."

J: "And then we played a bit."

Me: "So it got better?"

J: "Yes. I guess it was OK. I hope Jack gets better soon."

You can imagine that if I had over-reacted when Jacob said, "I don't want to go to school any more," we could have had a major argument, I wouldn't have heard what his real problem was, and as a consequence he might not have shared his next problem with me.

I have also found that the better I get at active listening; the more richly I am rewarded for my efforts. Active listening, allows me glimpses into my children's world – how they see and experience their own lives, and the world around them – and I feel very privileged when they trust me enough to share this. You can get some excellent coaching in active listening by reading *Parent Effectiveness Training*.

Caring for the carer

One of the biggest lessons that I have learned as a mother is that I need to care for myself well if I want to care for my children well. It's obvious really: when we are stressed, we can't give our best and, in a family setting, things can slide from bad to worse very quickly.

Like our love languages, we all have different things that refill our nurturing tanks. As a triple Taurean I can't survive for long without a massage, and I use my regular massage to consciously thank every part of my body for all that it has done for me and my family. Time out is also important to me and I love a long bath, a good book or magazine, and time to keep in touch with myself through my journal.

But caring for myself doesn't always mean taking time out. There are also nourishing rituals that I can weave into my family life, such as using essential oils (lavender always relaxes me), listening to soothing music (or sometimes dancing to exciting music), walking with my family in nature, or simply sitting down for a few minutes with a cuppa. Cooking and eating my favourite foods nourishes me, as well as my family.

When I have been in especially intense situations, such as when my partner goes away, I have found it useful to write a list of things that will nourish me, so that I remember to keep my mothering tanks full. Similarly with food: a list of nice and healthy pick-me-ups is great, especially for a busy breastfeeding mother who may not remember what she likes or needs to eat! I also like to have on-hand a list of friends whom I can call for support, or who have offered help, for when I need it.

I suggest that we all prioritise our own self-care, as parents, and make a list of at least seven things that nourish us. We can post it somewhere visible and make sure we do at least one thing for ourselves every day!

Being a self-centred parent

When Emma was a baby, I worked hard to be "The Perfect Mother". My version of "The Perfect Mother" involved fulfilling all of my child's needs (often ignoring my own), and never saying "No". The attachment parenting that I did with Emma was wonderful, and involved a lot of devotion, but I was in real danger of being an unselfish and emotionally unreal mother with a selfish, spoilt child.

Emma's fiery "No" certainly challenged me to be more real, and as each child has come along, I have also learned to be more self-centred in my parenting. With four children, I have reached a better balance between meeting my own needs and those of my family, and that balance involves approaching situations from a more self-centred perspective.

Being a self-centred parent is not a popular image. Our culture still expects us to be martyrs for the sake of our children, yet this is not healthy for us, nor for our children, who can only learn that it's OK to get their needs met at the expense of others – an attitude that seems to be growing in our society. Being a self-centred parent teaches my children to be respectful of my needs, and the needs of others, and gives us both good practice with saying "No". Being self-centred has made me a much stricter mother, in many ways, compared to my early mothering years, but my children are not selfish and spoilt, and are in fact more flexible and accommodating than I could have imagined.

Being a self-centred parent also helps me to keep my boundaries as clear as possible. In the language of PET, it helps me to know when the problem belongs to me (and I need to take action) and when it belongs to my child (who needs to take action, with my support if necessary).

For example, if my children leave their rooms untidy, my self-centred response is "How does this affect me?" If it has no real impact, then it is their problem, and they can live with the consequences, if any. If, however, I feel that I don't want to go in to put their washing away because I might trip over, or because I just don't like the mess, I could tell them, "I don't like going into your bedroom, so I am not going to put your washing away. You will have to collect it yourself from the laundry." In this way, I have owned my part of the problem, and trusted my child with the decisions and actions (or inactions) that affect them.

Self-centredness also saves us from the resentment that can come when we over-stretch ourselves in fulfilling our children's needs. This is not uncommon for attachment parents, especially for those who did not get their needs met as children, and who therefore can overcompensate with their own children. If you have difficulty with saying "No" to your children, as I did, this may be an issue that you need to look at.

Sometimes I lose my self-centeredness or I am unsure what is the right decision: do I go out of my way to do what my children want, or do I say "No" and live with their disappointment or anger (which is usually short-lived, in my experience)? At these times, I make my decisions based on how I imagine I will feel afterwards. If I think that, for example, tidying my children's room, reading yet another book, or breastfeeding my toddler, will leave me feeling tired or resentful, this gives me the extra resolve to say "No". Feeling resentful and blaming our children for what we have agreed to do for them is not healthy for either of us!

I leave some final words on self-centred parenting to Rachana, my wise teacher who has taught me so much about motherhood. As well as introducing me to PET, Rachana gave me a mothering mantra – a phrase that helps me to centre and come back to myself when things are difficult. The mantra is: "Because I love myself..."

This mantra reminds me that the core of my mothering is my self, and that the more I love myself, the more I am available to love and care for my children. Because I love myself... I can be loving and truly in love with my children, my family, my friends, and the world that we all share.

Putting gentle discipline into practice

Now that we have laid some strong foundations for gentle discipline through loving relationships; through active listening; and through being a self-centred, inconsistent, and imperfect parent (!), we can begin to build some skills and habits that will support a thriving and loving family life – and help us with discipline too.

Negotiation

Emma (14) is setting the table and she wants to sit next to her father. Jacob (nine), who actually doesn't have the right to decide who sits where (which goes with the task of setting the table), complains that he wants to sit next to Dad. He comes to me saying, "It's not fair…"

I ask, "Can you work it out?" and they argue heatedly. Eventually they agree, with a little input from me, that Jacob can sit next to Dad, if he finishes Emma's job for her, which also includes helping with dinner.

In our family, we call this "working it out" or "doing a deal"; other people might call it win–win. It means that two people (or more) can come to an agreement whereby all are happy, and none consider that they have been disadvantaged.

This approach may take some practice and a lot of faith, especially at the start, but it is another aspect of discipline that is vital, I believe, if we want a happy and harmonious family life. As with active listening, we need to trust that our children can devise their own solutions, although they may need help, especially in the beginning, to negotiate with each other.

As with active listening, the role of the parent in "working it out" is to listen and reflect back what the children are saying, and to support those who are less articulate. For example, this might be our conversation in the above example:

Jacob: "I want to sit next to Daddy…"

Emma (interrupts): "But it's not his night, he can't decide!"

Me: "Yes, you are right, it's your night to decide."

Emma: "Yes, it's my night – see, Jacob!"

Jacob: (scowls).

Me: "Is there a way you can work it out?"

Emma: "No."

Me: "Maybe Jacob could help you."

Emma: "No."

Me: "Is there any deal you could do?"

Emma: "No!" (Then thinks:) "Maybe Jacob could finish my job and I could go back on MSN (email)?"

Me: "Do you have [computer] time left?"

Emma "Yes, ten minutes. How about that, Jacob?"

Jacob: "Yeah, maybe."

Me: "Jacob, would you agree to help Emma if she lets you sit next to Dad?"

Jacob: "I guess so."

Emma: "And I want him to help with the salad too."

Me: "What do you think about that, Jacob?"

Jacob: "Yeah, OK."

The role of the parent may include: suggesting some win–win alternatives if necessary; reminding participants of the family's commitment to working it out; and having faith in the process, even when it seems impossible. As I mentioned in relation to active listening, sometimes no solution is reached, but the process can still be very helpful: a solution may come later, or else the tension may be diffused and the issue may simply evaporate. In other situations, I will repeatedly ask: "How can we work it out?", which helps to remind us all of our commitment to negotiation.

When things are difficult, or issues are complex, we might refer things to the family meeting, which is our weekly (or so) time to organise and discuss issues pertaining to family life. At family meetings, we can also decide rules and consequences such as the one above: whoever sets the table gets to choose where everyone sits.

Win–win also applies to us as parents. For example, if Zoe wants me to sew something for her, I can ask her to help with another of my jobs, or to do me another favour. We can trade assistance (as above); favours (for example, she gave me a massage

303

in return for helping her with a job); or material things (which sometimes has included money changing hands), as long as both parties are happy. This is also a very useful skill when teenagers ask to be driven places. For me, such a win–win deal is very different to bribes or rewards, which imply an imbalance in power and outcome, or an element of control and manipulation by those on one side, usually the parents.

If the deal that the children have worked out between themselves seems unfair to me, I might point out the disadvantages, as I perceive them, to the person involved. I can even ask the other person directly about their motivation, so that the deal is obvious to all parties. However, in this process, I need to fundamentally trust the children's own judgment about what is right for them. If, after a while, someone is unhappy about what they agreed to, then they have learned more about what they want for next time!

Negotiation is possible even with young children. Just today Maia, aged four, asked if she could help me (with packing up to go camping) in return for going to the toilet with her (which she can actually do by herself). "Working it out" equips children with excellent negotiation skills and, perhaps more importantly, they develop the creativity and confidence to reach a happy solution, without exploitation or hardship for anyone involved.

Praise, rewards and punishments

In our culture there has been a welcome shift away from parenting using physical punishments, and it is no longer acceptable (and in some places actually illegal) to use brute force to discipline children. However, we have not lost the mind-set attached to this behaviour, and it is still widely believed that discipline is only possible using punishments and rewards.

My beliefs and experiences contradict this rather pessimistic view of parenting. I believe that it is possible, and in fact much more effective, to parent without punishment or rewards. Like Thomas Gordon, author of *Parent Effectiveness Training*, I believe that using punishments (and even rewards) produces an exaggerated and unnecessary power imbalance between parent and child. In effect, the parent becomes the police, with the child at risk of becoming resentful, defiant, rebellious, retaliating, deceitful, over-ly submissive, and/or withdrawn, just as many adults are in the face of overblown authority figures.

Gordon also points out that eventually the parents will run out of authority and will lose the ability, for example, to send a child who is bigger than themselves to their room for "time out". Like Gordon, I wonder if some of the difficulties that we encounter with our children in the teenage years may reflect a rebellion against our over-use of authoritarian techniques and punishments, earlier in childhood.

Parenting without punishments may be easy to understand, but what about rewards? "Surely," many people ask, "rewards will help my child to behave well and help me to avoid the need for punishment." This is a more complex issue but my own feeling is that when we offer children rewards, we are presuming that they need external forms of motivation to do "the right thing". In my experience this is not only untrue, but also rather disrespectful to children who are intrinsically self-motivated and will always have good reasons for their behaviour, if we look deeply enough. (See also "More on difficult behaviours" below).

Another problem with using rewards is that they can actually create a dependence on such motivation. Even praise, if used as a reward rather than as a genuine expression of a feeling, can, I believe, create a need in the child for ongoing praise and instill a need to please others. Alfie Kohn, author of *Punished by Rewards: The Trouble with Gold Stars, Incentive Plans, A's, Praise, and Other Bribes*[7] quotes research that has found that children who are praised in one task will stumble over the next unpraised task, which they do less well than children who were not praised.

This does not mean that we can't say nice things to our children, but I feel that there is a difference between words that genuinely express our appreciation, and words that are designed to elicit or reinforce specific behaviours, or to discourage other behaviors.

Another way to look at it is to consider how it would be to receive rewards or praise from our partner or friend, when we did what they considered to be "the right thing". After a while, it might wear thin and we might start to doubt the genuineness of their words. In fact, we might even begin to suspect that our partner actually wanted to control our behaviour in an underhand sort of way, which is how our children can experience praise and rewards. It is far better, I believe, to be open and honest about what we want from our children and why, and to negotiate from that position, with faith that we will be able to work it out between us.

Putting it into practice

Parenting without punishment or rewards sounds good, but how do we do it, especially in the heat of the moment, or when conflict arises, and we really want our child to change their behaviour NOW?

Let's look at an example that will probably be familiar, at least in terms of the feelings that arise, and our urge to do something.

Your older child has a new bike, and the younger child now wants to ride it, or maybe just to push it around. A physical fight has ensued and both are crying and still angry with each other.

First, if the situation is very heated and the children are beyond reason, I recommend that any negotiation or discussion be delayed until everyone has cooled down. For this to happen, you may need to allow the children emotional expression, as outlined below, and in fact this may be all that is needed if the real need was for emotional release.

Whenever discussion becomes possible, I recommend that the parent involved make an effort to keep a neutral position. This means not making a premature judgment about a situation and, in our example, not taking sides even if it seems that one child has hurt the other. This doesn't mean not comforting a hurt child – in fact these issues are usually best resolved with the children physically close to us. At this stage we can use active listening and ask each child to tell their side of the story without interruption. We can use feedback to help the child to clarify their feelings; for example, "So you felt angry because he wouldn't give you the bike back?"

Along with this, we can encourage our children each to share their feelings, whether by word or action. This may involve some active emotional release, as below, especially in young children, or there may be words that will help a child to express their emotions. Again, active listening, our language of acceptance, is a great tool for helping our children to express themselves, and our patience and loving intent to help is often all that is needed to reach a resolution through telling the story.

After we have heard the story, or stories (which may not be consistent), it is still important not to make judgments about the behaviour, unless it is extreme. If it is extreme, sharing our own emotional reaction – for example, admitting, "I felt scared that you would hurt your brother, because you are so much bigger" – will be more effective than blaming or punishing.

Remember also that, in heated situations, anger may arise (our own or our children's) but it may actually be a cover for deeper (also called "primary") feelings such as fear, jealousy, embarrassment, disappointment or grief. Identifying the primary emotion, in our children and ourselves, can point us in the right direction towards resolution.

By this time, hopefully the issue will be much cooler, and negotiation, if appropriate, will be possible. As above, my favourite phrase here would be, "How can we work it out?" If you feel that further action is necessary to avert a repeat of the situation, I again recommend an explanation of your own feelings and fears, followed by open discussion and negotiation.

For example, you could say, "I am worried that you might hit your sister again over her bike. How can we work it out?" Maybe the children can negotiate with each other to share at particular times, or "do a deal" with each other, as described above. As I mentioned in relation to negotiation, even young children are very inventive and flexible, and very capable of reaching win–win agreements.

Pre-verbal children may be able to "work it out" through agreeing (or not) with the suggestions that we make, for example "How about I find a bike your own size to play with?" It is also possible that, as parents, we need to add other options; in this scenario, the younger child may actually be tired and need to be put to sleep, or at least kept close by.

When the problem is a more straightforward misdemeanour – in other words, our child has done something that they wanted to do, but we didn't want them to do – I recommend a similarly neutral attitude (or at least as neutral as we can manage at the time). As above, jumping in with blame, anger, judgment, and punishment will make it harder to understand the child's motivation, and will not help to build trust. In this, we can simply state the problem, and share what we didn't like about it.

For example, if my child has taken a book from my bedroom and left it lying on the floor, I could say, "I didn't like you taking my book, as it is precious to me and I don't want it to get lost or damaged." Similarly, we can ask (or try to figure out, if the child is pre-verbal) what was good about this action for the child, who obviously had some reason to act in this way.

Aletha Solter has a useful list that we can use in this situation. She suggests we ask ourselves first "Does my child have a legitimate need?" for example for sleep, food, or attention. Second, we can ask if our child is acting this way because they lack information; in the above example, my child may not understand the difference between their own books and my books. Third, we can consider that our child may be feeling upset for another (possibly unrelated) reason or may have an accumulation of stress and may need emotional release.

If we find the behaviour very puzzling, or repeated, we can look more deeply, as outlined below. (See "More on difficult behaviours".)

Consequences and feedback

This is another rather controversial area in parenting today. There is a move towards using consequences as a means of discipline, and some writers differentiate between "logical" and "natural" consequences. Personally I find this distinction a little confusing, and I suspect that "logical consequences" may be used as another means of punishment. However, I do believe that it is important that children experience the real consequences of their behaviour. For me, a better way to look at it is to say that we can help our children with their choices by helping them to get feedback, either while decision-making or after the event.

For example, today Maia and I bought a shower cap and she wanted to wear it into a shop. I told her, "Yes, that's fine, but people might look at you as though you look funny." She decided to take the risk and the woman who served us told her she looked cute! Similarly, if my teenage daughter decides to go out dressed in a very short skirt, I can tell her the reaction she might get, giving her more information to base her decisions on. If I feel strongly about it, I might advise her not to do it and she will often (but not always) take my advice.

With younger children, we may need to provide very tangible feedback rather than just words. For example, when we want our child to understand the concept (and the word) "hot", we can touch their finger against something that feels hot (but obviously won't hurt them). Personally I found this very useful when my toddler began struggling against being "clicked up" in a vehicle child restraint. I decided to let her feel why we use the restraint and to understand what it means to "go bang". I drove slowly in our driveway, with her protesting and unrestrained, and stopped suddenly so that she was propelled a short distance out of her seat and fell back with a bang. After this, she could understand that if she wasn't clicked up she might "go bang", and she was usually happy to comply.

I believe that exposing her to the reality of the situation was helpful, but, as with all aspects of parenting, we can choose our own level of comfort. I have allowed my children to take risks that other parents may be uncomfortable with, provided that we are both fully informed and I feel that I can trust their judgment. This philosophy has been successful so far, with no broken bones and few significant mishaps. I also notice that my children are very responsible, perhaps because I have allowed them to take more responsibility. You can read some interesting cross-cultural perspectives on allowing risks in childhood in *The Continuum Concept*.[8]

Feedback, as above, can be a useful learning tool after an event. I encourage my children to reflect on their decisions and learn from both their successes and mistakes. For example, if Jacob spends his pocket money on a cheap plastic toy, which breaks fairly quickly, I might remind him next time he is considering buying similar toys. Here again, I make an effort to keep my position neutral, so that I'm not imposing my own opinion or judgment, and giving him the space to come to his own conclusions.

Feedback might also include sharing how I feel, and the effect that their behaviour has on me, and on my willingness to help them. Perhaps this is close to the idea of "logical consequences", but my view is that if I do lots of things for them, I expect them to reciprocate and to help me to the best of their abilities. For example, I need them to help by "clicking up" in the car even when they are tired and hungry after school. If they help me, then I am more willing to take them places, have friends over, and arrange activities at a later time. Conversely, if they refuse to help me, I might also refuse to help them with their activities. For me, this is part of being respected for my role and appreciated for the things I do, which I believe is important for all parents.

More on difficult behaviours

At times, all children behave in ways that we find difficult or even strange. As well as doing our best to react in a loving and non-judgmental way, as described above, we can also use these times to find out more about our children and how they see their world.

One approach that I have found very helpful, in response to such behaviour, is based on the work of Melbourne child psycho-therapist Ruth Schmidt Neven, who suggests that we ask ourselves these questions when we want to understand our child (and their behaviour) more deeply:

- Why now?
- What is the child trying to tell me?
- What was happening for me when I was this age?

I suggest that we add another question:

- What is happening in the rest of the family or environment?

Using these questions helps us to see the situation more widely. When we ask "Why now?" we can begin to see the world from our child's perspective, at their age and stage, and to realise, for example, that they may be having a major adjustment to the arrival of a sibling. In my first example, my children may be arguing about positions at the table because they are hungry, or perhaps because they haven't seen much of their father for a few days.

The second question, "What is the child trying to tell me?" helps us to see the behaviour as a means of communication (rather than as a plot to annoy us), and to understand more of our child's world. It also helps us to appreciate that the behaviour may be the only language that a small child has, or may be an expression of something that is otherwise difficult to communicate.

Through asking the third question, "What was happening when I was this age?" we can realise that there are often uncanny parallels between our own childhoods and those of our children. For example, I have found myself experiencing more conflict when my children reached age four. Looking back, I can see that this was a difficult time in my own childhood as well. I have also known friends who went through major relationship problems when their same-sex child was the same age as they were when their parents separated.

This parallel-parenting phenomenon, which I have observed many times, does not have a logical explanation. My own belief is that life is kind to us, and gives us the opportunity to re-experience and resolve issues from our own childhood as we go through those years with our own children. The key for us, as parents, is to be aware and to give ourselves some space to really feel our own feelings that are triggered by our child's behaviour. To put it more positively, "It's never too late to have a happy childhood."

Finally, we can ask, "What is happening in the rest of the family or environment?" This helps us to realise that our children are very sensitive creatures, and very attuned to their emotional environment. Stresses that are not conscious, or not discussed, are, in my experience, particularly liable to be picked up and acted out by our children.

An example using this approach is the recent behaviour of my son, Jacob. I noticed that he was very irritable towards the end of the summer holidays, and was irritating his younger sister and making her squeal. I pondered these questions, and came to realise (after he returned to school and everyone told him how much he had grown) that he was having a growth spurt. I asked if he was hungry and he said, "Yes, all the time!" Together we found foods that would be good to fill him up.

I also considered that he might be reflecting our family's shock at coming home, after a holiday filled with friends and freedom, to the confines of our nuclear family. I also wondered if, as discussed in part one, his love tanks may not be full, and that he might need some dedicated gift-giving to let him know how much we value him, and went out of my way to buy him a thoughtful gift.

Whether I was right or not, he was much happier after I took those actions. If I had branded his behaviour as difficult, and moved towards punishing him, I would have missed the opportunity to get to know him better, and our relationship may have lost some trust.

Emotional expression

This is another potentially challenging aspect of parenting, because our culture is not comfortable with open expression of emotions, especially anger. Whether it is our partner, our child or even we ourselves who experience this strong emotion, our reaction is usually to prevent its expression, by one means or another.

However, emotional expression is a healthy and necessary part of life. In our culture we have sadly lost the skill to encourage healthy emotional expression, so that it can be an act of release, rather than something that is suppressed or judged and that can cause ongoing tensions (as well as emotional eating, smoking, alcohol abuse, and other addictions). Dealing with our children's emotional release can be very challenging, but strong emotions, like violent weather, will always pass, and when they do, we will be rewarded with a clear and bright child – and perhaps even a rainbow.

How does this work? Put simply, we agree to be present for our child's emotional storm, either holding the child or staying close by, until it has passed. For a small baby, this might involve holding them while they cry, without trying to stop the crying (presuming that there isn't a physical problem that needs attention). With a toddler, we can hold them securely, ensuring that they don't hurt themselves – or anyone or anything else – and allow them to physically express their rage. This might involve kicking and screaming, so we need to also ensure that we are not hurt in the process.

With an older child, we may simply be sitting close by, at their level, being emotionally present and giving the message that we love them and care about them, even when they are angry. This is a very powerful message, and one that will be internalised, so that our child will learn to be compassionate with themselves and others when they are angry.

I have found this invaluable with my fourth child, as I mention above, and wish I had known more about it when Emma, my equally fiery first, was a toddler. Even my more placid children have benefited from this approach: as Aletha Solter – whose work is dedicated to this form of release and healing – reminds us, we all have frustrations and difficulties that need healthy release. If we do not allow our children (and ourselves) some form of release, we will build up stress and tensions, which can affect our physical and mental wellbeing. These techniques are especially useful when there have been major changes, traumas, or stresses in the child's or family's life.

Other forms of release that children, and many adults, naturally use include imaginative play, laughing, and rough-and-tumble play. If you suspect that your child has some pent-up feelings, you can safely and easily encourage them into a game that includes these elements. You might even have fun, and lose some tensions yourself!

I highly recommend that you read some of the books and articles in the resources section before you decide either way about these techniques. They may seem radical in our culture but have the capacity, I believe, to create powerful and loving reconnections between parents and children.

Cooling off

As I imply above, it is not only our children who will get emotionally heated in the course of family life. All parents, at some times, will become angry, frustrated, overwhelmed, indignant, and generally cranky, as my children sometimes describe me. If we accept that this is a normal part of parenting, our responsibility shifts to the way that we manage our heated emotions.

Although all of this can be immensely challenging, I also believe that this is part of what makes parenting such a profound spiritual practice. Our children will always push us to our limits, and our goal is to be constantly moving beyond this. As my friend and mentor, Jeannine Parvati Baker, says, "Our children make us a whole lot better than we ever wanted to be."

One tool that I have found very useful in this is Heartmath.[9] Heartmath offers some very simple, well-researched tools for cooling down, which centre upon reconnecting with our hearts in the heat of the moment. Other tools that I have found useful include time out for myself in my bedroom, or a walk up our long driveway. All of these help me to reconnect with myself and see the bigger picture. I notice also that the wider the perspective I am able to have on the situation, and the more I can connect with my heart, the less my anger impacts on my children. In fact, they laugh at me sometimes, and I do too!

Raising gentle children

We are all trying to be the best parents we can and, as every parent knows, this is easier some days than others. As described, being an imperfect parent is normal and perhaps even necessary: when we stuff up, lose the plot, or act in ways that we later regret, we get the opportunity to apologise to our child and to learn from our mistakes. This keeps us both humble and human to our children.

Gentle discipline, by my own definition, has the aim of being both loving and effective in the short, medium and long terms; this applies to ourselves as well as our children. Through our own self-love, and acceptance of our imperfections, we teach tolerance, acceptance and honesty. By our sincere commitment to our children, and to gentle parenting, we can contribute towards gentle, loving, and effective approaches in family life, and in our society as a whole.

This article was first published, in two parts, in Natural Parenting *no 8, spring 2004, pp 24–9 and no 10, autumn 2005 pp 35–9, 45.*

Resources

1. Gordon T. *Parent Effectiveness Training.* New York: Penguin, 1975.
2. Sears W, Sears M. *The Discipline Book: Everything You Need to Know to Have a Better-Behaved Child – from Birth to Age Ten.* Boston: Little Brown, 1995.
3. Solter A. *Helping Young Children Flourish.* Goleta CA: Shining Star Press, 1989.
4. Solter A. *Tears and Tantrums.* Goleta CA: Shining Star Press, 1998.
5. Solter A. *The Aware Baby: A New Approach to Parenting.* Goleta CA: Shining Star Press, 2001.
6. Chapman G, Campbell R. *The Five Love Languages of Children.* Chicago: Moody Press, 1997.
7. Kohn A. *Punished by Rewards: The Trouble with Gold Stars, Incentive Plans, A's, Praise, and Other Bribes.* Boston: Houghton Mifflin Company, 1999.
8. Liedloff J. *The Continuum Concept: In Search of Happiness Lost.* Boston: Addison Wesley, 1986.
9. Childre D, Martin H. *The Heartmath Solution*: HarperSanFrancisco, 2001.

Acknowledgements

First I thank my beloved parents, Nola and Tim, who loved and supported me through my rather tempestuous and precocious childhood, encouraged me through my studies, and who continue to love and support me and my family.

Second, I am grateful beyond words to my own children, my best teachers, Emma, Zoe, Jacob, and Maia, who have given me such deep and rich experiences of pregnancy, birth, and mothering. Thank you too for the space you have given me for my writing, and for the new understandings you bring to me every day.

Equally, I thank Nicholas, the love of my life, for his love, support, tolerance, and sense of humour, and for walking alongside me for 15 years on this wild and wonderful path of parenting.

I am grateful to all the women in my "advanced women's mysteries" circle, based in Melbourne, who provide such a solid foundation for my work. Thanks especially to Rachana, circle leader, teacher, wise woman, and friend, who has been a true midwife to me, and to so many others. Thanks also to my many other supporters and mentors, including Michel Odent, Joseph Chilton Pearce, and Deva Daricha, whose work on the cutting edge of consciousness continues to inspire me.

A special dedication also to my dear friend and teacher Jeannine Parvati Baker – midwife, yogini, astrologer, herbalist and mother of freebirth – who is critically ill as this book goes to press. Jeannine's extraordinary 'word medicine', which you will see referenced throughout this book, has inspired, challenged, supported, and awoken so many of us around the world, and her work has expanded the realms of the possible family: thank you, dear Parvati.

Thanks to all my women friends, my homebirth and midwife friends, and the Brisbane Home Midwifery Association circle, who help to keep alive the spirit and love of birth and babies. Thanks especially to my faithful moon circle, Suzanne, Georgina, Susan, and Mary.

ACKNOWLEDGEMENTS

Appreciation to the people who have supported my writing and speaking, especially Ashisha at *Mothering*, Jan Tritten at *Midwifery Today*, Kali Wendorf at *byronchild*, Veronika Robinson at *The Mother* magazine, and Susan Stark at *Natural Parenting*. Thanks also to Leilah McCracken at birthlove.com, Sue Cookson from Homebirth Australia, and Margaret Horton from APPPAH (Association of Prenatal and Perinatal Psychology and Health), who have helped to bring my words to a wider audience.

Thanks to all those who have been my email community for this book: your availability, support, and encouragement have meant so much to me. Thanks also to the growing global network of birth activists; women and men of incredible courage and commitment, who are all working to heal birth in our culture. (That includes you, Bruce!)

On a more personal note, thanks to those superb practitioners who have supported my health and my body, so that I can do the work of mother and writer, especially my masseur Narelle Clark, homeopath Patricia Hatherly, and naturopath and cranio-sacral therapist Claire Brassard.

The process of birthing this book has been easier because of my excellent editor, Soni Stecker, and all of my friends who have generously given me feedback and support. I have enjoyed immensely the "women's work" that has been a cornerstone and joy in this project, including the photography (thanks to Deirdrie Cullen) and illustration (thanks to Durga Bernhard for the artwork and Nickole Webb for my rose and moon).

Lastly, gratitude to all my readers – mothers, fathers, families, and professionals worldwide – for your feedback, appreciation, and patronage, and for giving me the opportunity to bring together my mothering heart, my scientific mind, and my love of writing.

Blessings on your journey.

Sarah Buckley, Brisbane, August 2005

Photograph by Deirdrie Cullen.

Recommended Reading

A comprehensive and updated list of books and websites is available at: www.sarahjbuckley.com

Pregnancy, gentle birth

Suzanne Arms, *Immaculate Deception II: Myth, Magic and Birth* (Berkeley, CA: Celestial Arts, 1996)

David Chamberlain, *The Mind of Your Newborn Baby* (Berkeley, CA: North Atlantic Books, 1998)

Deepak Chopra, David Simon & Vicki Abrams, *Magical Beginnings, Enchanted Lives: A Holistic Guide to Pregnancy and Childbirth* (New York: Three Rivers Press, 2005)

Common Knowledge Trust, *The Pink Kit method for better birthing* (video and booklet). Available from: www.birthingbetter.com

Joan Donley, *Joan Donley's Compendium for a Healthy Pregnancy and a Normal Birth* (Auckland: Joan Donley, 2003)

Pam England & Rob Horowitz, *Birthing From Within: An Extraordinary Guide to Childbirth Preparation* (Albuquerque NM: Partera Press, 1998)

Murray Enkin, Marc JNC Keirse, James Neilson, Caroline Crowther, Leila Duley, Ellen Hodnett & G Justus Hofmeyr, *A Guide to Effective Care in Pregnancy and Childbirth*, 3rd edn (Oxford, Oxford University Press, 2000)

Anne Frye, *Holistic Midwifery; A Comprehensive Textbook for Midwives in Homebirth Practice*, vol I: *Care During Pregnancy* (Portland, OR: Labrys Press, 1998)

__, *Holistic Midwifery; A Comprehensive Textbook for Midwives in Homebirth Practice*, vol II *Care of the Mother and Baby from the Onset of Labor Through the Hours after Birth* (Portland, OR: Labrys Press, 2005)

Ina May Gaskin, *Ina May's Guide to Childbirth* (New York: Bantam, 2003)

Henci Goer, *Obstetric Myths vs Research Realities* (Westport, CT: Bergin & Garvey, 1995)

__, *The Thinking Woman's Guide to a Better Birth* (Perigee, 1999)

Breck Hawk, *Hey! Who's Having This Baby Anyway* (End Table Books, 2005)

Sunni Karll, *Sacred Birthing: Birthing a New Humanity* (Victoria, BC, Canada: Trafford Publishing, 2003) www.sacredbirthing.com

Sheila Kitzinger, *The New Pregnancy and Childbirth: Choices & Challenges* (London: Dorling Kindersley, 2003)

__, *Rediscovering Birth* (London: Little Brown, 2000)

__, *The Politics of Birth* (London: Elsevier, 2005)

318

Leilah McCracken, *Resexualizing Childbirth: A Collection of Essays* (Coquitlam BC: Birthlove 2000) www.birthlove.com

Francesca Naish & Janette Roberts, *Healthy Parents, Better Babies* (Dublin: Newleaf, Gill & Macmillan, 2000). Published in Australia as: *The Natural Way to Better Babies: Preconception Health Care for Prospective Parents* (Sydney: Random House, 1996) Published in USA as: *Healthy Parents, Better Babies* (Berkeley, CA: The Crossing Press, 1999)

__, *Healthy Lifestyle, Better Pregnancy* (Dublin: Newleaf, Gill & Macmillan, 2000). Published in Australia as: *The Natural Way to a Better Pregnancy* (Sydney: Doubleday, 1999)

__, *Healthy Body, Better Birthing* (Dublin: Newleaf, Gill & Macmillan, 2001). Published in Australia as: *The Natural Way to Better Birth and Bonding* (Sydney: Doubleday, 2000)

__, *Healthy Mother, Better Breastfeeding* (Dublin: Newleaf, Gill & Macmillan, 2002). Published in Australia as: *The Natural Way to Better Breastfeeding* (Sydney: Doubleday, 2002).

Elizabeth Noble, *Primal Connections* (New York: Simon & Schuster, 1993)

__, *Essential Exercises for the Childbearing Year* (New York: Simon & Schuster, 1993)

Michel Odent, *The Scientification of Love* (London: Free Association Books, 2001)

__, *Birth Reborn*, 3rd edn (London: Souvenir Books, 2005)

__, *The Caesarean* (London: Free Association Books, 2004)

Peggy O'Mara, *Having a Baby, Naturally: The Mothering Magazine Guide to Pregnancy and Childbirth* (New York: Simon & Schuster, 2003)

Laura Kaplan Shanley, *Unassisted Birth* (Westport, CT: Bergin & Garvey, 1994)

Penny Simkin, Janet Whalley, Ann Keppler, *Pregnancy, Childbirth and the Newborn: The Complete Guide – Expanded and Updated* (Minnetonka, MN: Meadowbrook Press, 2001)

David Vernon (ed), *Having a great birth in Australia* (Canberra: Australian College of Midwives, 2005)

Marsden Wagner, *Pursuing the Birth Machine: the Search for Appropriate Birth Technology* (Camperdown, NSW, Australia: ACE Graphics, 1994).

Waterbirth

Janet Balaskas, *The Water Birth Book* (London: Thorsons Element, 2004)

Beverley Lawrence Beech, *Choosing a Water Birth* (London: AIMS, 1998)

Ethel Burns & Sheila Kitzinger, *Midwifery Guidelines for the Use of Water in Labour*, 2nd edn (Oxford: Oxford Brookes University, 2005)

Susanna Napierala, *Waterbirth: A Midwive's Perspective* (Westport, CT: Bergin & Garvey, 1994)

Michel Odent & Jessica Johnson, *We are all Water Babies* (Surrey: Dragon's World, 1994)

Lotus birth

Jeannine Parvati Baker, *Lotus Birth information pack*. Available from: www.freestone.org

Shivam Rachana (ed), *Lotus Birth* (Yarra Glen, Vic, Australia: Greenwood Press, 2000)

Third stage

Nadine Pilley Edwards, *Delivering Your Placenta: The Third Stage* (AIMS for British Maternity Trust, 1999)

Homebirth

Ina May Gaskin, *Spiritual Midwifery* (Summertown, TN: The Farm Publishing Co, 1990)

Ingrid and Paul Johnson, *The Paper Midwife: A Guide to Responsible Homebirth* (Sydney: AH & AW Reed, 1980)

Sheila Kitzinger, *Birth Your Way. Choosing Birth at Home or in a Birth Center* (London: Dorling Kindersley, 1999)

David Miller, *Birth at Home* (Sydney: Doubleday, 1990)

Marjorie Tew, *Safer Childbirth? A Critical History of Maternity Care* (London: Chapman & Hall, 1990)

Healing from birth trauma

Benig Mauger, *Songs from the Womb: Healing the Wounded Mother* (Dublin: Collin's Press, 1998). Published in USA as *Reclaiming the Spirituality of Birth – Healing for Mothers and Babies*, (Healing Arts Press, 2000)

Ultrasound, prenatal diagnosis

Lachlan de Crespigny with Meg Espie & Sophie Holmes, *Prenatal Testing – Making Choices in Pregnancy* (Melbourne: Penguin, 1998)

Lachlan de Crespigny with Rhonda Dredge, *Which Tests for my Unborn Baby? Ultrasound and other prenatal tests*, 2nd edn (Melbourne: Oxford University Press, 1996)

Barbara Katz Rothman, *The Tentative Pregnancy* (London: Pandora, 1998)

Down syndrome

Martha Beck, *Expecting Adam: a true story of birth, rebirth and everyday magic* (New York: Berkley Books, 1999)

Cynthia Kidder, Brian Skotko, *Common threads: Celebrating life with Down syndrome* (Rochester Hills, MI: Band of Angels Press, 2001)

Mitchell Kuckoff, *Choosing Naia: A family's journey* (Boston: Beacon Press, 2002)

Vicki Noble, *Down is up for Aaron Eagle* (New York: Harper Collins, 1993)

Breastfeeding

Norma Jane Bumgarner, *Mothering Your Nursing Toddler* (La Leche League Intl, 2000)

Jill Day, Australian Breastfeeding Association, *Breastfeeding Naturally* (Melbourne: ABA, 2004)

Hilary Flower, *Adventures in Tandem Nursing* (La Leche League Intl, 2000)

Patricia Hatherley, *The Homeopathic Physician's Guide to Lactation* (Brisbane: Luminoz, 2004)

Kathleen Huggins, *The Nursing Mother's Companion*, 5th edn (Harvard Common Press, 1999)

Patricia Stuart-Macadam & Kathleen Dettwyler (eds), *Breastfeeding; Biocultural Perspectives* (New York: Aldine de Gruyter, 1995)

Sleeping and co-sleeping

Debra Jackson, *Three in a Bed: the benefits of sharing your bed with your baby* (Bloomsbury, 1999)

William Sears, *Night Time Parenting* (La Leche League Intl, 1999)

Meredith E Small, *Our Babies, Ourselves* (New York: Random House, 1998)

Tine Thevenin, *The Family Bed* (Knoxville, TN: Avery Publishing, 1987)

Elimination communication

Ingrid Bauer, *Diaper Free!, The Gentle Wisdom of Natural Infant Hygiene* (Saltspring Island, BC: Natural Wisdom Press, 2001) www.natural-wisdom.com

Laurie Boucke, *Infant Potty Training: A gentle and primeval method adapted to modern living* (Lafayette, CO: White-Boucke Publishing, 2002)

Pregnancy yoga

Jeannine Parvati Baker & Frederick Baker, *Conscious Conception: Elemental Journey through the Labyrinth of Sexuality* (Monroe UT: Freestone Publishing Co /Berkeley CA: North Atlantic Books, 1986) www.freestone.org

Jeannine Parvati Baker, *Prenatal Yoga and Natural Childbirth*, 3rd edn (Monroe UT: Freestone Publishing Co /Berkeley CA: North Atlantic Books, 2001) www.freestone.org

Kaur Khalsa Gurmukh, *Bountiful, Beautiful, Blissful: Experience the Natural Power of Your Pregnancy with Kundalini Yoga* (London: Penguin, 2003) www.GoldenBridgeYoga.com

Swami Gurupremananda Sarasvati, *Mother as First Guru* (Swami Gurupremananda Sarasvati, 2002)

Gentle parenting

Robin Grille, *Parenting for a Peaceful World* (Sydney: Longueville Media, 2005)

Jan Hunt, *The Natural Child: Parenting from the Heart* (Gabriola Island, BC, Canada: New Society Publishers, 2001

Myla and Jon Kabat-Zinn, *Everyday Blessings: The Inner Work of Mindful Parenting* (New York: Hyperion, 1997)

Marshall Klaus, John Kennell & Phyllis Klaus, *Bonding: Building the Foundation of Secure Attachment and Independence* (Reading, MA: Addison-Wesley, 1996)

Jean Liedloff, *The Continuum Concept: In Search of Happiness Lost* (Reading, MA: Perseus Books, 1997)

Pinky McKay, *Parenting by Heart: Unlock Your Intuition and Nurture with Confidence* (Port Melbourne, Australia: Lothian Books, 2001)

Peggy O'Mara, *The Way Back home: Essays on Life and Family* (Santa Fe, NM: Mothering magazine, 1991)

__, Natural Family Living: *The Mothering Magazine Guide to Parenting* (New York: Simon & Schuster, 2000)

Tiffany Palisi (ed), *Loving Mama: Essays on Natural Parenting and Motherhood* (Tucson, AZ: Hats Off Books, 2004)

Joseph Chilton Pearce, *Magical Child: Rediscovering Nature's Plan for Our Children* (New York: Dutton, 1977)

William Sears & Martha Sears, *The Baby Book: Everything You Need to Know About Your Baby from Birth to Age Two* (Boston: Little Brown, 2003)

Gentle discipline

Doc Childre & Howard Martin, *The HeartMath Solution* (San Francisco: HarperSanFrancisco, 1999)

Thomas Gordon, *Parent Effectiveness Training* (New York: Penguin, 1975)

William & Martha Sears, *The Discipline Book: Everything You Need to Know to Have a Better-Behaved Child – from Birth to Age Ten* (Boston: Little, Brown & Company, 1995)

Aletha Solter, *The Aware Baby: A New Approach to Parenting* (Goleta CA: Shining Star Press, 2001)

__, *Tears and Tantrums* (Goleta CA: Shining Star Press, 1998)

__, *Helping Young Children Flourish* (Goleta CA: Shining Star Press, 1989)

Index

ORDER FORM

Please send me

_____ copies of *Gentle Birth, Gentle Mothering*

     A$36.95 per copy (includes GST) _____

     postage and handling:
     A$5.50 per book in Australia _____
     A$12.00 per book international _____
     A$6.00 per book US/Canada _____
     Total amount _____

Name _____

Address _____

_____

_____

Email/phone number _____

Payment enclosed

☐ Cheque made out to One Moon Press

☐ International Money Order made out to One Moon Press

☐ Credit card no. _____

    ☐ Mastercard   ☐ Visa

    Expiry date _____ / _____

    Name on credit card _____

    Signature _____

Please mail to   One Moon Press
                245 Sugars Road
                Anstead QLD 4070 Australia

Phone   61 7 3202 9052

Fax (Australia)   07 3202 5851